RIDING IN THE ZONE ROUGE

RIDING IN THE ZONE ROUGE

THE TOUR OF THE BATTLEFIELDS 1919 CYCLING'S TOUGHEST-EVER STAGE RACE

TOM ISITT

WEIDENFELD & NICOLSON

First published in Great Britain in 2019 by Weidenfeld & Nicolson
an imprint of The Orion Publishing Group Ltd
Carmelite House, 50 Victoria Embankment
London EC4Y ODZ

An Hachette UK Company

10 9 8 7 6 5 4 3 2 1

The author and publisher are grateful
to Getty Images Ltd for permission to
reproduce photographs on pp. 113 and 129.

A CIP catalogue record for this book is
available from the British Library.

ISBN (Hardback) 978-1-4091-7114-0
ISBN (eBook) 978-1-4091-7116-4

Typeset by Input Data Services Ltd, Somerset

Printed and bound by CPI Group (UK) Ltd, Croydon, CR0 4YY

MIX
Paper from
responsible sources
FSC FSC® C104740
www.fsc.org

www.orionbooks.co.uk

CONTENTS

ACKNOWLEDGEMENTS

The bit no one reads. But if you are reading this, I wanted to extend my thanks to:

Emma (my poor wife), for putting up with all of this.

Michael (my father-in-law), for his encouragement and translation services.

Servanne (my French friend), for her help with translating old newspapers.

Phil (my cycling friend), for his *domestique* services and cheery encouragement.

George, Joe and Harry (my sons), for their help and support.

And, obviously, my mum (a pretty decent author herself).

PREFACE

The Circuit des Champs de Bataille in 1919 was one of the most extraordinary bicycle races ever staged. In cataclysmic weather the riders raced across the battlefields of Belgium and northern France just a few months after the First World War had ended, enduring 300km-long stages, often on roads that no longer existed in the normal sense. It was such a tough race that it was never held again as a multi-stage event, and it all but disappeared from the records.

As a result, the primary source material is limited to brief reports in the organising newspaper, *Le Petit Journal*, reports in sports newspapers such as *L'Auto* in France and *Sportwereld* in Belgium, and the briefest of mentions in a couple of cycling history books. The event was clearly so horrific for the organisers and most of the participants that they never mentioned it again.

With this in mind, I cannot know what the riders said, what they thought, or how they felt as they raced across the battlefields of Flanders and the Somme. So I have drawn on contemporary accounts of the battlefields in the immediate aftermath of the First World War in order to paint a picture of the conditions they endured. And I have drawn on accounts of bike racing immediately before and after the war to build up a picture of the men involved, the bikes they rode, and the tactics they used.

A full bibliography of sources can be found at the end of this book. The facts of the race are correct, but the dialogue and some scenes (in the lighter print) are the product of my imagination, based on what I know about those early racers. I hope you will forgive the small amount of literary licence employed to help bring these extraordinary men, and their astonishing achievements, to life.

Tom Isitt
London, 2017

MAP OF THE COURSE

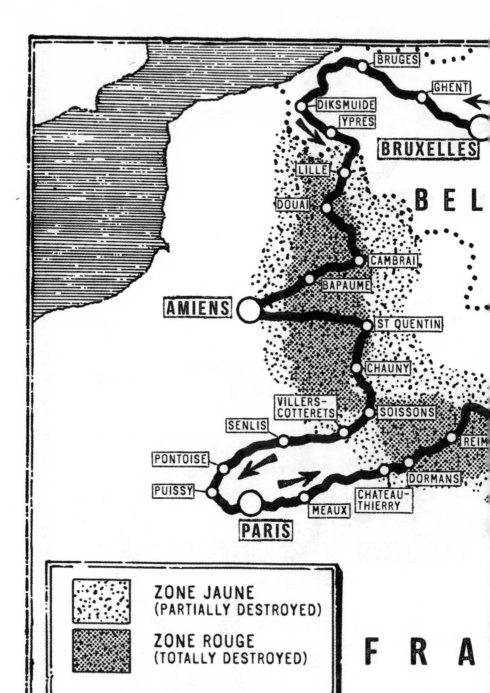

PROLOGUE

2 May 1919

Lecomte took a lantern from a hook by the door, and stepped outside. Pulling his hat down against the flurries of sleet and rain borne on a biting wind, he peered into the night. Nothing. No sign. Where the hell were they? They should have been here hours ago. He lifted the lantern, as if hoping its modest glow would summon the riders from the gloom. Still nothing.

Out on the road, Charles Deruyter battled on. He was cold. Frozen to the core by the relentless wind and rain. And utterly exhausted. He had been riding since before dawn, and still had 70km to go. He hadn't seen any other riders for hours, and only one of the commissaires' cars. All he had witnessed was the destruction and chaos of the battlefields. And, through the gathering darkness, hastily dug graves amongst the shell-holes and the wire. It was hard to pick a good line through the ruts and mud when you were shaking uncontrollably from the cold. The sleet whipped around him as he slipped and skidded on the treacherous muddy surface. Deruyter's lonely suffering stretched to the endless bleak horizon; he wondered if feeling would ever return to his fingers and toes.

Returning to the light and warmth of the Café de L'Est in the centre of Amiens, Lecomte stamped his feet and shrugged off his thick overcoat. '*Il pleut encore*,' he muttered to his fellow Race Commissaires, gathered around a table near the fire. Degrain checked his pocketwatch and wondered, not for the first time, whether this race across the battlefields of the First World War, only a few months after the armistice, really was such a good idea.

A few miles behind Deruyter, Paul Duboc was locked in his own world of suffering. De-mobbed from the army only a few weeks earlier, the 35-year-old was a veteran of five Tours de France, and Deruyter's senior by six years. Those five Tours meant he was no stranger to long, arduous race stages, but this was different. This was infinitely worse. He was chilled to the bone, and completely exhausted. Darkness was falling, and with no lights on his bike and no moonlight, Duboc would soon be riding blind, squinting through the rain and sleet to make out the road ahead. It was barely a road at all . . . more an endless succession of smashed cobbles, potholes and shell craters, bridged with slippery wooden planks or partially filled in with whatever had come to hand.

Duboc cursed as his front wheel slid sideways and dumped him, for the umpteenth time, into the cold wet mud. Better that, he thought to himself, than to end up in one of the ditches either side. Since Cambrai he had become aware that the roadside ditches were filled with the most appalling detritus – burned-out vehicles, rusting barbed wire, clothing, broken weapons, the bones of long-dead mules and horses. And all around were stacked piles of unexploded munitions, gathered up by the labour battalions clearing the battlefields. A dank, rotting smell of death and mud and rust oozed from the brutalised, lifeless earth.

While Deruyter and Duboc were struggling across the Somme, Van Lerberghe and Anseeuw, an hour behind, had sensibly teamed up and were negotiating their way through the ruins of Cambrai, now a sprawling pile of scorched masonry, charred wood and weeds. Van Lerberghe had ridden the Paris–Roubaix race, subsequently nicknamed 'The Hell of the North', two weeks earlier so he had some inkling of what to expect. For the young Anseeuw, the utter desolation he saw here, and in the parts of Belgium they had already traversed, was profoundly shocking.

'My God,' muttered Anseeuw, 'look at this place!' The Germans had set the town on fire when they pulled out six months earlier, leaving huge swathes of burned and collapsed houses. Here and there small shacks had been erected amongst the ruins by returning refugees, the only signs of life in this once-vibrant town.

'The bastards didn't spare the matches, did they?' answered Van Lerberghe as they slowed to negotiate another large, badly filled shell crater in the road. Up ahead, an elderly couple, dressed in shabby clothes and wearing rough wooden clogs, were pushing an old pram piled high with salvaged wood through the rain. Every few metres the uneven road surface would cause an avalanche of timber to cascade around their feet and they would stop and gather up their cargo. They paused in their Sisyphean labours to watch as Van Lerberghe and Anseeuw rode by.

Skirting the rusting remains of a tank on the outskirts of town, and a particularly pungent crater filled with God-knows-what, Van Lerberghe and Anseeuw exchanged weary glances and rode on, hoping to make it to Amiens at some point that night. But the weather was so bad, and the road so difficult, that it wasn't until after 1 a.m. that they made it to the finish of Stage 3, nearly 21 hours after they had set off from Brussels. The remaining riders still out on the road abandoned their attempts to get to the finish that evening, and spent the night shivering with cold in various trenches, dug-outs and pill-boxes on the Somme and Cambrai battlefields. For riders such as Maurice Brocco, de-mobbed from the army only a month before the race, this wasn't the first night he had spent trying to sleep in a cold, damp dug-out on a battlefield.

29 April 2016

If Stage 3 was the nadir of the Circuit des Champs de Bataille for the riders, the low point of my attempt to follow the route of the race came nearly a century later. It wasn't when I crashed on some Belgian cobbles and cracked three ribs, it wasn't when I got hopelessly lost in the snow of the Ardennes forests, and it wasn't when my rear derailleur cable snapped on a Sunday afternoon in the middle of Rural Nowhere. No, my low point came on the road from Liège to Brussels – a dead-straight, gently rolling A-road lined for mile after depressing mile with second-hand car dealers, furniture warehouses, car-washes, and brothels.

A fierce headwind blew freezing rain straight in my face, black clouds scudded low overhead, and huge trucks threw bow-waves of filthy water over me as they passed. I had been soaked to the skin for several hours and suspected that the trench-foot that had developed over the last couple of days was not going to clear up any time soon. To ensure my cup of misery was filled to overflowing, the crappy concrete-slabbed cycle paths caused a mind-numbingly repetitive *thur-dunk thur-dunk* as the wheels bumped over the gaps between the slabs. *Thur-dunk thur-dunk, thur-dunk thur-dunk.* Consulting the sat-nav, I noted the temperature was a chilly 6 degrees, and my speed had slowed to a 12mph crawl thanks to the bloody awful headwind.

That morning had been spent slogging up and down brutally steep hills and valleys in the Ardennes forests while the poxy sat-nav attempted to determine where the hell we were. I had then crossed a desolate snow-covered plateau, encouragingly called Malchamps (Bad Fields), before getting hopelessly lost (again) in the decaying post-industrial wastes of Liège thanks to the endless roadworks. As the sleet turned to rain I hauled myself up the Côte de Saint-Nicolas (the final serious climb of the Liège–Bastogne–Liège bike race) and set off west towards Brussels, 60 miles away. The sat-nav informed me I'd already ridden 65 miles and climbed 5,000ft that day.

Squinting through the rain, I could just make out something in the road ahead, at the top of the endless incline I'd been riding up for several miles. It looked like some kind of soggy, dirty old rope, the far end of which was lying in a puddle beneath the awning of a closed tanning salon. I pulled over and stopped to have a look. Ah, I thought I recognised it . . . It's the END OF MY BLOODY TETHER! I'm freezing cold, soaking wet, exhausted, dispirited, hungry and suffering a slight sense-of-humour failure.

So I did what any self-respecting pro cyclist does when faced with crappy conditions and seemingly insurmountable odds. I cheated. I stopped in Sint-Truiden and got the train for the last

35 miles to Brussels. No, don't give me that 'you're not doing it properly' crap. In the early days of bike racing it was standard practice to hop on a train or load yourself and your bike into the back of a truck the minute the commissaires turned their backs. It was against the rules, but everyone was doing it (fast-forward 90 years and you'll find pro cyclists still using that as an excuse to cheat). Anyway, at 6 p.m. I found myself shivering uncontrollably in the ticket office of Sint-Truiden station, feeling not one ounce of remorse, as a dirty puddle formed around my feet.

THE IDEA

As the guns fell silent all along the Western Front in November 1918, plans were being made to stage an extraordinary bicycle race across the First World War battlefields in the spring of the following year. The Circuit Cycliste des Champs de Bataille (the Tour of the Battlefields) was to become known at the time as the toughest race in cycling history, but the extraordinary efforts of the riders, who raced across the fields of Flanders, the Somme and Verdun barely five months after the armistice, have been all but forgotten these days.

If you Google 'the toughest bicycle race ever' you pretty quickly come up with a list that includes the Tour Divide, the Race Across America, the Transcontinental, and a whole host of modern ultra-endurance events that seem to involve cycling halfway round the globe without stopping (or shaving). While I applaud these certifiable lunatics for their courage, determination and endurance, these aren't 'proper' bike races. Well, not in the sense that they have set stages, team cars, *soigneurs*, doping, publicity caravans, scandals, rest days and all the other things we associate with professional bike racing.

Similar internet searches might produce a list of Tours de France, or the Italian equivalent, the Giro d'Italia, that were also particularly challenging. Received wisdom says that the 1914 Giro d'Italia was the toughest of all Grand Tours on account of the horrendous weather and barbarically long 400+km stages. But the only major climb was the slog up to Sestriere. Horribly hard on a 1914 bike that weighed half a ton and only had two gears, no doubt, but how does that compare to tackling the Telegraphe, the Galibier, the Tourmalet and the Aubisque, as the riders of the 1911 Tour de France were forced to do? Yes, but at least the Tour riders had decent weather on their 5,000m-a-day Alpine climbs. Swings and roundabouts.

But with a 2,000km route in seven stages across the war-torn roads and battlefields of the Western Front in horrific weather, a mere couple of months after hostilities ceased, the Circuit des Champs de Bataille took suffering on a bike to a whole new level. On the stage that ran across the battlefields of Flanders, Artois, Cambrai and the Somme, in the sleet, snow and storm-force winds, only one rider finished on the same day he set off, one rider took 39 hours to complete the stage, and almost half the field abandoned the race. That was a properly tough bicycle race.

So why did anyone think this race was a good idea? Well, as was usually the case in those days, the Circuit des Champs de Bataille was an attempt to sell more newspapers for the organisers, *Le Petit Journal* in Paris. Most of the big races in cycling began life as promotional events for the newspapers that organised them – the Tour de France, the Giro d'Italia, the Tour of Flanders, and a host of others. In the absence of TV and radio at the beginning of the twentieth century, daily papers were the only source of news for those who were literate, and so any newspaper organising a popular sporting event over the course of a few weeks could expect a significant increase in circulation as readers bought the paper to catch up on the latest news of the event.

Le Petit Journal, one of France's biggest newspapers, first experienced this phenomenon in 1891 when it organised the Paris–Brest–Paris, a spectacularly bonkers non-stop cycle race of 1,200km that was won by Charles Terront in a time of 71 hours. It was a huge success that led to a significant bump in sales for the paper, but the logistics were so complicated that they decided to hold it only every ten years. Amazingly, it still takes place, but has become an amateur event held every four years.

In 1903 the sports newspaper *L'Auto* launched the Tour de

France, and during the race the circulation went from 20,000 copies per day up to 65,000. By 1910 *L'Auto* was selling 200,000 copies a day during the Tour. Organising sporting events was a potentially lucrative business.

Delighted with the success of the Paris–Brest–Paris race, *Le Petit Journal* organised a running race from Paris to Belfort (a distance of 380km) a year later, and again saw a rise in circulation. Next they put on what they claimed to be the world's first motor race in 1894, from Paris to Rouen. Amusingly, the average speed of these early motor races was only 2kmh faster than the bikes in the Paris–Brest–Paris race three years earlier.

By 1900 *Le Petit Journal* was selling 2 million copies a day, but being a conservative paper, they made the mistake of adopting an anti-Dreyfus stance in the turmoil of the Dreyfus Affair (Dreyfus was a Jewish officer in the French army who was framed for spying by the establishment). The *Dreyfusards*, and there were many of them, abandoned *Le Petit Journal* for the staunchly neutral *Le Petit Parisien*, and *Le Petit Journal*'s circulation began a long decline from 2 million copies in 1900 to just 400,000 in 1919.

It's easy to see why, at the end of 1918, *Le Petit Journal* needed a boost in its fortunes. And it's easy to see why a programme of sporting events might be the way forward – it had worked in the past, it might work again. There was another aspect, too. Since their humiliating defeat at the hands of the Germans in the Franco-Prussian war of 1870–1, and the loss of Alsace and Lorraine as a consequence, the French had become obsessed with their perceived physical weakness and a steady decline in the birth rate. The great and the good of French society (who were doubtless the epitome of athletic prowess themselves) bemoaned the feeble state of the nation. Henri Desgrange, the man who ruled the Tour de France with an iron fist, described his pre-war fellow countrymen as 'tired, without muscle, without character, and without willpower'. His answer, in common with many of the French chattering classes, was basically to prescribe cross-country runs and cold showers.

So organising a series of sporting events immediately after the First World War seemed like a good way to boost circulation and celebrate French manliness in their victory over the Germans. There was also the perception that fit and healthy youngsters would make better soldiers in any future conflict. The Tour had proved to be the golden goose for *L'Auto*, the Giro for *La Gazzetta dello Sport*, and *Le Petit Journal* wanted its own version. But what? And where? And how?

A month after the armistice, in December 1918, *Le Petit Journal* published a short news item:

An Easter Festival of Sport

Let us simply announce that all sportsmen . . . aviators, cyclists, automobilists, footballers, boxers . . . all without exception will be interested in a series of events including a Tour of The Battlefields which will pass through the whole of Alsace, the whole of Lorraine, through martyred Belgium, through all those places whose chains have been broken by Victory.

Over the next few weeks the paper drip-fed the readership with more details of this Easter Festival of Sport. The events would be centred on Strasbourg and the newly reclaimed regions of Alsace and Lorraine where nearly 2 million additional potential readers lived. There would be a swimming race on the river at Strasbourg, there would be a cross-country running race around Strasbourg, as well as a football tournament for teams from liberated regions. There would also be a high-profile boxing match, some rugby, an athletics meeting, a motor race, and an air-race around the battlefields, as well as the cycling Circuit des Champs de Bataille, starting and finishing in Strasbourg.

Since losing Alsace and Lorraine to the Germans in 1871 the French, as a nation, had become fixated with getting them back. The loss of these parts of France was an outrage, a stain on the honour and pride of France. Alsace-Lorraine had also accounted for a significant percentage of France's industrial output (coal,

The front page of Le Petit Journal *from 5 January 1919, announcing the route of the Circuit des Champs de Bataille*

iron, steel and textiles) in the 1870s, so maybe the outrage was as much political and financial. Certainly, the majority of people of Alsace and Lorraine didn't seem too bothered one way or the other. They were given the choice in 1872 of staying put and becoming German citizens or remaining French citizens and being forced to emigrate. One and a half million stayed and became Germans, around 100,000 left and remained French.

The fact is that the French had taken Alsace and Lorraine from the Holy Roman Empire of the German Nation in the 17th and 18th centuries, so these areas were culturally more German than French. And barely 10 per cent of their population spoke French as their first language.

The upshot is that the French wanted Alsace and Lorraine back, and they got them in 1918. They were delighted and set about celebrating their return with visits from the Prime Minister and a rapid reintegration into French cultural life, part of which involved *Le Petit Journal*'s Easter of Sport. Of course, organising anything in the days immediately following the armistice was a tricky business. Millions of men were still in the army in early 1919, many great sportsmen and athletes had died or been seriously injured on the battlefields, and communications with distant parts of the country were extremely difficult.

But Alsace and Lorraine had remained relatively unscathed during the First World War, and Strasbourg was a big enough city to host sizeable sporting events. Football, rugby, swimming and athletics would not be a problem. But a bicycle race across the battlefields would be another matter entirely. That required a level of planning and organisation that would dwarf the Paris–Brest–Paris race, last held in 1911. A route needed to be decided upon and reconnoitred, checkpoints needed to be arranged, the cycling federations of France, Luxembourg and Belgium needed to be consulted, and the logistical problems of getting riders, commissaires, food, accommodation and reporters in the right places at the right times needed to be considered. Organising a two-week stage-race was a mammoth undertaking; organising one across a war zone with barely four months' notice was optimistic, to say the least.

We don't know precisely how the route for the Circuit des Champs de Bataille was decided upon because there is no documentary evidence to tell us. But it's reasonable to assume that basically it would be a race along the Western Front, from Nieuwport on the Belgian coast to Mulhouse near the Swiss border, but also taking in the newly liberated regions of Alsace and Lorraine. It's also fair to assume that the organisers wanted the race to take in the battlefields that were of major importance to the French, but they also wanted to include Belgium and Luxembourg in the *parcours* (race route). Whether the inclusion of Belgium and Luxembourg was a show of solidarity with others who had been occupied by Germany, or whether it was an acknowledgement that they needed riders from those countries to augment a severely depleted post-war French peloton, is hard to know.

Whatever the truth, the organisers came up with a rough anticlockwise route, starting and finishing in Strasbourg, and taking in Alsace, Lorraine, Luxembourg, Belgium, and the battlefields of north-eastern France. But no one back at *Le Petit Journal* in Paris had any real idea of what the roads were like in north-eastern France and Belgium at the end of the war. The roads prior to the war had been pretty poor, and after four years of warfare were only likely to be worse.

It's hard to imagine just how bad the roads were 100 years ago. We cyclists moan about potholes, chip-seal road surfaces, sunken drain-covers, over-banding, raised manhole-covers and all the other things local councils do to make our lives just that little bit more exciting, but really we have it very easy compared to our grandfathers or great-grandfathers.

In the early years of the twentieth century, when cycling and motor cars were in their infancy, the roads were built for horses, carts, wagons and pedestrians. In towns the roads were mostly cobbled (or *pavé* in French), while the main roads between towns and villages were usually macadam (hard-packed layers of road stones), which were not too bad if properly made and well maintained. Most minor roads were unmade, hard-packed dirt and gravel, which were OK for traffic that never went above walking-pace, but in bad weather turned into quagmires of mud, and in dry weather threw up clouds of choking dust.

The war zone was strictly off-limits until the end of 1918, and it was only in early 1919, when newspaper reporters accompanied Eugène Christophe (one of the great pre-war bike racers) on a recce for the Paris–Roubaix race in April 1919, that the full horror of the war zone became apparent. With only a week to go before the Circuit des Champs de Bataille started, it was too late for *Le Petit Journal* to cancel the race because riders had signed up, sponsors had committed, and cancelling it would have been a costly loss of face for the newspaper.

*

My interest in this long-forgotten bicycle race started when I stumbled across a very brief mention of it in a cycling history book. Having a love of cycling and a curiosity about the First World War (my great uncle Jack was killed at Passchendaele, and my grandfather fought on the Somme and at Ypres), I was intrigued and set about trying to find out more. The only information appeared to be in contemporary French and Belgian newspaper reports from April and May 1919, which described a race quite unlike anything else before or since.

Being a freelance journalist, I wrote a story about the Circuit des Champs de Bataille for *Rouleur* cycling magazine and as part of my research I mapped out the entire route on an online route-planner. I also read a lot about the First World War battlefields to try and get a feel of what it must have been like to race a bike across them only a few months after the armistice. As I looked at the route map the kernel of an idea began to form . . . By riding the route myself I could visit places where my relatives fought, I could see some of the lesser-known battlefields of the Western

Front, and I could cycle in the wheel-tracks of some of cycling's most extraordinary riders.

I was also curious to find out more about the Zone Rouge, the area of northern France designated by the French government immediately post-war as being so badly damaged by gas and shells during the war that it would never again be fit for habitation or cultivation. In 1919 the Zone Rouge covered 1,200km² of northern France, and it was across this devastated and deserted land that the Circuit des Champs de Bataille was raced. And although the Zone is smaller these days, there are still areas of northern France that are out of bounds due to the huge amount of unexploded ordnance, poisoned soil, and unrecovered bodies.

For the sake of verisimilitude I wanted to ride the route at the same time of year as the riders did it (late April to mid May). It might have been nicer to do the trip in summer, but somehow that felt like a bit of a cop-out. With around 2,000km to cover there was no way I was going to be able to manage it in the seven stages of the original race, so I needed to think about how to divide the route up into manageable pieces that would also allow time for visiting the battlefields. I also needed to think about how much time I could take, where I would stay, and what I needed to take with me on this unsupported trip.

PREPARATIONS

With the outline plan of the Circuit des Champs de Bataille decided upon, *Le Petit Journal* set about the complicated business of making it happen. Although they had experience in organising major sporting events before the war, things had changed radically in the last decade – communications, roads and transport were much improved, stage-racing had become more refined, and strong trade teams run by bicycle and tyre manufacturers had come to the fore. By 1914 *L'Auto* had organised 12 Tours de France and there had been six editions of the Giro d'Italia. Stage-racing was definitely here to stay.

The paper continued drip-feeding the readership details of the race, along with giving details of how to enter, how to apply for the relevant racing licence, and endless reminders to riders to bring their passports with them. The big news was the prize-money, announced at the beginning of January 1919. The winner would receive a whopping 6,000 French Francs, there would be 4,000FF for second place, 3,000FF for third, 2,000FF for fourth, down to 200FF for tenth place. The winner would receive 1,000FF more than the winner of that year's Tour de France, a race that was twice the length of the Circuit des Champs de Bataille. There were also cash prizes offered for each stage, with the stage winner getting 1,000FF, second place receiving 400FF, down to tenth place winning 100FF. Additionally, each rider would receive 10FF a day to cover their expenses.

In total, the official prize money amounted to 39,300FF. That was a huge sum in post-war France. The average wage for an unskilled manual labourer at the time was around 5FF a day, so the winner would get the equivalent of four years' wages, plus around nine months' wages per stage win. There were also additional prizes, both cash and in-kind, offered along the route by local councils and businesses. Even today, the best climber in the Arctic Race in Norway wins 500kg of salmon, stage winners at a recent Tour of Britain won a wheel of local cheese, and back in the 1970s a rider entered the Tour of Flanders specifically because there was a washing machine on offer for the first person over the Edelareberg, and his mum wanted one (which she got). Other odd prizes have included winning your own weight in beer, and in Haribo sweets.

With the French economy on its knees by the end of the war, having lost much of its industry in the north-east of the country and having spent $24 billion on the war effort, the prospects for young men coming out of the army were often pretty bleak in the short term. With the menfolk at war, many farms had barely functioned, or had lain fallow, so the farmers hurried back to their farms. Factory workers returned to work if their factories still survived and hadn't been turned over to the war effort, but French industry was in tatters. Although everyone was in a hurry to get back to the way things had been in 1914, that often wasn't possible.

Le Petit Journal knew that attracting riders might be a struggle, given the circumstances, hence the lavish prize fund. For those who didn't have to be back on the family farm or in the family business, the idea of earning three or four years' wages in the space of two weeks just for racing a bike would have been hugely appealing. There were other factors, too. The pre-war peloton had not fared well on the battlefields of France, and over 60 professional riders had died fighting for their country, including several Tour de France winners. Among the big names were Lucien Petit-Breton, François Faber (actually a Luxembourgois fighting in the French Foreign Legion), Octave Lapize, Henri Alavoine, François Lafourcade, Emile Engel and Camille Fily.

Maybe this was a chance for some of the lower-ranked riders who had survived the war to step up. There were also the riders who had been too young to join up, but were now old enough to race.

Behind the scenes *Le Petit Journal* contacted the Belgian and Luxembourg cycling federations to drum up interest in the race and to assist in arranging Stage starts and finishes, signposting, accommodation, checkpoints, provisioning, and suchlike. There was a huge amount of organisation needed, and *Le Petit Journal*'s limited experience with events like Paris–Brest–Paris just wasn't enough.

So the editor of *Le Petit Journal*, Marcel Allain (an extraordinary man who, as well as editing one of France's biggest newspapers, penned more than 400 novels, mostly in the hugely popular Fantômas series), did the sensible thing and approached Alphonse Steinès for help with the organisation. Steinès was Henri Desgrange's right-hand man at *L'Auto* and had experience organising the Paris–Roubaix race and the Tour de France. If anyone could help organise the Circuit des Champs de Bataille, it was Steinès.

Except that Steinès was a bare-faced liar and a bit of a sadist. He is most famous for persuading Henri Desgrange that the Tour de France should visit the high mountains of the Pyrenees. Desgrange was not convinced, so Steinès went off to recce a route for the 1910 Tour. It's a famous story, the gist of which is that he went to the Pyrenees, got lost on the rough tracks of the Tourmalet mountain, fell in a snow-drift in the dark, nearly froze to death, got rescued, then sent a telegram to Desgrange the next morning saying that the route was perfectly suitable for a cycle race. It really wasn't, because the 'roads' were tracks and the gradients were steeper than almost anyone could manage on a 1910 bike, but the Tour went there anyway. The following year Steinès took them over the Galibier in the Alps, a 33km slog rising 1,900m to an altitude of nearly 2,800m.

But Steinès was a big cheese in French cycling before the war. He was president of the Paris Cyclists' Union (one of the premier cycling clubs in France) and his work on the Tour meant that he had excellent contacts all over France and with national cycling federations around Europe. His work on the Paris–Roubaix race through north-eastern France meant he knew this area (and its cycling clubs) very well. On the face of it, Steinès seemed to be the perfect man for the job.

It is in some ways quite strange that Desgrange allowed his right-hand man to help organise a stage-race for another publication, albeit not a direct rival. But maybe Desgrange had pragmatic reasons to allow this – his Tour de France was going to resume in July 1919 and perhaps Steinès' reconnaissance for *Le Petit Journal* could be put to good use by *L'Auto*. Also, Desgrange had a financial interest in Le Parc des Princes, the outdoor velodrome in Paris where Stage 4 of the Circuit de Champs de Bataille was scheduled to finish. If that were full of paying customers, Desgrange would profit handsomely.

I also wonder whether Desgrange encouraged Steinès to plan a *parcours* so difficult that the race would be a total failure, thus preserving the prestige of the Tour and keeping *L'Auto* at the top of the pile. Desgrange may have been worried that the big teams might jump ship to the Circuit des Champs de Bataille if it proved to be a success, not least because multi-geared bikes were allowed (they wouldn't be allowed in the Tour until 1937), and the bike manufacturers were keen to expand this sector of the market.

By February 1919 *Le Petit Journal* was beginning to publish details of the rules for the race. Again, Steinès probably had a hand in this as a senior member of the Union Vélocipédique Française (the French national cycling federation) and president of the Paris Cyclists' Union. As was the norm in those days, the rules were draconian and the stage lengths were immense (300+km), which ensured that most races were horrendous tests of endurance.

Early bike racing was supposed to be a test of the individual man and his machine against the other competitors, the terrain and the elements, and the racers were therefore expected to be self-sufficient. Generally speaking, they had to carry out all repairs to their own bikes and were not allowed any outside help, even from other members of the same cycling team. In those days more than a few highly rated racers owed their success as much to their abilities with a spanner as to pure athletic prowess. Being the fastest rider is not much use if it takes you 20 minutes to change a tyre.

The rules laid down by *Le Petit Journal*, in association with the French, Belgian and Luxembourg cycling federations, were pretty much in accordance with how other races at the time were controlled. The important ones were:

- The winner would be decided on the shortest elapsed time. (Between 1906 and 1912 the Tour de France had been decided on a points system, but then reverted back to timings.)
- Riders had to start and finish on the same bike. A numbered lead seal was attached to each bike frame to ensure no swapping went on.
- Riders could not accept any help from anyone else, even from those on the same team, 'whether organised or fortuitous'.
- They could only mend their bikes with whatever they had with them.
- Riders were permitted to use bikes with multiple gears, unlike in the Tour de France, where riders only had two gears (changed by removing the back wheel and flipping it round to a different-sized cog on the other side of the wheel).
- There would be equal provisioning for all riders, laid on by the organisers, at a *parc fermé* set up midway through each stage. They had five minutes in which to eat their allotted refreshments (six slices of bread with cheese, two mutton chops or chicken drumsticks, and some fruit). In addition to refreshment in the *parc fermé*, riders were given two *bidons* of drinks and 'solid provisions' to consume *en route*.
- The organisers laid on mechanics in the *parc fermé* to assist riders. This was the only outside help allowed.

- The pacing of other riders was banned, but they were allowed to exchange tyres, food and drink amongst themselves.
- And NO Germans, NO Austrians, NO Hungarians. 'We saw too much of them during the war. Our prizes will be reserved for our lads, the cyclists of France, and for their friends and allies,' proclaimed the paper.

As was the norm, the rules were there to make sure that each rider effectively rode a solo race and had to rely on his own strength, endurance and mechanical abilities. *Le Petit Journal* also did its best to close the gap between the powerful sponsored teams and the independents (*isolés*). Before the war the big teams supplied their riders with far better food (and performance-enhancing drugs) than the *isolés* had, and weren't above bending the rules on pacing and assistance. They were big advertisers with big budgets, so they rarely got properly punished. Not that *Le Petit Journal* needed to worry too much, since in 1919 none of the big French bike or tyre manufacturers was in a position to fund teams, so Alcyon, Armor, Automoto, Clément, La Française, Gladiator, Griffon, Hurtu, Labor, Liberator, Peugeot and Thomann all joined forces to form one super-team – La Sportive, which sponsored most of the French professional peloton until it was disbanded in 1922.

Henri Desgrange at *L'Auto* fought an ongoing battle to prevent the big teams, such as Alcyon and Peugeot, monopolising the Tour de France and detracting from the spectacle. (He moaned later, in 1929, that his race 'has been won by a corpse', Maurice Dewaele, such was the level of assistance given to him by his Alcyon team, and by other riders who helped in exchange for a brown envelope of cash at the end of the day.) But *Le Petit Journal* was more concerned with signing up enough riders to make it a race. Racing bicycles and tyres were in very short supply, many riders still had not been de-mobbed from the army, and very few riders were in any condition to undertake a tough two-week race, having spent four years on the battlefields.

By the middle of February, the race had attracted just ten entrants, which must have been a worryingly small number as far as the organisers were concerned. However, one of those ten was Jean Alavoine, a man who had six Tour de France stage wins on his *palmarès* before the war. He was a very successful racer, a climbing specialist who had ridden for the Alcyon, Armor and Peugeot teams pre-war, and was signed to the Bianchi-Pirelli team in 1919. His brother, Henri, was also an accomplished racer pre-war but had been killed in a flying accident in 1916. Interestingly, although many army regiments had cycling battalions made up of lightly armed but extremely mobile troops, very few pro cyclists enlisted in them during the First World War. Instead many of them became pilots in the Service Aéronautique, or dispatch-riders for their local regiments. Other cycling pilots who perished in the war included Tour-winner Octave Lapize, François Lafourcarde, Leon Hourlier, Aimé Behaeghe, Leon Comès, Albert Delrieu, Emile Quaissard and Emile Guyon.

Alavoine was something of a coup for the organisers, a big-name rider who had finished on the podium twice at pre-war Tours. Other racers who had signed up were the Belgian hotshot Charles Deruyter and the eccentric Tunisian Ali Neffati, but the rest were relative unknowns. The slow uptake for the race was probably due to the demobilisation process of the French army. Although the armistice of 11 November 1918 brought a halt to hostilities, a state of war would continue to exist until the Treaty of Versailles was actually signed (which eventually happened on 28 June 1919). If the Germans refused to sign, then hostilities could break out again, and France did not want to be caught napping for a second time. But there were still 5 million men desperate to get home to their former lives.

The solution for the French army was to de-mob the older soldiers first, so by April 1919 everyone aged 30 or over, as well as those with six or more living children, had been de-mobbed. Everyone under 30 was obliged to remain in the army until the Germans signed the peace agreement. That included a significant proportion of the pro peloton, many of whom weren't released until the autumn of 1919. Not that a rider necessarily had to be de-mobbed in order to race. Although most racing was suspended during the war, some still took place, and some riders were given leave from their army or air force units in order to compete.

So it's hardly surprising that by mid February 1919 only a few riders had signed up. Most were not sure when they were likely to be de-mobbed, or if they could get their hands on a suitable bike, or if they could attract any sponsorship. Even the well-established Tour de France struggled to attract a decent field that year, with just 65 riders taking to the start line in July. Nonetheless, *Le Petit Journal* redoubled its efforts, and its column-inches, in an effort to attract more entries.

There was also, it would appear, some chicanery going on in the cycling world. *Le Petit Journal* makes reference to 'tendentious rumours circulated by colleagues' about the race. It seemed that there were people who didn't want the Circuit des Champs de Bataille to be a success. We can't be sure who those people were, but we can assume that the organisers of other races (the Tour, Paris–Roubaix, the Tour of Flanders, etc.) didn't want one of the largest French newspapers muscling in on their territory. The word 'colleagues' would seem to confirm that. These nefarious colleagues may even have put pressure on the cycling-team managers not to support the event, for fear of being excluded from other, more high-profile, races. There was certainly a whispering campaign against the Circuit des Champs de Bataille, with rumours circulating throughout February and March that the race was going to be cancelled. With hindsight, maybe it should have been.

In a desperate effort to attract more riders and to get the bike manufacturers on-side, *Le Petit Journal* made an announcement in the middle of March that they were adding another prize: a constructor's trophy for the marque that finished first. And the prize was for 12,000FF. Except that it wasn't a cash prize, it was 12,000FF worth of advertising in *Le Petit Journal*. The paper attempted to dress this up as a big deal, and as a way of levelling the playing field for the smaller manufacturers, but it was a prize that effectively cost them nothing at a time when they were struggling for advertising revenue anyway. That said, for impoverished bike manufacturers working hard to get their businesses going again, this was certainly an incentive, and by late March the number of entries was up to 40. Admittedly they were mostly over-30s or Belgians, but momentum was growing.

By modern standards, the early professional riders (and the enthusiastic amateurs) were an extraordinary bunch of tough, determined eccentrics, but then early racing was tough and eccentric. The massively long stages, poor roads, primitive bikes, and stringent regulations meant that road racing was the preserve of the hardy and resourceful. Take, for instance, Eugène Christophe. When his forks snapped on the Tourmalet in 1913 he carried his bike seven miles down the mountain to a black-smith's forge where he mended them himself (although he was penalised for allowing the blacksmith's assistant to operate the bellows for him). After he missed out on a Tour win for the third time, again thanks to snapped forks, the Tour organisers had a whip-round for the unfortunate Christophe among the readers of *L'Auto*. It raised over 13,000FF, more than twice what he would have got for actually winning the Tour.

While everybody loved Christophe, almost no one liked Henri Pélissier, a garrulous racer during the 1920s who was constantly arguing with anyone and everyone. His long-suffering wife eventually shot herself, and shortly afterwards his mistress used the same gun to shoot Pélissier dead.

Henri Van Lerberghe was another marvellous eccentric, a Belgian well known for his doomed solo breakaways. During the 1919 Tour of Flanders he took so many drugs, and drank so much alcohol, that he finished the race unable to ride, or stand unaided. He still won by 14 minutes. While leading the 1919 Paris–Roubaix, Pélissier was held up by a stationary train at a railway crossing. With the peloton closing in behind, he shouldered his bike, climbed through a carriage full of people, dropped down the other side, and carried on racing. He won.

Few of those early racers were mentally tougher than Lucien Buysse. His daughter died while he was away riding the 1926 Tour, but he was persuaded by his family to keep riding. He missed his daughter's funeral, but won the Tour.

When Paul Duboc was handed a poisoned drink on the 1911 Tour he collapsed into a ditch with vomiting and diarrhoea. A race official stayed with him by the side of the road . . . to make sure he didn't get any outside assistance. Gustave Garrigou, suspected of the poisoning, had to ride through Duboc's home town of Rouen wearing a disguise because fans had been known to attack and beat the rivals of their favourite rider. Indeed, the fans in those days were a lawless bunch who thought nothing of resorting to violence to aid their hero or hinder a competitor. On several occasions in the early days of the Tour the commissaires had to fire shots in the air to disperse angry crowds trying to attack riders with clubs and rocks. During an early Giro d'Italia the organisers used whips to disperse belligerent spectators.

The early days of bike racing were pretty extraordinary. Without the all-seeing eye of TV and a million mobile phones, cheating and chicanery were much easier to get away with. On stage races there were usually a couple of commissaire's cars on the route, and there were checkpoints set up (usually near a railway station so that officials could get around the course), but it was possible to go for hours without seeing a commissaire. So getting a tow from a car, or hitching a lift in a lorry, wasn't likely to be seen by race officials, although there were sometimes semi-official spies posted along the course.

Cheating was also made possible by the horribly early start times. As most races were organised by newspapers, they needed stages to finish by late afternoon so that the results could be published in the following day's paper. But because stages were routinely more than 300km long and often took 12 hours to complete, they often started in the early hours of the morning, before sunrise. Usually the peloton rode *piano* (a steady, relaxed pace) behind the lead commissaire's car until it got light, before the attacks started, but it wasn't uncommon for riders to use the darkness to cover their shortcuts, tows and trips to the train station (Maurice Garin was stripped of his 1904 Tour win for completing most of one stage by train). Nor was it uncommon for riders to carry a handful of carpet tacks for use in slowing down a competitor closing from behind.

But one thing that wasn't considered cheating was the use of performance-enhancing drugs. Everyone was using drugs of one sort or another in those days, often in cocktails that make today's steroid-abuse in sport look like child's play. Take, for instance, the *Pot Belge*. This was a mixture of some, or all, of the following: alcohol, cocaine, caffeine, amphetamines, heroin, analgesics, morphine, and even strychnine. It was usually swigged from a small bottle that the rider carried with him, and most often used in the final hours of a stage for a bit of extra ooomph. Tying an ether-soaked handkerchief around the neck was another way of dulling the pain.

During the 1925 Tour the ever-argumentative Henri Pélissier, and his brother Francis, abandoned after yet another row with Desgrange and gave an interview to a newspaper reporter. 'We run on dynamite,' they said, and to illustrate their point they produced a stash of pills and potions. 'Cocaine for our eyes, chloroform for our gums, and horse-liniment for our knees . . . At night, in our rooms, we can't sleep. We twitch and dance and jig about as though we're doing St Vitus' Dance.'

The glazed, vacant, 1,000-yard stare that you see in the faces of bike riders from those days is the product of extreme exhaustion and truly epic quantities of drugs. To make matters worse, riders in those days thought that water inhibited their digestion, so they drank very little compared to modern sportsmen, and what they did drink was usually alcoholic (it was much safer to drink than the water generally available at the time). The rest days, which came between each stage, must have been spent trying to recover

27

from the worst hangovers imaginable. A handy side-effect of taking these drugs was that not only could the riders race for 14 hours a day, but the drugs also made the riding conditions more bearable. The dust, ruts, mud and potholes that predominated were rendered more manageable when the riders were basically anaesthetised.

In mid March 1919, *Le Petit Journal* got a telegram from Steinès, who was out reconnoitring the *parcours* and arranging checkpoints. In classic Steinès fashion he wrote: 'The roads are possible, but very hard. The winning bicycle will be a machine outside the normal mould.' This wasn't the big fat lie of the 1910 Tourmalet episode, but it didn't really offer a fair assessment of the conditions along the route.

Steinès wasn't the only one out looking at the roads of north-eastern France. Eugène Christophe, possibly the most famous cyclist to survive the war, along with a couple of journalists, went to recce the route of the 1919 Paris–Roubaix race due to take place on 20 April. That race would have to skirt the Somme battlefield, traverse the battlefields of Artois, and ride through the remnants of Arras and Lens. Roubaix had been behind German lines throughout the war, but that didn't stop them looting anything of value and destroying the stuff they couldn't steal, including the old velodrome. *Le Petit Journal* reported:

> From Doullens onwards the countryside is nothing but desolation. The shattered trees look vaguely like skeletons, the roads have collapsed and been potholed or torn away by shells. The vegetation, rare, has been replaced by military vehicles in a pitiful state. The houses of villages are no more than bare walls. At their foot, heaps of rubble. Eugène Christophe exclaimed: 'Here, this really is the hell of the North.'

Another report, by Victor Breyer at *L'Auto*, stated:

> We enter into the centre of the battlefield. There is not a tree,

everything is flattened! Not a square metre that has not been hurled upside down. There's one shell-hole after another. The only things that stand out in this churned earth are the crosses with their ribbons of blue, white and red. It is hell.

To give you an idea of just how bad things were, of the 40 motor vehicles accompanying the Paris–Roubaix race in April 1919, only 5 made it to Roubaix. Unsurprisingly, that year's race was the slowest in its history, such was the terrible state of the roads. Nine of the top 25 finishers had already signed up for the Circuit des Champs de Bataille, along with at least two riders who abandoned the race somewhere between Amiens and Doullens.

The Circuit des Champs de Bataille was due to start a week later, and included some of the Paris–Roubaix route plus the battlefields of the Marne, Aisne, Flanders, Argonne, Verdun, Saint-Mihiel and the Vosges. As they struggled into Roubaix after a gruelling 12 hours racing across the battlefields, those riders who had signed up for both races must have been wondering what the hell they were letting themselves in for.

By 27 April 1919, most of the riders who had registered for the Circuit des Champs de Bataille had arrived in Strasbourg. Most, but not all, because 49 of the 138 who had signed up didn't have a valid racing licence or hadn't been de-mobbed, and were therefore not allowed to take to the start line. Considering that the paper had published almost daily reminders that riders had to have an appropriate racing licence, clearly many of them took no notice. The organisers also needed to see proper documentation regarding each rider's military status. Those who had been de-mobbed had to prove it, and those who hadn't needed official permission to ride in the race. But at least 14 of them subsequently got their collective act together and had their paperwork complete before scrutineering (a technical inspection of their bikes) in Strasbourg the day before the race was due to start. There was also a pretty high drop-out rate – only 87 turned up in Strasbourg with their bikes and paperwork in order.

Jean Alavoine   Urbain Anseeuw   Maurice Brocco

Lucien Buysse   Charles Deruyter   Oscar Egg

René Guénot   Hector Heusghem   André Huret

Charles Kippert   Séraphin Morel   Ali Neffati

Ernest Paul   José Pelletier   Jules Van Hevel

Henri Vanlerberghe   Alois Verstraeten   Marcel Allain

It seems likely that the reports, and experiences, of the Paris–Roubaix competitors may have caused a few riders to rethink, and the organisers must have become increasingly worried as the full extent of the challenge became clear.

★

They weren't the only ones. What had seemed like a good idea six months previously, in a vague pub-plan sort of way, was becoming a slightly daunting reality. As a not-particularly-fit 55-year-old MAMIL (Middle-Aged Man In Lycra), 1,400 miles in 3 weeks would be hard, but not impossible. I'd ridden over 100 miles in a day on a couple of occasions, and I regularly ride 60 miles from London to Cambridge to visit my mum, so I knew I could do that much, but 70 miles a day, day after day? Various non-cycling friends thought I was mad, but it really shouldn't be that difficult to ride those sorts of distances in the space of a day.

With the original route mapped out on my online route-planner of choice (ridewithgps.com), I set about planning my trip in chunks of about 75 miles a day. That would give me a decent amount of time to meander along, stop and see the sights, and still get to a hotel by late afternoon. By staying in cheap hotels and B&Bs I didn't have to do the camping thing, and I could hope for washing facilities and a decent night's sleep.

The first problem was that many of the roads they used in 1919 have since become major A-roads, dual carriageways, and even motorways. I wanted to stick as closely as I could to the original route, but not at the expense of becoming a bonnet-ornament for a speeding Renault van, so quite a lot of time was spent looking at alternative roads and cross-checking on Google Street View to see whether I was choosing a dirt track, a pleasant B-road, or a horrible HGV-infested short-cut.

Stage 1, from Strasbourg to Luxembourg, proved surprisingly simple. No motorways or terrifying A-roads, no need for diversions, just a stop for the night in Sareguemines and Metz, and the job's a good 'un. Stage 2 was less good, with the N4 from Arlon to Bastogne being four lanes of speeding traffic and no hard shoulder or cycle path. The alternative was through the hills and valleys to the east, adding many extra miles and a shed-load more climbing, or by getting an early-morning train for 20 miles west to Neufchâteau and riding a relatively flat route from there.

Several days were spent in this way, checking elevation profiles and distances, zooming around Google Street View, and searching for cheap hotels in obscure parts of eastern France. And I have to admit, I loved it. I'm a planner. I like a plan. And I like to pore over maps. I think it's a middle-aged-man thing. I haven't quite got to the stage of discussing, at every social gathering, the best route to get from home to the venue of said social gathering, but it won't be long now.

Anyway, after a few days I had a route that was as close as possible (within reason) to the original route, and which also featured three 'rest days' where I would get to sleep in the same bed for two nights running and mooch around on my bike without my luggage. Brussels, Paris and Verdun were to be my days off, although the Brussels rest day would be spent riding some of the iconic cobbled climbs of the Tour of Flanders, and the Verdun rest day would include 50 miles of battlefield touring.

I also threw in a couple of diversions to go and look at things that weren't on the 1919 route. The original *parcours* had to skirt around a couple of areas that were particularly badly affected by the war, but which I wanted to visit – the Chemin des Dames battlefield east of Soissons, and the Champagne-Argonne battlefields between Reims and Verdun. In 1919 no proper roads existed any more in these areas and the race was forced to bypass them.

With the route pretty much planned, the dates decided upon (late April to mid May, to roughly match the time of year of the race) and cheap hotels and B&Bs provisionally booked, I turned my attention to hardware and softwear – the bike and clothing. There's a popular expression amongst cyclists that the correct number of bikes to own is N+1, where N equals the number of bikes currently owned. I don't subscribe to this at all. I have three bikes, and that's all I need (or want). One is a crappy old single-speed clunker made from bits I found lying around in the shed, which I'm happy to leave locked up in public, knowing it's very unlikely to get nicked. Another is my mountain bike, which I use for getting muddy and taking the dog for a run. And the other is my proper bike, the result of careful thought and consideration, and a desire for one bike to rule them all.

Clearly, I wasn't going to ride round Europe on a 15kg single-speed home-made Frankenbike. Nor was I going to ride an MTB for 1,400 miles in 3 weeks. No, I was going to go touring on my titanium-framed 7.5kg 22-speed Spin Spitfire MkIII race bike, because that bike and I have history. We've done stuff together, we have a bond. Well, *I* have a bond, *it's* just a collection of metal, carbon-fibre and plastic parts. But when I look at it I don't just see a lovely-looking bike, I'm transported to the places we've been and the experiences we've had – a dusty afternoon on the Carrefour des l'Arbres, a beautiful summer's morning on the Col d'Aspin, sweltering days slogging up the Alpe d'Huez and Mont Ventoux, a joyous swoop down the slopes of the Tourmalet, grinding up the Stelvio in the snow. For me, the Spin is a repository of joyful memories shared with friends and family, and I wanted to add the Circuit des Champs de Bataille to our *palmarès*.

Given that I wasn't about to attach panniers and a rack to the Spin, I needed to think about alternative ways of carrying some luggage. I'd previously done a four-day trip in France with a friend using just a backpack, but it was pretty tough on the shoulders and not particularly satisfactory. For a three-week trip I would want more stuff than I could comfortably fit in a backpack, so I needed something else. The answer came from the mentalists who take part in races like the Transcontinental – bikepacking. Originally a means of lightweight off-road touring on mountain bikes, bikepacking has expanded to road cycling and offers a modicum of carrying capacity but without the bulk and weight of a full touring 'rig'. Essentially bikepacking means fitting a large saddle-bag on the back of the bike and a bag strapped to the handlebars, plus maybe a frame-bag as well.

After a fair bit of internet searching, reading reviews, and asking questions, I opted for kit from Apidura, a British company making good-quality bikepacking equipment at reasonable prices. I got their mid-size saddle-bag and their compact bar-bag, giving me 23 litres of storage, in addition to my small 15-litre Kriega backpack. The Apidura bags are designed to be water-resistant rather than completely waterproof, due to the way they are stitched, so I also bought a couple of lightweight drybags that are completely waterproof and allow you to compress everything down to its smallest size before being rammed into the Apidura bags.

The author's Spin Spitfire in touring trim, with Apidura bikepacking bags

Obviously I needed to go on a shake-down run with my bike and kit a month or so before I was due to do the real thing. I needed to find out what worked and what didn't, whether consecutive 75-mile days were manageable, and what else I might need to take with me. Which is how I came to be lying in a muddy puddle beside a canal outside Birmingham in the rain.

Six weeks before heading for France I left my home in north London to visit my kids – one was at university in Birmingham, one was at university in Manchester, and one works as a junior doctor in Lancaster. I could spend one night with each of them, stopping off to stay with some old friends near Nottingham en route. I could even do most of the leg between Birmingham and Nottingham on canal tow-paths. Sweet.

London to Birmingham was absolutely fine, but Birmingham to Nottingham turned out to be one of my most calamitous days on a bike. For a start, the sat-nav (in cahoots with my online route-planner) contrived to direct me around parts of central Birmingham that I hope never to see again, in search of the correct canal tow-path. When I eventually found it, and was heading in roughly the right direction, I had the good fortune to share it with a number of interesting people. Some of them were drinking Tennant's Extra at 9 a.m., some were asleep on (or at least near) benches, and some were just getting their crack-pipes fired up for the first hit of the day. A couple of young Peaky Blinders with the nearest thing I've ever seen to Cerberus, the three-headed devil-dog, eyed my shiny expensive bike in a disturbingly acquisitive manner. I was reminded of the adverts for small hand-guns that used to run in the cycling press in the early days – 'The Cyclist's Friend, No Rider Should be Without One, I Fear No Tramp, 12 shillings including 100 Rounds of Ammunition'. As Cerberus strained at his leash (a chain of Brunelian proportions) and the two lads leered menacingly at me, I pedalled on with unseemly haste, wishing I was packing my Cyclist's Friend.

Once out of Birmingham, the scenery changed from deserted grey factories and graffitied flyovers to overhanging trees and damp leafy greenery. Being March, the tow-path was pretty waterlogged and quite muddy, but my 25mm road tyres seemed able to cope quite well and I squelched along at a fairly decent pace. Until I rode through a larger-than-usual puddle which, I later discovered, contained a brick. The bike stopped dead and I was launched into the air, performing a mid-air flip that would have scored me straight 4.9s from the judges, had I not fluffed my landing. Instead I came down like a sack of spuds with a sort of splat-oooff noise. *Sploooff!*

In my younger days I used to be a motorcycle journalist, and I learned that when you crash (as you most assuredly will), you need to take a moment before you get to your feet. There's a curious thing that happens when you crash, to do with your perception of time and space. At first everything seems to be in slow motion, and you seem to be viewing your crash as a slightly detached observer, then in a flash you're back in your body and going straight to the scene of your accident, with broken stuff flying in all directions. When you think it's all stopped, count to ten before getting to your feet. This is to stop you from standing up while still travelling at 20mph, or from jumping to your feet only to discover you've broken both your ankles.

So I lay in the mud for a few moments, reflecting on my own stupidity and wondering how badly damaged the bike was. As far as I could tell I was mostly unscathed, but I really hoped I hadn't broken the bike in any significant way. As it happened, all I had were a few bruises and the bike was fine except for a front puncture. I brushed as much mud off myself as possible, replaced the front inner tube with a spare, and carried on as before. And it was all very pleasant – countrysidey, not on the nearby A38, and with the occasional canal boat, moorhen and lock to look at as I passed.

This bucolic idyll lasted nearly 15 whole minutes before I became aware of a hissing noise from the front tyre. Arse! Another puncture, this time from a thorn. I used the final spare inner tube, but wasn't particularly worried because I had multiple patches I could use if I was unlucky enough to get a third puncture. Which happened half a mile later, except this was both tyres punctured.

What I hadn't realised was that the council had been along the canal tow-path fairly recently and cut back the hawthorn hedges with a giant strimmer that had scattered thousands of thorns across the path. For miles and miles.

I fished out my two punctured inner tubes with a view to patching them and carrying on, but it was at this point I realised my basic, but catastrophic, error – no bike pump. I generally use CO_2 canisters and an inflator nozzle to pump up tyres after a puncture (quick and easy compared to a manual pump), and use my floor-standing track pump to inflate tyres at home. Now I had four punctured tubes, only two CO_2 canisters left, no way to find out where the tubes were punctured, and thus no way of fixing them.

Like a total idiot I spent several minutes blowing furiously into the valves, trying to get enough air into them so that I could then dip them in the canal to identify the punctures from the stream of bubbles. Not enough air, no bubbles, frozen blue hands, red sweaty face. Swearing. 'HOW COULD I BE SO STUPID?' I shouted. I consulted the sat-nav and discovered that a couple of miles along the tow-path was a canal-side pub and a main road. I then called Joe, my middle son at Birmingham University, and asked him if he could sack-off work on his dissertation and meet me at the pub with a few spares.

An hour later Joe arrived in the pub car park with a bootful of bike stuff. As well as bringing a track pump and a handful of CO_2 canisters, he'd also cannibalised his Cannondale to bring me four intact inner tubes. By the time my bike was back in one piece it was mid afternoon and I was hours behind schedule, so Joe gave me a lift another 30 miles up the road in the car. It was now pretty much dark and it was pouring with rain as I covered the last 20 miles on firm, smooth, unthorny tarmac. Joy.

From Nottingham to Manchester it just rained and rained and rained, but I discovered which of my waterproof stuff worked and which didn't. From Manchester to Lancaster was clear blue skies and chilly, and I learned that my bike was quite heavy when it came to climbing short, steep ascents through the Forest of Bowland.

Back home in London, I considered my set-up. The Spin runs Campagnolo 11-speed Chorus with a compact chainset and a 12/29 cassette (for the non-cyclists, that means it has 22 gears, which range from low enough to get me up just about any mountain to high enough not to spin out below 35mph). The 34 × 29 bottom gear would easily get me over the climbs I would encounter on the trip, primarily the Ballon d'Alsace in the Vosges mountains, so there were no concerns there.

I have three sets of wheels for the Spin – winter, spring/autumn/mountain, and summer. The summer ones are beautiful Spin 40mm carbon rims, but not ideally suited for lugging an extra 8kg of luggage around. The winter ones are a bit basic and heavy, but the spring/autumn ones are absolutely lovely – H Plus Sons Archetype rims, Chris King R45 hubs, and Sapim CX Ray spokes (24 front, 28 rear) built up by Strada down in Worthing. I would definitely use the Archetypes, and I had spare spokes (front, drive-side and non-drive-side) in case of any incidents.

I was going to use my winter tyre of choice (Continental 4 Seasons) because they are pretty sturdy and puncture resistant, but without losing suppleness and 'feel'. After the tow-path debacle I did contemplate running tubeless tyres, but in the end decided against it. I was certainly not planning on going anywhere near a tow-path any time soon, and in the event of a tear in a tubeless tyre you need to replace the whole thing or run it with an inner tube.

The only other change was to the pedals. I planned on doing a fair amount of trudging around battlefields, which isn't ideal in a pair of road shoes with SPD-SL cleats (the clips on the bottom of the shoes which clip into the pedals). So I bought some MTB shoes with two-bolt SPDs and fitted some cheapo touring pedals to the bike. The Spin now weighed in at 7.7kg, and around 15kg with luggage.

Compared to a race bike from 1919, this is incredibly lightweight and efficient – the difference between a Sopwith Camel and a Cessna Citation. In 1919 the race bikes were big, heavy old things by modern standards. They were made from steel, had big frames with a high bottom-bracket (the bit where the pedals attach to the frame) for ground clearance and rarely had more than two gears. The wheels used wooden rims, usually maple, and were normally laced with 32 steel spokes at the front and 40 at the back to withstand the intense pummelling they got. Tyres were pneumatic tubulars (where the inner tube is sewn inside the tyre, and the tyre is then glued to the rim), and the brake blocks were made from cork.

But it's the gearing of those old bikes that is the killer for us modern cyclists. My Spin's 22 gears give me a range of gear-inches (the distance travelled forward with one rotation of the pedals) from 31.7 inches in the lowest gear (34×29) to 112.5 inches in the highest gear (50×12). By contrast, most 1919 bikes usually ran something like a 48×17, giving around 75 inches. This was a horrible compromise that meant climbing at a shockingly slow cadence and spinning furiously on flat, smooth roads. Some riders used bikes with two cogs on each side of the rear hub, giving four gears, but even then they couldn't use a wide range of ratios because they didn't yet have the technology to tension the chain correctly (a bit of fore and aft adjustment at the horizontal rear drop-out was the limited solution).

Because the roads in the early twentieth century were pretty bad, race bikes tended to be engineered to last, and thus were weighty machines. They usually tipped the scales at around 12kg unladen, but then the rider would have to carry enough tools and spares (chain links, spoke key, etc.) in his bar-bag to fix his bike as he raced, as well as several spare tyres looped around his shoulders and a *musette* (bag) over his shoulder for carrying food, drugs, carpet tacks and maybe a pistol. The total weight of the bike was sometimes as much as 20kg, compared to my 15kg all-up weight, and the 6.8kg that the modern peloton is limited to. The riders' personal effects, such as they were, were transported by the race organisers in trucks and could be collected at the end of each stage.

The riding gear was also unbelievably primitive by modern standards. These days we have padded, multi-panel Lycra bib-shorts (shorts with shoulder-straps to keep them up), wicking base-layers, breathable mid-layers and Gore-Tex outer layers that keep the rain out. In 1919 they had a cotton base-layer, a woollen jersey or two, and a pair of lightly padded woollen cycling shorts. If they were lucky they might also have a waxed-cotton jacket and some waxed-cotton mittens. Some, particularly immediately post-war, wore long-johns and puttees, much as they did in the trenches. That was it. If it got wet it got heavy, it got misshapen, and it offered little in the way of protection or on-bike comfort.

My riding kit for the trip would consist of a short-sleeved base-layer, a short-sleeved jersey, bib-shorts, fingerless gloves (bizarrely called mitts in cycling), socks and riding shoes. On the bike I planned on fitting a tool/spares *bidon*, drinks *bidon*, sat-nav, lights and luggage. Into the saddle-bag would go one set of civvies (T-shirt, trousers, underwear, socks, trainers), spare bib-shorts, a long-sleeved jersey, a long-sleeved base-layer, knee-warmers, warm socks, overshoes and warm gloves.

Meanwhile, in the handlebar-bag would be a waterproof jacket, more spares (inner tubes, CO_2 canisters, pump and spare spokes), carb and protein bars, chargers, plug and adaptor, chammy cream and toiletries. Finally, in my small Kriega back-pack would go my passport, phone, wallet, medical kit, small USB power-bank, Kindle, snacks and small bottle of water.

This was the set-up I used for my Tour des Enfants (except for the pump, obviously), and it had worked pretty well. I had just enough different clothing to make sure I could wear something clean and dry in the evenings while that day's riding kit was washed and drying, but not so much as to add too much bulk and weight. The abysmal weather had allowed me to test a variety of clothing options, and for wet weather I eventually opted for my long-sleeved Castelli Gabba jacket with the rather odd Rapha soft-shell base-layer underneath on the grounds that almost nothing will keep the rain out for 8 hours, so at least keep warm while you're wet. Assos bib-shorts and Castelli NanoFlex leg-warmers worked well for the bottom half, and Castelli over-shoes kept my feet reasonably dry.

For drier weather I had the option of long-sleeved base-layer and long-sleeved jersey, or short-sleeved base-layer and short-sleeved jersey. Come rain or shine, 10°C to 30°C, I pretty much had it covered.

The Apidura luggage and SeaToSummit drybags combo proved to be absolutely brilliant – easy to attach, very well made, 100 per cent waterproof, and reasonably solid once mounted. Fully loaded, the saddle-pack does move slightly from side to side (it attaches to the saddle-rails and around the seat-post) as you pedal, but it's only noticeable if you get out of the saddle and pedal hard, and even then it's not exactly a problem.

By mid April the bike was fettled and anything that might wear out in the next 1,500 miles had been replaced (tyres, chain and cassette). The long-range forecast for north-eastern France and Belgium predicted changeable conditions but temperatures be-tween 12°C and 17°C, which meant I wouldn't be needing any deep-winter riding gear. The folly of that particular decision would only become apparent in the snow of the Ardennes a week or so later.

The final piece of the jigsaw was booking myself and my bike onto the Eurostar to Paris and then a TGV to Strasbourg, the departure point for the Circuit des Champs de Bataille. Booking the Eurostar is a doddle, but getting your bike onto a TGV is incredibly complicated because you get passed around several different departments of the SNCF (the French national train line) before ending up back where you started. SNCF used to have an office in Piccadilly, which was brilliant because you could sit down face-to-face with a real person and they would book and print your tickets there and then. Sadly, the office has gone, and now you have to do it over the phone with someone in France who'd rather not be dealing with complicated booking requests from stupid Englishmen.

After much faffing about, being put on hold, and transferred to different departments, I finally spoke to someone who explained that bikes are not generally allowed on TGVs (unless dismantled and put in a big box), but one operator had a limited number of trains that could accommodate me and my bike to Strasbourg. The booking was made, and finally I was ready to go.

STAGE 1

Strasbourg to Luxembourg

275km

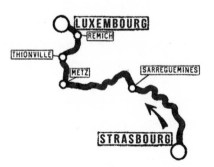

28 April 1919

The scene inside the Grand Café de l'Univers in Strasbourg's Place Broglie was chaotic. Although it was 5 a.m. and still dark outside, the lights inside were blazing and dozens of bike racers were jostling and queuing to sign in and get their *dossards* (race numbers) from the commissaires seated at the far end. The windows dripped with condensation and the air was thick with tobacco smoke, muttered conversations, and greetings shouted across the crowd. At the bar, groups of riders took a glass or two of brandy to keep out the cold, and discussed the events of the previous weekend's Paris–Roubaix race.

'Anyone know why Defraye abandoned after Amiens?' asked one.

'Not really his kind of race, is it? He's better in the mountains than he is on the flat stuff,' replied another.

'And where are the Pélissier brothers?' asked someone else. 'I thought they'd be here.'

'I heard that their bastard manager, Baugé, wouldn't let them race. He wants to save his top riders for the Tour.'

'Nah . . . they're doing the Grand Prix de l'Heure in Paris, along with Christophe and Barthélémy.'

Standing slightly off to one side, alone, Ernest Paul stared blankly through the fogged-up window at the crowds gathering outside. They look cold, he thought to himself. It's going to be a cold day. His thoughts returned to his half-brother François, wishing he could have been here for this race. The great François Faber, winner of the 1909 Tour de France. It had always seemed faintly ridiculous to Paul that his kid brother by six years was the hulking giant of the peloton, a man standing nearly two metres in height and weighing over 90kg, not your usual pro cyclist. But Ernest Paul had been proud of him, and was quietly proud that he'd now been nicknamed 'Faber' as a tribute to his dead brother.

Even now, four years later, no one really knew what had happened to François. He'd fought with distinction in the Battle of the Marne in 1914, in the French Foreign Legion, and was promoted to corporal. He'd had to join the Foreign Legion because he was a Luxembourgois who chose to fight for his adopted country. François was last seen on 9 May 1915 when his battalion went over the top somewhere between Carency and Berthonval Farm, on the western approaches to Vimy Ridge.

Four battalions of the Foreign Legion attacked alongside the Moroccan Division (part of Pétain's 33rd Corps) on that cold, wet day. While the divisions on either side made little progress, the Moroccans and the Foreign Legion made astonishing advances, pushing the Germans aside and sweeping up Vimy Ridge itself. They managed to advance 4.5 kilometres in 90 minutes. Having outstripped the divisions on either side, the Moroccans and Legionnaires took withering fire from both flanks and were forced to retreat back down the ridge. Three of the four Foreign Legion battalion commanders were killed and the 33rd lost two-thirds of its men, François Faber among them.

All that Paul knew was that his brother had been hit during the attack, and had fallen, wounded. As the fighting died down, several of François' friends (including Charles Cruchon, a fellow pro cyclist) had crawled out among the bodies and the shell-holes to look for him, but they found no trace. In the relentless bombardments during the day many of the dead and the dying on the battlefield were blasted into unrecognisable pieces. Like tens of thousands of other soldiers, François Faber still lies somewhere in the fields north of Arras.

'Ça va, Faber?' came a gentle voice at his elbow. He turned to see the slender figure of Jean Alavoine, dressed in his Bianchi-Pirelli team kit.

'You look tired, Gars Jean,' said Paul, smiling weakly and acknowledging his own nickname by using Alavoine's.

'We all look tired,' replied Alavoine, looking around the crowded café. 'Most of us have only been back in *La Vie Civile* a couple of weeks. Except for those Belgians,' he nodded in the direction of a group of muscular-looking Flandrians huddled in a corner, chatting away in their harsh, unintelligible tongue. 'But it'll be good to get back to racing again.'

They lapsed into a momentary silence. The heat and noise of the café were oppressive, but they'd be out in the cold soon enough.

'Sorry to hear about your brother,' said Alavoine, placing a friendly hand on Paul's shoulder. 'He was a good rider . . . and a kind soul.'

'Thanks.' A pause. 'I was sad to hear about your Henri. That was in the summer of '16, wasn't it?'

'Yeah . . . the family took it very hard . . . I miss him. We all do.' Another pause.

'Remember at the Tour,' said Paul, 'how he would sometimes pick an argument with Desgrange when we came to a big hill? And how Desgrange never seemed to notice that all the while they were arguing, Henri was holding onto Desgrange's car, getting a tow to the top.'

'Yeah, I remember,' chuckled Alavoine. 'He was a smart kid, was Henri.'

It was 5.45 a.m., and the café began to empty out into the square, riders gathering up their *bidons* and bags, adjusting their clothing and making sure their *dossards* were securely attached. '*En y va,*' said Alavoine, draining his glass and heading for the door. Paul followed him out into the cold morning air.

The Place Broglie was filled with people. Thousands had turned out for *Le Grand Départ*, eager to see the cycling stars and grateful to have something to think about other than unemployment and shortages. It had been a long, cold winter, but now spring was here and there was a general feeling of optimism. The Boche had been vanquished, Alsace and Lorraine had been returned to France, and now maybe everyone could get back to something approaching normal. Strasbourg hadn't seen anything like this in years, so the town was *en fête*. Thousands of people had arrived by train, buses and cars, and one fan even arrived in his own private plane, landing it in the Tivoli park. Despite the cold, and the early hour, thousands packed the square and lined the route out of town towards Haguenau.

Alavoine and Paul, having collected their bikes from the *parc fermé*, joined the other riders in the start area. Looking around, they could see Oscar Egg, the great Swiss rider; Van Lerberghe, winner of the Ronde van Vlaanderen the previous month; Paul Duboc, the veteran of six Tours; and the rising Belgian stars Anseeuw, Buysse and Dejonghe. 'Maurice! Maurice! Coco!' shouted Paul, gesticulating to a rider further back. Maurice 'Coco' Brocco pushed his way through the crowd of riders and embraced Paul.

Back in the 1911 Tour, when François Faber suffered a mechanical problem and was in danger of missing the time-cut, Brocco paced him back up to the front of the peloton, knowing that if he was caught he'd be thrown off the race. Brocco was caught, but was also handsomely rewarded by the Fabers' team. He might even have even got away with it had he not put in an exceptional performance the day after in the Pyrenees and won the stage by 34 minutes. At the time Desgrange sneeringly referred to Brocco as a *domestique*, a name now universally used in the peloton to denote a rider who gives his all for his team-mates or team-leader, and promptly disqualified Brocco for so obviously having sold his services the day before. But Brocco and François had become firm friends.

'Ernest! Great to see you!'

'You too, Coco. You made it through, then?'

Brocco grinned his goofy trademark grin. 'Yep. Just about in one piece.' Many people misjudged Brocco. He was small and had a curiously medieval appearance, part jester and part gargoyle. He often wore a woollen skull-cap, beneath which his ears stuck out in a rather comic fashion. Many saw him as a figure of fun, but the comedic exterior hid a steely determination, physical strength and mental toughness.

At the age of 17 Brocco had left the family farm in the Marne and joined the French Foreign Legion (he was part-Italian), ending up in North Africa where the merciless training regime turned him from a callow farm-hand into a tough fighting soldier. One night, when he was supposed to be on sentry duty, he had an encounter with a young Arab woman 'with a face that would stop the heart of any man, and eyes like the Sahara stars'. Unfortunately for Brocco, he was caught *in flagrante* by his sergeant and as punishment was posted to the worst, most distant, fly-blown Legion outpost in Algeria. After six months there, in terrible conditions, he became so ill with fever (probably ty-phoid fever) that he was discharged from the Legion and went back to France to recover.

But his tough Legionnaire's training stood him in good stead in his new career as a professional cyclist, and before the war he'd been a very successful Six Day track racer and a pretty decent stage racer. At the outbreak of hostilities he joined the regular French army and became a motorcycle despatch rider for his battalion. His bravery won him the Croix de Guerre and the Médaille Militaire, and although wounded in the shoulder he'd made it through the war relatively unscathed.

'And the farm?' enquired Paul, referring to Brocco's family home outside Fismes, between the Marne and the Aisne.

A look of sadness passed over Brocco's normally cheery features. 'Gone. The fighting last August flattened the town, and the Germans destroyed everything before they withdrew. My parents are staying with family in Languedoc, but we don't know when they'll be able to go back. Or even if they'll be able to go back. They're getting on a bit now, and I'm not sure if they're up to starting again.'

'Maybe if you win this race you'll be able to help them. The prize money's enough to give any of us a good leg-up.'

At that moment Marcel Allain, editor of *Le Petit Journal*, stood up on the dais outside the Hotel de Ville and addressed the crowd through a loud-hailer. He gave a short speech about the glorious victory of the French, about the newspaper's motives for organising the race, and called on everyone to observe a minute's silence in memory of the fallen. All of the riders had either lost someone during the war, or at least knew someone *mort pour la France*. A respectful hush fell over the crowd.

At 6 a.m. precisely Allain fired the starting pistol and 87 riders rolled slowly out of the Place Broglie, to the enthusiastic cheers of the crowd, en route to Luxembourg 275km away. As was the norm in those days, the riders were led by a couple of the organisers' cars to light the way, and were followed by dozens of enthusiastic amateur cyclists. The roads weren't closed for racing in those days, so sundry punters could drive, or ride, alongside the racers for as long as they were able. For the first few miles there was a party atmosphere as the race rolled along, and it was only when it started to get light that the racing proper got under way.

★

As I rolled out of the Place Broglie the crowds, such as they were, seemed more interested in getting to work on time than celebrating the departure of some bloke on his bike. Not that I paid them much attention either, because the cobbles and tram-lines were occupying my immediate thoughts. Specifically, why do they have to have both? I like trams, and I like cobbles, but the combination is lethal to cyclists, and I really didn't want to crash before I was even out of sight of the start line. So I picked my way nervously (trams approach with a terrifying rumble and screech of brakes, and stop for no one, ever) north through the rush-hour traffic towards Haguenau.

My trip to the start point in Strasbourg had been remarkably pain-free considering the level of faffing required to buy the right tickets for me and my bike. The Eurostar was a breeze, I only got slightly lost riding from the Gare du Nord to the Gare de l'Est (a distance of about half a mile), and I got on the correct train to Strasbourg, which even had part of a carriage dedicated to cyclists and their bikes. I shared the carriage with a chap, prob-ably in his late 60s, who had with him an elderly steel touring bike covered with panniers and bags, and who had spread a large map out on the table in front of him and was clearly making plans. I wondered if I was looking at my future self, ten years from now.

Leaving from Place Broglie in Strasbourg, starting point of the toughest race in history

Like many French towns over a certain size, Strasbourg has a delightful historic centre, but gets progressively crappier as you ride out of town. My first few miles were cycled at a tentative pace thanks to endless delivery vans and the reluctance of their drivers to look, indicate, or even give a damn about anyone else. Ugly 1930s housing gave way to ugly '50s housing, ugly car-lots and ugly furniture shops. And then suddenly it's all behind you and you're briefly in the countryside.

The sky was a uniform grey as I pedalled north, and the temperature surprisingly low. Despite assurances from every weather app available for iPhones that it was going to be a spring-like 11°C, it wasn't. It was, according to my sat-nav, an annoyingly chilly 5°C, with a stiff westerly blowing. After Haguenau the road started to climb gently. The surface was good, the traffic was light, and by late morning I was in Reichshoffen and ready for a small diversion I had planned in order to get a battlefield under my belt. This part of the world saw a lot of action in the Franco-Prussian war, and the battle of Reichshoffen / Frœschwiller / Wörth (the French and Germans had different names for the same battles) in early August 1870 was a painful defeat for the French.

I turned off my route to have a quick look at the Frœschwiller battlefield, 250ft above Reichshoffen. The road through the trees rose at a steady 6 per cent, I passed a heinously ugly 1970s Franco-Prussian memorial made from blocks of streaked and stained concrete, and as I emerged onto the plateau at the top, a light sleet began to fall. There was nothing to see apart from a few woods and fields, and a plaque stating this was the site of the battle. My sat-nav said 3°C, my stomach said lunchtime, and my brain said sod this, time to go. The town of Bitche was less than 20 miles away, so I should be able to get an amusing photo and a late lunch there.

The sleet stopped. It turned into rain and redoubled its efforts to chill me to the bone. By the time I got to Bitche I didn't care for an amusing selfie at the city-limits sign, I just wanted warmth and food. Fortunately it only took an additional 20 minutes of riding around in the rain to find the only open restaurant, so that was good. The place was rammed, but they managed to find me a table *'pour un, seulement?'* right in the middle of the dining room so that I immediately became the focus of everyone's attention, more so when my schoolboy French singled me out as English.

As I self-consciously shovelled beef stew and potatoes (delicious) into my starving maw, a puddle of rainwater formed on the quarry-tiles around me. A waitress, scurrying from the kitchen to another table with a tray of starters, slipped in the puddle, regained her balance, and threw a dozen snails over me. I tried not to scream as boiling garlic oil spattered the side of my face and the back of one hand. It was quite painful, but the smell was divine. Needless to say, the entire restaurant, including the waiting staff, thought it was absolutely the funniest thing they'd ever seen. A cheery fellow at the next table said something to the waitress about '*plat du jour – rosbif avec l'escargots*'.

The good news was that after another hour or so the rain had washed most of the garlicky green slime off me. The bad news was that my inexplicable failure to pack my waterproof overshoes (what the hell was I *thinking?*) or anything longer than knee-warmers (seriously, what the hell *was* I thinking?) meant that I lost all feeling below the knees. My lightweight long-fingered gloves had also ceased to offer any form of protection, and a muddy, icy, slush-puppy had accumulated in my crotch.

*

And it wasn't much better for the riders on the Circuit des Champs de Bataille. They too encountered stiff winds and freezing rain as they rode north and then west, battling the heavy macadam roads and the horrible weather. Despite the rain, the locals of Bitche turned out in force to wave and cheer as the soggy riders slogged by. The town, or rather the huge Napoleonic fortress above the town, held out during the Franco-Prussian war until long after the fighting had stopped elsewhere, finally surrendering at the end of March 1871.

By this point the race was beginning to split up. A lead group of around 20 riders had broken away from the rest of the peloton and were making pretty good progress. Among their number were Oscar Egg, Jules Van Hevel, Jean Alavoine and Henri Van Lerberghe, all of them hardened, experienced racers. As they began the sharp, steep climb out of Bitche, Jean Alavoine punctured.

Although the roads during the first two stages were heavy going, at least they had had not been obliterated by shell-fire

Pulling over to the side of the road, he grabbed his tools out of the handlebar-bag and then flipped the bike over so it rested on the saddle and handlebars, beneath a tree. No axle wing-nuts were allowed in this race, so he took a spanner to the wheel nuts and whipped out the front wheel. With practised hands he ran a flat-head screwdriver around the rim on both sides of the tyre and then started the agonisingly slow wrestle to remove the tyre from the rim. It was hard enough in a warm, dry workshop, but by the side of the road, in the cold and wet, it was hard going.

With the tyre off, Alavoine took a rag and cleaned the rim thoroughly, drying it as best he could. He then applied glue to the rim, struggling to keep the rain off. Unwrapping a spare tyre from around his shoulders, he partially inflated it and eased it onto the rim. It was a difficult and messy procedure, but once it was seated to Alavoine's satisfaction, he then pumped it back up.

Normally he would leave the glue to 'go off' for at least 24 hours before riding on the tyre, but he didn't even have 24 minutes. It should be fine in a straight line, but he'd have to take it easy in the corners so that the tyre didn't roll off the rim if the glue hadn't set strongly enough.

Alavoine wrapped the punctured tyre around his shoulders, along with the other spare, put the wheel back in, tightened the nuts, and put the bike back on its wheels. The whole process had only taken five or six minutes, but he'd now lost contact with the lead group. Back on his bike, he set about trying to reel them in. The terrain, untouched by the war, consisted of rolling country with fields in the valleys and pine forests on the hillsides. It would have been quite pleasant, had it not been for the freezing rain and the icy cross/headwind.

At least the roads were in decent condition, even if the weather was becoming increasingly awful. This entire area had been German before the war, and now the new (old) border lay just a couple of kilometres to the east. What little traffic the racers did encounter was exclusively military, as France reinforced her borders and occupied parts of Germany, waiting for the Versailles peace treaty to be signed. With a state of war technically still in existence, the French were understandably anxious about the security of their borders.

They were also anxious about war reparations. Millions of people had been displaced, great swathes of north-eastern France had been destroyed, and the economy was crippled and heavily in debt. All eyes were on Paris (the peace negotiations were actually carried out in Paris, and signed at Versailles) as the two sides thrashed out a treaty, waiting to see how much Germany would have to pay to get France back on her feet. All across north-eastern France people were returning to their homes, often to find them destroyed by shell-fire or burned and looted by the retreating Germans. Compensation claims were lodged at the local town halls, sometimes for slightly grander buildings than had actually existed before the war. And why not? The Germans had forced people from their homes, stolen their possessions, and robbed them of ways to make a living. Germany should pay.

By the end of April the negotiations in Paris were well under way and the initial demands had been made – the return of Alsace and Lorraine, demilitarisation, the loss of Germany's overseas colonies, the immediate payment of 20 billion gold Marks ($5 billion in today's money), and Allied military occupation of the Rhineland and Ruhr. The Germans were outraged by what they perceived as excessively harsh penalties, having conveniently forgotten the Treaty of Brest-Litovsk in 1918, whereby the Russians sued for peace and the Germans demanded the Baltic states (3.3 million square kilometres of land that accounted for over 50 per cent of Russia's industrial output) plus 6 billion gold Marks.

Germany also seemed to have forgotten the Treaty of Frankfurt of 1871, whereby they took Alsace and Lorraine from the French and also demanded 5 billion gold Francs. The French paid up and stuck to the terms of that treaty until the outbreak of war in 1914. In 1919 Germany was unable to pay, and honoured only a tiny fraction of her obligations under the Treaty of Versailles. Even as the ink was drying on the Treaty, Germany had already breached it by secretly re-forming her army's General Staff, against the explicit terms of the Treaty.

None of which was of immediate concern to the riders as they dodged military vehicles on the roads next to the border. As a lone rider, Alavoine faced a real challenge to catch back up to the leading group. Although pacing each other wasn't allowed, a group of 20 riders naturally took turns on the front of the group and thus travelled faster than a lone rider. But mile by mile Alavoine was catching them, clawing back time as he pushed on. By the time they came to the checkpoint at Sarreguemines, where the River Saar forms a natural boundary with Germany, Alavoine was once more back with the lead group after a huge effort to get back in.

★

My own slog to Sarreguemines, under similar weather conditions, was not a lot of fun either. The scenery passed in a grey blur of rain and spray, the wind blew in my face, and I shivered with cold. The fact that I was having 'an authentic' Circuit des Champs de Bataille experience was (literally) cold comfort. To alleviate the misery I took a short diversion to look at Fort Casso, built in the late 1930s as part of the Maginot Line. I hoped to get out of the wind and rain for a while and see how the French were determined never again to be invaded by the Germans. The Maginot Line turned out to be entirely useless, and Fort Casso turned out to be entirely shut.

The last few kilometres to Sarreguemines were agony – slow, tiring, miserable, cold and very wet. I rolled to a stop outside an unprepossessing semi in the suburbs of Sarreguemines, my B&B for the night, and rang the doorbell. A middle-aged chap regarded me with a look of alarm, followed by a look of extreme disappointment when I announced that I was a guest for the night. *'Bien sûr,'* he muttered, motioning me to a side door before disappearing inside. I went round to the side door and waited. And waited.

Christ, it's cold. Hurry up! Maybe he's having second thoughts and is just going to leave me outside. By the time my host opened the side door into the kitchen, I was visibly shaking and desperate to get out of the rain. But despite this rather inauspicious start, my stay turned out to be utterly delightful. The couple running the place, once they'd recovered from the shock of receiving a wet and dirty Englishman into their home, were charming and showed me to my room . . . a shed in the garden. I kid you not. OK, it wasn't so much a shed as a huge wooden Wendy-house on stilts, perfect for keeping the *rosbif* away from the rest of the paying customers.

But my Wendy-house was fabulous. It had a terrace out the front, and the interior contained a large double bed, a couple of chairs and a desk, and a huge bathroom area. Never has a hot bath been so welcome, and before long my riding kit was washed and hanging up to dry, turning this bijou accommodation into something that looked like an East End slum laundry from the 1890s. With my cycling shoes drying on the radiator, it probably smelled like one, too.

Next I needed food. Lots of food. So I asked my hosts about local eating establishments. The news was not encouraging – I could have pizza delivered, I could walk for 15 minutes in the rain to McDonald's, or I could get a cab into town. But it's Monday, so everything is shut except for the Casino Brasserie on the river. My hosts phoned for a taxi to take me there. Exactly *who* they phoned I'm not sure, because a man called Claude arrived in a large white Transit van and took me to the Brasserie in that. He even declined immediate payment, saying I could pay him when he came to take me back later.

After 70 miles of cycling in horrible conditions, I was tired. But the dinner was good. I had beef cheeks and the cheapest bottle of red wine on the list. Then I had a mountain of cheese and some more wine. When I woke up the waitress was tapping me gently on the shoulder, telling me my driver was waiting at the bar. Back at the B&B, Claude would not accept a cent over €10 for the return trip into town, and I collapsed into my bed, my room a steamy fug of hot, damp clothing.

The next morning dawned grey and drizzly. Not quite as bad as yesterday, but not exactly what I was hoping for. Breakfast, though, was more than I ever could have dreamed of . . . it was huge! Croissants, pains-au-chocolat, bread, cheese, ham, cereal, yoghurt, coffee, juice, fruit. What I couldn't force down my gullet was wrapped in paper napkins and stowed in my bag for lunch. As I bade farewell to my hosts and pedalled off down the road, Mr Creosote in Lycra, it suddenly occurred to me that maybe this epic feast had been laid out for all the guests, not just for me. No, surely not. Oh well.

Cyclists have a very specific list of things we dislike. We may not place all the things on the list in the same order, but they are all there on all of our lists. Here are some of mine: headwinds, sucky road surfaces, false flats, white vans, tram lines, mini-cabs and punctures. For one reason or another, these things are sent to try (or kill) us. And as I set off from Sarreguemines to Metz, I had a 20mph headwind and horribly sucky road surfaces that seemed to drag all the speed from my wheels. The combination was like cycling through treacle. But at least the rain was slackening off. I stopped at a Super U supermarket outside Forbach and bought myself a pair of expensive fleece-lined leather gloves, something I'd been fantasising about for the last 24 hours. Oooh . . . nice. And a snip at only €45!

Heading west in my toasty new gloves, I followed the French/ German border for a few miles, although at one point I was surprised to see a sign saying *Welcome to France*. Eh? So where the hell had I been all morning? The road was one long succession of the usual stuff – tyre and battery centres, closed cafés, second-hand van showrooms, dingy-looking bars, Monsieur Bricolage shops – sometimes there was a bike path (where the locals like to park their cars and store their broken glass), mostly there wasn't. But by midday the clouds parted briefly and I even got some sunshine as I made another diversion off route, this time to visit the Lorraine American Cemetery at Saint-Avold. This entirely Second World War cemetery is the biggest of its kind in Europe, and a beautifully cared-for place. I sat in the sun, out of the freezing wind, and ate my breakfast contraband while considering the sacrifice these men made in a country far from home.

At this point the sat-nav had one of its periodic glitches and turned itself off for no apparent reason, wiping the morning's data and refusing to reboot. It was like an annoying child having a tantrum, so I chose to ignore it for half an hour until it decided to behave itself. The afternoon was spent traversing open rolling countryside and cursing the ever-present chilly headwind. But even though it was cold and windy, it was better than Monsieur Bricolage and crappy take-away pizza places. There were woods, and farms, and flowers in the hedgerows. Or to be more precise, flowers on the verges, because the hedgerows were ploughed up in the 1970s.

As I neared Metz the number of Franco-Prussian war memorials increased dramatically and the weather deteriorated equally dramatically. Dark rainclouds gathered overhead, so the bloody sat-nav decided to take me into Metz via a network of cycle paths through some very rough-looking housing estates full of vandalised cars and fly-tipped rubbish. Malevolent, shaven-headed kids on stolen mopeds and BMX bikes interrupted their wheelie practice and drug-taking to watch me pass. Then they followed me for a bit, whistling and making cat-calls. I was lost, slightly nervous, and having to rely on the crappy sat-nav to get me out of there.

Fortunately I came upon six lanes of speeding traffic, rammed with lorries, and with no cycle path or hard shoulder. *That'll do,* I thought to myself, bouncing off the kerb and into the traffic. Better a swift and relatively painless death beneath the wheels of a speeding truck than slowly bleeding to death from stab wounds by the dustbins on a housing estate, while some 12-year-old thug does wheelies on my bike.

I arrived at my hotel just as the sleet started to come down again. I had every intention of going out to eat somewhere in Metz, which has a rather interesting historic centre, but after the usual shower and hand-washing of my riding kit I really couldn't be bothered. I'd only just warmed up, and had zero intention of wandering around getting cold and wet again. I ate in the hotel, then sat in the bar drinking beer (purely for rehydration purposes, obviously), staring at football on the telly. It had been a surprisingly gruelling day, even though I'd only covered 65 miles.

★

By the time the riders reached Metz, 182km into the first stage, the pace of the leaders and the horrible weather had blown the race apart. At just after 1 p.m. a group of five riders – Alois

Verstraeten, Oscar Egg, Jules Van Hevel, Basiel Matthys and Henri Van Lerberghe – arrived at the Metz checkpoint. They had exactly five minutes to eat whatever the organisers had laid on for them, check over their bikes, and fill their *bidons* with whatever hot drinks were available. Then, when the time-keeper signalled, they were off again, heading north to Luxembourg.

Refreshment stops were often brief and chaotic. This was taken at the Tour a couple of years later. Note the bloke drinking wine and the home-made knee-warmers of the chap on the left

Two minutes behind them was the lone figure of Lucien Buysse. His brother, Marcel, would normally have been by his side but had been unable to get his paperwork sorted out in time, and had to withdraw shortly before the start. But Lucien's brother-in-law, Urbain Anseeuw, was in the race and not too far behind him. Buysse battled on, a tough Belgian who would go on to become the first '*super-domestique*' in cycling. At the Automoto team in the mid 1920s, when a rule change allowed members of the same team to help each other, Buysse became Ottavio

Bottechia's right-hand man, always ready to protect his leader, take a turn on the front, or pace Bottechia back to the bunch after a puncture. A *super-domestique* is often a rider who would be a team-leader on a lesser team, and is the one whose sole purpose is to get his team-leader to the finish as quickly and easily as possible. Buysse's potential was fully realised on the Tour, an event that Bottechia shunned, when he won it in 1926.

A further 12 minutes down came a group of six, including Pelletier and Chassot, the leading French riders on the road. Already the strength and better condition of the Belgians was beginning to show. According to *Le Petit Journal* huge crowds turned out to greet the riders despite the snow that was now falling. The commander of the Metz garrison allowed his men to leave their posts to watch the riders pass. They were even permitted to applaud.

By modern standards, a 12-minute gap is pretty much unbridgeable, such are the tiny margins by which bike races are won and lost these days. But in the early days of bike racing these huge gaps were quite common, and it was possible to gain or lose an hour without significantly affecting your place in the race. So when Brocco and Duboc arrived at the checkpoint 20 minutes down on the leaders, they were probably not unduly concerned.

Just as Brocco and Duboc were preparing to leave, having wolfed down their lunch, Alavoine and a couple of other riders rolled in. Of the 87 starters, only 73 made it as far as Metz. Many riders were amateurs using old, pre-war bikes and old, poor-quality tyres, which meant that some suffered mechanical issues they just couldn't fix by the roadside. The weather, too, was having a devastating effect on the peloton. As many of the French riders had come straight from the army and had suffered four years of poor food and terrible conditions, they were in no fit state for a two-week stage race. Also, few had done any training, and the combination of lack of fitness, poor-quality machinery and terrible weather meant that the rate of attrition was high.

From Metz the *parcours* took the riders north along the west bank of the Moselle River as far as Thionville, then north-east to the border of France, Germany and Luxembourg at Schengen, following the Moselle for most of the way. In 1919 this was a heavily industrialised region, with factories lining the road on one side and docks and barges on the Moselle River on the other. It was also a time of turmoil as the French took over the factories from German ownership and expelled more than 100,000 German citizens who had settled in Alsace-Lorraine between 1871 and 1914. As the race passed, a few of the factories and steelworks were beginning to get up and running, and groups of men gathered by the side of the road to watch the riders pass.

Twelve kilometres north of Metz, as the leading four (Verstraeten had been dropped) pushed to extend their lead, a dog ran out into the road and brought Oscar Egg crashing to the ground. It only took him a moment or two to gather himself up, straighten his handlebars, and remount, but the moment they saw what had happened, the other three attacked. Egg was now riding solo between the leaders and the chasing bunch, cursing his luck and riding like fury to catch back up. These days it's frowned upon to attack when one of the favourites suffers a mishap, but in those days it was perfectly normal.

And it seems that getting knocked off by a dog has become a fairly normal occurrence, too, because cycling history is full of such incidents. In the 1981 Paris–Roubaix Bernard Hinault was knocked off his bike 13km from the finish by a dog called Gruson, Joaquim Agostinho died during the 1984 Tour of the Algarve after crashing into a dog, and wayward canines have caused Marcus Berghardt, Philippe Gilbert, Sandy Casar, Davide Rebellin and Stephan Schumacher all to come croppers.

Before the war, the delightfully named Oscar Egg had been a prolific racer, both on the track and on the road. Between 1912 and 1914 Egg had engaged in a titanic struggle with Marcel Berthet to hold the cycling Hour Record (interestingly, Henri Desgrange of *L'Auto* was the very first Hour Record holder). Berthet set the new record of 41.52kmh in 1907, which Egg took from him in August

1912 with a distance of 42.12km. Berthet took it back in August 1913 with a distance of 42.74km. That record stood for only two weeks before Egg rode 43.52 kilometres in an hour. That record survived just one month before Berthet took it back with a distance of 43.77km. A year later, just after the outbreak of the First World War, Egg retook the record with a distance of 44.27km, a record that stood until 1933. To this day, Chris Boardman is the only other rider to equal Egg and Berthet's achievement of taking the Hour Record three times.

As a neutral, Egg spent most of the First World War racing. He'd done reasonably well in the 1914 Tour, with two stage wins and a 13th place overall, and he won Paris–Tours that year. With most racing suspended in late 1914, Egg went to America in 1915 to take part in the Chicago Six Days, which he won, partnering Francesco Verri. Six Day racing was a big deal in those days, and successful riders could earn a very good living at it. But it was notoriously tough. Taking it in turns with a team-mate, riders rode day and night for six days round a velodrome. Needless to say, drugs were a major factor in Six Day racing, but the financial rewards made it worth doing.

The following year Egg was back in America, this time at Madison Square Gardens in New York for another Six Day race. He won that as well, this time with French partner Marcel Depuy. Depuy was subsequently banned for life for racing in America rather than joining the army, but he and Egg scooped the equivalent of €100,000 for their win. In 1917 Egg went to Italy and joined the Italian Bianchi team. He did well, with some race wins and top-three placings, well enough to extend his contract with Bianchi into 1919, when he teamed up with Jean Alavoine and Alois Verstraeten for the Circuit des Champs de Bataille.

Oscar Egg was fit and strong, compared to most of the peloton, and he had a genuine shot at winning the race, but no matter how hard he rode, he couldn't see the leading three in front of him. He would no doubt have considered sitting up and waiting for the chasing group, but with no real idea how far they were behind, he kept going. At the checkpoint in Remich he was astonished to find he was the first to sign in.

It must have brought a smile to Egg's face to realise that his competitors had not benefited from his misfortune, and he now had an opportunity to put them to the sword and pay them back for their attack. He powered on alone with a 5-minute lead over Pelletier and a 9-minute lead over the Van Lerberghe/ Matthys/Van Hevel group which had ridden 5 kilometres along the wrong road before Van Hevel realised their mistake. With 240km covered, Egg's recent solo efforts would have meant that he was beginning to tire. Snow was now falling quite heavily as he heaved himself over the nasty little hill at a place called Rolling and headed into the final run-in to Luxembourg.

Egg had the lead and although it was slowly dropping, he managed to plough on through the sleet and snow to Luxembourg City. The roads by this time had turned into a muddy quagmire, and the sheer physical effort of riding was horrendous. Clad in soaking-wet wool and covered from head to foot in filth from the roads, they slipped and slid, crashed and remounted, churning through the mud.

On the run-in to the finish in Luxembourg City the organisers had erected large grandstands beside the Avenue Marie-Thérèse, and a significant crowd had turned out despite the cold to welcome the riders. Apparently 'all seats were filled with enthusiastic crowds, and there was a party atmosphere', according to Le Petit Journal. I suspect a bit of journalistic licence here, but perhaps the Luxembourgois really did sit around in the snow for a couple of hours waiting to see the riders come in. Certainly there was little else to occupy them in these austere post-war times, so maybe this was the only show in town. Besides, the band of the French 62nd RI (infantry regiment) was on hand to keep them amused.

Oscar Egg crossed the line at 16.58 that afternoon, having covered the 275km from Strasbourg in 10 hours 58 minutes at an average of 25kmh. He was delighted to have put some time into the Belgians. Seven minutes later the group of Van Lerberghe,

Matthys, Verstraeten, Van Hevel, Buysse, Heusghem and Dejonghe arrived together, and sprinted for the prize-money on offer. Van Hevel took second, Buysse third, Matthys fourth and Heusghem fifth, but all were in a tight group and so were awarded the same time, as is the norm in bunch-sprints both then and now. A minute later a group of six more riders came in together. Thirty minutes down was Joseph Rasqui, who won an extremely generous prize of 500FF (put up by the wealthy industrialist Paul Würth) for being the first Luxembourgois home. Jean Alavoine rode in 38 minutes down, accompanied by his friend Ernest Paul, Fernand Lemay, Charles Deruyter and Constant Ménager.

Abandoning their bikes at the *parc fermé* to be checked over by the commissaires, the riders stumbled into the warmth of the Café de la Paix and attempted, with frozen fingers, to sign in and hand over the official ticket on which was noted their finishing times. The earlier finishers were all there, drinking hot, sweet coffee and sipping brandy, trying to restore some feeling into their extremities.

'No sign of Brocco yet,' said Alavoine.

Paul looked around the café. 'He wasn't that far behind us, I think.'

Lemay hobbled over to join them. 'God, that was hard,' he grumbled. 'And those Flandrians are tough bastards, aren't they?' Lemay had been a despatch-rider during the war and knew about riding in tough conditions, but at least then he only had to ride from the command post back to regimental HQ, not 275km. He had started the Paris–Roubaix a week earlier, but abandoned when he realised there was no point exhausting himself or breaking his bike a week before a far more profitable race.

Alavoine grunted and went back to trying to massage some feeling back into his wrinkled white feet. He really hoped that whatever accommodation he'd been allocated for the evening had a decent bath.

Last man home that day was Louis Ellner, who rolled across the finish line just before 1 a.m. the next morning and won himself 50FF for being the *Lanterne Rouge*, the last-placed in the race. But

Stage 1 wasn't quite over. At 7.30 the next morning André Pérrès, with *dossard* number 14, crossed the finishing line, pushing his bike (as he had for the last 23km). Pérrès, a deaf-mute from Paris, had missed the time-cut by hours and was disqualified from the race.

★

Peering blearily out of my hotel window in Metz, I was pleased to see that the rain had cleared and the roads were dry. It still looked gloomily grey, and the people outside were warmly wrapped, so I picked my warmest, most waterproof ensemble for my 80-mile ride to Arlon, just beyond Luxembourg City. With the last of the available breakfast (bread, cheese, croissants, ham) pilfered and stuffed into my backpack, I set off north along the banks of the Moselle.

It was bloody freezing, and the scenery was pretty grim, but at least it was flat. Mile after mile of cheap housing, crappy take-aways, warehouses, scrap-yards and factories rolled by. On the right the succession of run-down shops and houses occasionally gave way to docks on the Moselle, cranes, goods yards, lorry parks and vast hoppers full of god-knows-what. It wasn't pretty, but at least there was employment and signs of life.

After an hour or so I arrived in Thionville where I'd planned a quick diversion to look at Groupe Fortifié de Guentrange, one of a group of defences built by Germany after the Franco-Prussian war to deter the French from trying to retake Alsace and Lorraine. Perched high on a hill above the town, a two-mile slog at over 7 per cent incline, the place is fascinating. Built on a monumental scale, and at that time commanding excellent views (sadly now overgrown with trees) over the town, river and railway, this collection of fortifications is an impressive sight. Although it is technically open to the public, you have to book a visit in advance, which obviously I hadn't. So I wandered around for a bit, marvelling at the massive massiveness of it. It looked more like a prison than a collection of forts, and I had the place entirely to myself. In fact it was so overgrown, it looked like no one had been there for decades.

Having spent too much time there already, I thought I'd better push on. So the poxy sat-nav immediately tried to send me down an overgrown footpath on the far side of the hill. I declined to follow its advice, so it sent me down a gravelly track. Which turned into an overgrown footpath. I turned back and tried another gravelly track, and guess what? Yep, another overgrown footpath. Sigh. Not for the first time, I was gripped with an urge to hurl the sat-nav to the ground and stamp on it to teach it a valuable lesson.

Like most men, I have a pathological hatred of retracing my steps. It's an annoying waste of time, and often an admission of having cocked things up. And it's worse on a bike because there has been physical effort involved. But I bit the bullet and retraced my steps into Thionville as the rain started again. At least it was a balmy 6°C, I thought to myself, as the first drips made their way down my back. By now I was well behind schedule and had a choice to make – stick to the original race route via Remich, or cut the corner and head straight to Luxembourg City, knocking 30 miles off the route. I hoped to make it to Arlon in time to visit the cycle museum there, so I sacked off Remich and the nasty little climb at Rolling, and headed due north for Luxembourg City.

The road was long and straight and boring. Even in nice weather it wouldn't have been particularly interesting. As the temperature dropped a few degrees and the rain turned to sleet, it was even less engaging. The temperature now displayed on the sat-nav was 2°C, my lovely new leather gloves had absorbed so much water that they weighed about a kilo each, and my hands and feet were chilled to the bone. For the first time I began to wonder whether this really was such a good idea. I'm all for a bit of authenticity, but this was ridiculous.

Just outside Luxembourg City I noticed a sign for a place called Itzig and remembered that Andy Schleck (retired pro racer and winner of the Tour) had recently opened a bike shop there. Maybe I could pick up some overshoes and a pair of decent gloves there. I might even get to meet a Tour winner. Either way, half an hour spent in an upmarket bike shop, away from the sleet and rain, seemed like an excellent idea, given my hypothermic state.

As the only customer on a wet and miserable mid-week afternoon, I was afforded a warm welcome by the man himself, was given a properly good cup of coffee, and was invited to peruse a huge selection of quality riding kit. Overshoes, check. Leg-warmers, check. Waterproof gloves, check. Energy and protein bars, check. I just couldn't give Andy my money quickly enough. He even asked what brought me here, and inspected my filthy, dripping bike with a professional eye. 'Very nice,' he said, nodding approvingly. While I looked for more warm things to buy, Andy sat at the computer and read my piece about the Circuit des Champs de Bataille online. He'd never heard of the race and seemed genuinely interested in it, so we spent a while talking about the lunacy of early bike racing and the folly of racing across impossible terrain in horrible weather. The more I told him about the men who raced, and the machines they raced on, the more astonished he became. 'It's incredible,' he said, shaking his head. 'Those guys were really hard men.'

Leaving Itzig and attempting a direct route into Luxembourg City, the sat-nav did it again. My greatly restored sense of well-being, brought on by coffee, energy bars and a warm welcome, evaporated immediately. The tiny country lane I was on turned into a track that descended gently through a wood. *No problem,* I thought, *the Spin can handle a bit of off-roading.* Even when it turned into single-track it wasn't too bad. *Hah,* I thought, *who needs an adventure bike or a gravel-grinder when the mighty Spin will do it all?* Except the single-track turned into virtually no-track and disappeared down a 50-degree slope through the trees. For this I needed a full-suspension mountain-bike and balls of steel.

I could have turned round and gone back. I should have turned round and gone back. But I didn't. I hate turning round and

69

going back. So I heaved the Spin over my shoulder and began an interminable scramble down through fallen branches, mud and leaves.

By the time I made it to the bottom of the hill and onto a small country road, I looked like something emerging from a swamp. My new leg-warmers were filthy, my new gloves were covered in mud, my shoes were covered in mud and twigs, my jacket was covered in mud, and I was sweating buckets despite the chill. I glowered at the beeping sat-nav, hoping by sheer force of will to make it behave. It turned itself off and sulked.

Luxembourg City looked rather nice, and I really wanted to stop for tea and cake, but I didn't because I wanted to get to the cycle museum in Arlon before it closed. At least the rain had stopped, and my impression of Luxembourg was one of well-groomed neatness and order. Not quite Swiss-neat, but not far off, and miles away from the industrial grot of the Moselle valley I had experienced that morning. I thought about Oscar Egg and his stage victory as I cycled up the Avenue Marie-Thérèse, and about André Pérrès the deaf mute who finished 14 hours behind Egg. The idea of having complete amateurs racing alongside the stars of the day is extraordinary by today's standards, but that's what happened. I idly wondered how I would fare if I rocked up at the Tour of Flanders and rode against the cream of the Classics riders. I'd probably finish 14 hours behind the winner, too.

The following 20 miles were spent churning into a chilly head-wind, hoping to make it to the cycle museum before the sleet started again. Obviously the museum was closed, and by the time I made it to my hotel on the outskirts of the town it was full-on snowing. Happily the hotel receptionist asked if I would mind putting my bike in my room, on account of a coach-load of old dears having monopolised the baggage storage room with gigantic suitcases (why do old people always travel with bags manifestly too big for them to carry/wheel/manage?). Of course I wouldn't mind . . . it would give me a chance to do a bit of routine maintenance.

So far the bike had behaved impeccably – no creaks, groans, squeaks or problems of any sort. I realised I'd barely given it a second thought since leaving Strasbourg, other than to squeeze the tyres every morning to 'check' pressures. After the daily ritual of shower, wash clothes, hang clothes up to dry, put shoes on radiator, I went to the hotel kitchen and scrounged some old rags. Wiping down the bike, I gave it a thorough once-over, secretly hoping to find something to tinker with. I couldn't, so I tried to mop up the puddle of water that had formed beneath it, lubed the chain, and then turned my attention to myself.

My decrepit 55-year-old body was standing up to the rigours quite well, although the ball of my right foot seemed to have developed a strange trench-foot-type thing. It was white, and pitted, and squishy. And it didn't smell too good, either. Hmmm . . . I wondered if it was actually trench-foot (authentic) or whether it was some kind of gangrene or necrosis. I'd have to keep an eye on it, and if it started to spread I'd have to take the multi-tool to it.

My biggest concern had been with my undercarriage. Chafing and saddle-sores can wreak havoc on a cyclist, so I'm particularly fastidious when it comes to washing, drying, and anointing my bits. Non-cyclists might find this a trifle strange, but it's something that assumes significant levels of concern if you're riding 80 miles a day. For a start, cyclists (as opposed to people who just scoot round town on a bike) ride commando. Yep, no underwear for us because it can get sweaty and cause chafing. And the seams can also be a problem. Before long rides we also slather our undercarriage in stuff called chammy cream (the chamois is the padded bit of your cycling shorts, between your legs) which prevents chafing and creates a not-entirely-unpleasant cool, slippery feeling when you first put on your shorts.

But I'm happy to report that my undercarriage was in fine fettle. Cold, and almost invisible to the naked eye much of the time, but not a cause for any concern or the source of any discomfort. And the rest of me seemed OK as well. My legs ached a little, but 200 miles in three days hadn't been too arduous. And the relative lightness of my backpack meant my back and shoulders didn't hurt.

Outside, it was now properly snowing, settling on the grass and looking all Christmassy . . . at the end of April! Once again I couldn't be bothered to head into town in the snow, so I had dinner in the hotel and then watched a couple of episodes of *Band of Brothers* on my phone (not perfect, but waaaay better than French TV). Tomorrow I was heading for Bastogne, at the heart of the Second World War Battle of the Bulge battlefields. In the snow. Authentic was just about to get much, much more authentic.

General Classification after Stage 1

	Rider	Time	Time gap
1	Oscar Egg (CH)	10hr 58min	0.0min
2	Jules Van Hevel (B)	11hr 05min	+7min
3	Lucien Buysse (B)	Same Time	+7min
4	Basiel Matthys (B)	ST	+7min
5	Hector Heusghem (F)	ST	+7min
6	Albert Dejonghe (B)	ST	+7min
7	Aloysius Verstraeten (B)	ST	+7min
8	José Pelletier (F)	11hr 06min	+8min
9	Albert Desmedt (F)	ST	+8min
10	Henri Van Lerberghe (B)	ST	+8min
11	André Huret (F)	ST	+8min
12	Charles Haidon (B)	ST	+8min
13	Urbain Anseeuw (B)	ST	+8min
14	Paul Duboc (F)	11hr 12min	+14min
15	Henri Hanlet (B)	ST	+14min
16	René Chassot (F)	11hr 28min	+30min
17	Ali Neffati (Tun.)	ST	+30min
18	Georges Gatier (F)	11hr 31min	+33min
19	Léon Despontin (F)	ST	+33min
20	René Guenot (F)	11hr 36min	+38min
21	Fernand Lemay (F)	ST	+38min
22	Jean Alavoine (F)	ST	+38min
23	Ernest Paul (F)	ST	+38min
24	Charles Deruyter (B)	ST	+38min
25	Constant Ménager (F)	ST	+38min
71	Louis Ellner (F)	18hr 50min	+7hr 52min

STAGE 2

Luxembourg to Brussels

301km

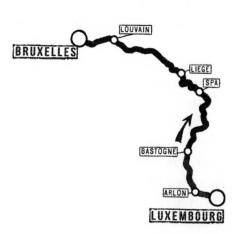

30 April 1919

At the end of Stage 1, Alavoine, Egg and Verstraeten, as members of the same prestigious Bianchi-Pirelli team, had collected their bags from the organisers' lorry and been driven to the house of Monsieur Hippert, a senior official from the Luxembourg cycling federation, where they were put up for two nights. Other riders were either put up on camp-beds in a local gymnasium, in modest hotels, or stayed with members of the Luxembourg federation. In the very early days of racing, the *isolés* often had to seek out their own accommodation and scrounge meals wherever they could, but with the increasing professionalisation of the peloton, this was becoming less often the case. Race organisers were becoming more concerned with the welfare of their riders and, more importantly, wanted to attract a decent number of entries to their races. In order to attract plenty of *isolés* they had to be a little more generous and accommodating.

For the riders, the rest day that followed each stage was spent sleeping, eating, resting, and carrying out maintenance on their bikes. The race organisers gave them 10FF a day to cover expenses, including on rest days, so they could afford a decent meal and a few drinks with fellow riders. There were various activities (a tour of the town, a concert, a civic reception with the Mayor, etc.) laid on if riders wanted, but most were content to eat and sleep. Except for Henri Van Lerberghe, who, according to *L'Auto*, declared, 'I'll sleep when I'm dead', and went out for a ride on his bike.

Meanwhile, the weather continued to deteriorate – sleet and snow showers during the day, hard frosts at night. Historical weather records show that in the last week of April and the first week of May, a metre of snow fell on France and Belgium. Conditions were horrendous, a terrible reminder to many riders of their time spent in and out of the trenches in the bitterly cold winter of 1916–17.

Given the toughness of Stage 1, and the continuing poor weather, it seems incredible that anyone actually turned up for Stage 2, but 70 riders arrived at 4 a.m. to sign in for the start. According to *Le Petit Journal*, even the organisers were surprised at this, expecting 60 riders at most: '*Les pronostiqueurs adoptaient un chiffre: soixante. Erreur! Tous les arrivés l'avant-veille prennent le départ.*' (The organisers proposed a figure: 60. Mistake! Everyone who arrived is taking to the start.) As it turned out, Albert Heux, Germain Titran and Louis Vanderborght took one look at the weather and withdrew from the race. And then there were 67.

Louis Ellner stood shivering in the cold of the starting area. Around him his fellow riders looked as cold and miserable as he did. That morning he had put on virtually every item of clothing he possessed in an attempt to stave off the misery he knew would be coming his way. Three hundred kilometres, in this? It didn't seem even remotely possible. But he was damned if he was going to give up now. Four years in the army had made him tough, determined, and accustomed to physical discomfort. He was the epitome of the *poilu*, the long-suffering French infantryman. But his slight build and four years of army rations meant he wasn't a strong rider, and as an *isolé* he had no support or back-up. He didn't even have a racing bike . . . he was competing on an upright gent's touring bike!

Stage 1 had not been kind to Ellner. As a club rider before the war he had never raced these kinds of distances before and the bike he was riding, a *routière*, was impossibly heavy and slow. Plus, his chain was too loose and kept jumping off the rear sprocket. With his mechanical issues, and his slow pace, he was now the *Lanterne Rouge* of the race, although the 50FF prize for being last was something of a bonus.

In the first stage he had lost 7 hours 52 minutes to the leader, and had arrived at the finish line having ridden for nearly 19 hours. Amazingly, the checkpoint was still open (it stayed open until 3 a.m.), and even more amazingly, the organisers had quite a generous time-cut, so he was still in the race.

'Morning, Louis,' said René Ameline, another *isolé* who had struggled badly on Stage 1 and with whom he'd ridden for a while.

'Morning, René. How are you today?'

Ameline chuckled mirthlessly. 'Been better. This bloody weather . . .' He squinted up at the dark sky, from which snowflakes continued to fall. 'At least the wind's dropped a bit.'

Ameline was 3 hours ahead of Ellner in the GC (general classification), but they were still the last two in the race. 'Let's hope to do a bit better today, eh?'

Ellner smiled a wan smile. 'Let's hope so, although some of the other guys were saying how tough some of the Ardennes climbs are.'

The snow continued to fall heavily as they got under way. It was 5.30 a.m., dark, and the peloton rode slowly behind the lead commissaire's car for the first hour or so. Despite the sedate pace, riders were slipping and sliding all over the road, crashing, re-mounting, struggling on. *Le Petit Journal* describes the conditions: 'thick snow, horrible cold, maddening rain, sticky mud on the roads and treacherous ice on the Belgian *pavé*'. They were concerned whether the convoy of trucks and cars would even make it to Brussels, let alone the riders.

Handing over their *cartes blanche* (travel permits given to each rider at the beginning of the stage) at the Belgian border, the peloton rode north through Arlon and on to Bastogne. In those days Bastogne didn't have the significance it does for us.

The Battle of the Bulge was still 25 years in the future, and the Liège–Bastogne–Liège bike race had not yet established itself as a premier cycling event. But this area had seen unspeakable savagery by the German invaders, who murdered thousands of unarmed civilians in this small corner of Belgium in August 1914.

Up to this point the roads had been poor, but manageable. From Houffalize the race climbed up to Baraque de Fraiture, at over 650m above sea level, one of the highest points in Belgium and nowadays home to a ski resort. On the rutted, snowy, frozen dirt roads this 15km climb must have been a nightmare, and at points where the gradient was over 7 per cent most riders were forced to dismount and push. The deep mud clogged wheels, brakes and chains, forcing riders to stop regularly to clear the mud. But it certainly broke up the peloton as the stronger riders pushed on and the weaker ones got left further and further behind. Going down the other side would, in some ways, have been even worse as the riders battled to control their descent on terrible slippery surfaces with very ineffectual brakes.

The endless climbing and descending took its toll, and at each town big enough to have a train station a couple of riders would admit defeat and climb off. At the back of the race Ellner waved goodbye to his friend Ameline, who just couldn't take any more. Ellner pedalled on, chilled to the core and only halfway through the stage, last on GC, and last on the road. But Ellner wasn't done yet. At the front, Lucien Buysse had dropped Matthys and Van Lerberghe, his two breakaway companions, and was riding hard.

Up to this point the *parcours* had been entirely behind German lines in the First World War, but as the riders approached Liège the signs of war became more obvious. In 1914 the German army, having violated Belgium's neutrality, had expected to sweep through Belgium without any significant resistance en route to northern France, hoping to encircle Paris as part of the Schlieffen Plan. But the Belgian army put up surprisingly stiff resistance for such a small fighting force, and the forts around Liège played a vital part in slowing the German advance.

The Liège forts stopped the Germans in their tracks, but not for very long. When they realised that small-calibre field guns weren't going to subdue the forts, the Germans brought up their train-mounted heavy artillery and proceeded to pound them to dust using 380mm- and 420mm-calibre shells that weighed over half a tonne each. It took several days, but those days were vital in giving the French and British time to block any German push to the Channel ports.

At the first checkpoint, in Liège, the estimated time of arrival had come and gone. But the organisers weren't too worried . . . the weather was bound to have an effect. Then, at 12.38 p.m., Lucien Buysse arrived at the *parc fermé* and signed in with trembling hands. He ate, he drank, he stamped his feet and flapped his arms to keep warm, and then he was on his way. Five minutes after he left came a group of seven containing Heusghem, Dejonghe, Nempon and Anseeuw.

'Oscar Egg crashed a few kilometres back,' Nempon told the commissaires. 'I don't know if he is continuing.' Quickly word spread and the crowd was buzzing with the news. Alavoine struggled in just before 1 p.m., with Duboc, Van Hevel and Deruyter rolling in just behind. They were 20 minutes behind Buysse, but there was plenty of racing still to do. Not that any of them really felt like riding another 120km, even if it was pretty much pan-flat all the way to Brussels. But the flat, straight nature of the road to Brussels gave the chasing group a distinct advantage over a solo rider. They pressed on as fast as they could.

A little while later Oscar Egg limped in to the checkpoint. His handlebars were badly damaged, and he was bleeding from an assortment of cuts and abrasions, as the result of crashing into a ditch just outside Liège.

He sat down on a bench and inspected his injuries, seemingly oblivious to the snow still falling. Someone found him a clean cloth and he made a half-hearted attempt to clean himself up. Then he went to the commissaires and told them that because he couldn't fix his handlebars he had to abandon. One of the best all-rounders of his

79

generation, and probably the rider in the best condition at the race, he withdrew due to an unfortunate crash on the second stage.

Meanwhile, Ernest Paul and Maurice Brocco were nearly 90 minutes down on the leader and struggling badly. They were riding solo, but caught and passed each other regularly, exchanging grunts of encouragement along the way, each immersed in his own world of cold and pain. In the report in *La Petit Journal* there is no mention of the arrival of Ellner at the checkpoint in Liège. Maybe he too had thrown in the towel somewhere in the Ardennes.

★

I almost didn't dare look out of my Arlon hotel-room window. It was snowing when I went to bed, surely it couldn't still be snowing? It's the end of April, for crying out loud! Astonishingly, it wasn't snowing. There was snow on the ground, but it wasn't actually snowing. There was even some blue sky and a bit of sunshine. My mood improved enormously as I munched my way through half a dozen croissants and pains-au-chocolat, swilled several cups of coffee, drank a litre of orange juice, and prepared to get on the road.

From a route-planning perspective, this next bit had me stumped. Apart from the N4, a horrible dual carriageway with no hard shoulder or cycle path, there was just no way to get to Bastogne without going a long way out of my way and/or involving a lot of climbing. I'd explored every possibility, but came up with nothing. So I went to the station in Arlon and rode the train 20 miles north-west to Neufchâteau. From there it would be a straight run on a quieter road to Bastogne, where I could pick up the race route again.

Just south of Neufchâteau, at Rossignol, the French army experienced one of its worst one-day defeats in the early days of the First World War. On 22 August 1914, during the Battle of the Frontiers, the 3rd Colonial Division (around 16,000 of the most experienced soldiers in the French army) was annihilated by two divisions of the German 5th Army. The French lost over 11,000 men in one day, including three battalion commanders killed in one burst of machine-gun fire, and two generals were also killed.

There's a perception about the First World War that the generals sat in their châteaux miles behind the front line, drinking brandy and plotting new stupid ways to kill their own troops. It's a perception that suits the lions-led-by-donkeys and *Blackadder* narrative, but the reality is very different. During the war 55 French generals, 71 German generals and 78 British generals were killed in action.

As I stood on the platform at Arlon station I thought about the 131 Belgian civilians who had been brought here in cattle trucks by the Germans from nearby Rossignol in August 1914. They were forced out of the wagons at gun-point and murdered beside the tracks. For the Belgians, this was just the start of a horrifically savage occupation.

Despite the cold, around 5°C, the weather was quite sunny, the road was almost empty, the undulating countryside was pleasantly farmy, and I was looking forward to not getting wet. I arrived in Bastogne in glorious sunshine and made my way to the Mardasson Memorial where the Americans commemorate the Battle of the Bulge. As I was to discover, the Americans like their memorials on an epic, monumental scale, and Mardasson is no exception. This huge star-shaped structure stands 40ft high and is inscribed with the states of the USA and with the names of the units that fought here in 1944–5.

It's an impressive memorial, but the nearby museum is even more so. It's a marvellous, sprawling interactive affair, thoroughly modern and very immersive. Even though none of this was relevant to my 1919 story, it was an hour well spent, and the café provided welcome relief from the coach-loads of Belgian school-kids and their smartphones. By the time I left the museum the sunshine had gone, the temperature had dropped, and dark clouds were looming. Oh joy.

A mile or so to the north, along a small country lane, I came across a memorial by the side of the road, on the edge of a wood, to E Company of the 506th Parachute Infantry Regiment, 101st Airborne Division. Anyone who's seen the *Band of Brothers* miniseries will know about Easy Company and their experiences in Bois Jacques, holding the perimeter around Bastogne. In freezing conditions and deep snow they held out against the Germans for weeks, living in foxholes in the woods under constant bombardment. That winter the temperatures dropped to as low as –28°C.

As I pulled into a layby in the woods, snow began to fall. I leant my bike against a tree and looked around. The snow was settling, and the scene was uncannily similar to the scenes from *Band of Brothers*. As I walked into the woods there was complete silence, the snow muffling all sounds. Here and there the remains of Second World War foxholes are still visible amongst the trees. I thought about the courage of the men who fought and died here, and the madness that it had happened all over again, barely two decades after the slaughter of the First World War. Being there, in this weather, was a profoundly moving experience, and I was lucky to have the place to myself.

Back on the road, the only sound was the hiss of tyres on the wet tarmac. On either side the woods were dusted with snow and couldn't have looked more beautiful, or more tragic. The snow stung my face, but I didn't care. I was in an extraordinary place, in extraordinary weather, and seething with emotions – sadness, gratitude, awe, anger, wonder, pity, indignation, compassion. Battlefields do this to me. I'd make a terrible historian because I feel completely unable to detach myself emotionally from what these men went through.

Back on the main road heading north to Houffalize, I felt slightly unstuck in time, a bit like Billy Pilgrim in Kurt Vonnegut's *Slaughterhouse 5*. For a while I had been transported back to the winter of 1944–5, then I was with the 1919 peloton, pushing north through the snow towards Liège, and now I was riding in the wheel-tracks of Bernard Hinault and Eddy Merckx in their epic editions of the Liège–Bastogne–Liège race. LBL is one of

Snow at Bois Jacques near Bastogne, scene of freezing conditions in 1919 and again in 1944 and 2016

the five Monuments of cycling, the five greatest one-day races on the calendar (the others are Paris–Roubaix, the Tour of Flanders, Milan–Sanremo and the Tour of Lombardy), and is arguably the toughest of the lot. They say it's possible to fluke a win in the other Monuments, but only the very strongest riders win LBL due to its length, weather and brutal terrain.

And as the riders of 1919 had discovered, the Ardennes are tough. Wherever you go the road is either going up steeply, or coming down steeply, as you slog through the pine forests. And it's cold here. Much colder than elsewhere in Belgium. In April 1980, 174 riders started the Liège–Bastogne–Liège in a snowstorm. After the first hour more than half the riders had abandoned the race, so cold and harsh were the conditions. Bernard Hinault, a tough little bastard from Brittany, ploughed on and won the race in just over 7 hours. He got frostbite in two fingers, and says they've never been the same since. Hinault won by over 9 minutes, and only 20 other riders finished the race that year.

These were the things I thought about as I rode on, although thankfully the snow stopped after a few more miles and by the time I arrived in Houffalize there were even patches of blue sky. I swung left at the bottom of the hill into town so that I could ride one of LBL's short, sharp climbs – the Côte de Saint-Roch. It's a funny narrow urban road up between rather grim terraced houses, and it seems so weird that this very ordinary road in a very ordinary Belgian town is one of cycling's most iconic climbs. But it is, so I slogged my way up it, agonisingly slowly. Then I came down and slogged up it another couple of times for the benefit of my camera and its self-timer. Then I stripped to my base-layer and allowed the massive amount of steam that I'd generated to escape. Seriously, I was actually steaming.

Another 30 miles passed in stop–start snow flurries, interspersed with sleet. The countryside is one of hilly pastures and pine forests, probably quite pretty in the summer, but bleak and cheerless in late April. I stopped at a *patisserie* somewhere for cake and hot chocolate, and to dry out my feet in front of the gas fire. I was about to take off my shoes when I remembered the curious smell of rotting flesh that came from my trench-foot, so decided maybe I'd leave my shoes on.

And so to Stavelot, scene of savage fighting in the Battle of the Bulge and scene of savage riding in the late 1960s. Eddy Merckx, the greatest cyclist of all time and five-times winner of LBL, monstered the opposition every time they came to the Côte de Stockeu on the edge of Stavelot. This evil little climb has no run-up to it and ascends the 1.1km hill on the edge of town at an average of 10.5 per cent, with pitches of over 20 per cent. Again, I couldn't ride past without giving it a go, and again I suffered like a dog hauling myself up it. I collapsed in a snivelling heap at the top, next to a very disturbing bas-relief sculpture of Merckx looking like some kind of demented hunchbacked ape. Surely the great man deserves better than this? I may look like a hunch-backed ape on a bike, but not Eddy.

That night I checked into my B&B in Malmedy and went through the usual routine of hand-washing my riding kit, hanging everything up to dry, getting dressed in my increasingly crumpled civvies, putting my riding shoes on the radiator, opening a window to avoid asphyxiation, and heading into town to find something to eat. I was in luck . . . there was a small Italian restaurant with a wood-fired pizza oven. After 65 miles and over 5,000ft of climbing, mostly in the snow, I deserved this. I ordered a *pichet* of vin rouge and a pizza, and demolished the bread-basket (well, the bread inside the basket, obviously) in about two minutes. Then I ordered more bread to go with my pizza. And another *pichet*.

The following morning I snapped one of the clips on my saddle-bag while over-tightening it. Crap! Now I couldn't do it up properly. Bugger. Now what? A bodge using zip-ties and a bit of wire I found in my room (which may have been a coat-hanger). Over a breakfast of croissants and coffee (for a change) I called home and spoke to middle son Joe. He was about get the Eurostar to Brussels that afternoon, along with his bike, so that he could join me for a couple of days' riding. He offered to call Apidura and ask them to send a spare clip for the bag out to my hotel in Brussels, where I'd be spending two nights. After a week on the road I wanted a day off, and Joe and I had planned on spending it riding the final climbs of the Tour of Flanders.

And so began a really shitty day. The minute I left Malmedy the bloody sat-nav took me up a bruising climb above the town at a steady 12–14 per cent. With no time to warm up my muscles or digest my breakfast, this was horrible. Then I turned a corner two-thirds of the way up and the tarmac turned abruptly into a rocky track and disappeared up the mountain at an even more vertiginous angle. I was just considering giving it a go when a bloke on a full-suspension mountain bike came down it, covered from head to foot in mud. He looked at me as if I was mental.

I rested my forehead on my handlebars and took a minute to compose myself.

Back in Malmedy I could skirt this mountain to the east or the west. I chose the east, which turned out to be the much harder, longer and snowier option. If the Ardennes had been tough yesterday, today they really made me suffer – steep and long on the way up, icy and slippery on the way down. And it never bloody ends – up, down, up, down! The only thing that took my mind off it was fantasising about the way I would exact my revenge on the sat-nav. Crush it slowly in a vice, or smash it with a sledgehammer? Rest it on a golf tee and take a seven-iron to it? Blam it into the sea with a cricket bat? Strap half a dozen bangers to it and blow it to pieces?

As if to spite me, for the first 2 hours the sat-nav constantly tried to get me to ride up muddy lanes, along fire-breaks in the forests, in fact almost anywhere except where I wanted to go. I stopped and altered the sat-nav's preferences from 'take me where the hell you want' to 'stick to the bloody tarmac you useless piece of junk'. This improved things immeasurably and I went for several miles without getting lost. And although the snow lay deep and crisp and even, at least it wasn't falling from the sky at the moment.

I stopped for coffee in one of those village bars where you find locals drinking spirits at 9 a.m. By now it was 11 a.m. and the local, a rather hippyish lady in leather fringes and tie-dye, was already two-thirds of her way through the bottle of white wine on the bar. There followed a conversation which I would have many times over the three weeks of my trip:

Drunk Hippy Lady: Are you going far?

Me: To Brussels.

DHL: On your bike?

Me: Yes.

DHL: Noooo!

Me: Yes.

DHL: Today?

Me: Yes.

DHL: Noooo!

Me: Yes. And then to Lille, Paris and Strasbourg.

DHL: On your bike?

Me: Yes.

DHL: Noooo!

Me: Yes.

I should probably mention my linguistic abilities at this point. Basically, I pretend to speak French, and French people pretend not to understand me. It works perfectly. For a long time I used to think that all French people were dullards, with their furrowed brows and looks of blank incomprehension. Then I realised that it was only the ones I was speaking 'French' to who looked like that. But I do like a bit of lexicographic adventurism, and speaking French allows me to plumb new depths of inappropriate tenses, mangled syntax and malapropisms.

I once asked a French petrol-pump attendant to fill my car up with 'petrol without feathers' (*sans plume*, instead of *sans plomb*). I thought he was actually going to injure himself laughing. And once when I met Robert Pires, the French footballer, I tortured him for a full five minutes. '*Vous êtes un footballeur fantastique,*' I gushed. '*Allez les cannoniers! J'aime beaucoup les rouges et blancs.*' (Go, the Gunners. I love the Red and Whites.) The look on his face was a picture. Eventually I shook his hand and left him with this *mot juste*: '*Votre gilet de sauvetage est sous votre siège.*' (Your lifejacket is under your seat.) He couldn't get out of there fast enough.

Anyway, Drunk Hippy Lady and I spent a cheerful 15 minutes chatting away, neither of us understanding much of what was said. Once I'd thawed out I set off for Liège, several hours behind schedule and casting a worried eye at the dark clouds forming overhead. This was day five of my trip and I had yet to experience one without getting soaked. But as I descended from the Ardennes the snow disappeared and the weather warmed up to a balmy 8°C.

By the time I reached Liège it was lunchtime, I seemed to have pissed away the morning at an average speed of 8mph (how the hell did that happen?), and I was hopelessly lost in the post-industrial horrors of south Liège. This really is a grim place, with its disused factories, boarded-up terraced houses, broken glass, graffiti, rubbish, and blacked-out Beemers cruising slowly around the housing estates. Endless roadworks and road closures caused the sat-nav to flip-out yet again, but I finally made it to the Rue Bordelais, known in the cycling world as the Côte de Saint-Nicolas, the final significant climb of the LBL. It's 1km in length and 11.1 per cent average incline, and it's another lung-busting, leg-sapping grind up through inner-city terraced housing, round an ugly tower-block, and on through more terraces. It may not be a beautiful or long climb, but for cycling fans it's imbued with history and drama. I loved it, and was pleased to be able to add it to my *palmarès*.

As I pedalled through Liège on my way to Brussels, the rain that had been threatening for most of the morning started to fall. I stopped at Fort de Loncin, one of Liège's defensive fortifications. Like pretty much everything else I tried to visit, it was shut.

*

As the race headed west towards Brussels the riders passed just a hundred metres from the huge pile of brick-and-concrete rubble that had once been Fort de Loncin. It was blown to pieces in mid-August 1914 when a direct hit on one of its magazines set off 12 tonnes of munitions. Around 350 men disappeared in that explosion, and it signalled the final collapse of Liège's resistance. But they had held out just long enough to enable the French and British forces to get organised.

An unfortunate consequence of the Battle of Liège was that everyone assumed that, in the face of 380mm and 420mm ultra-heavy artillery, forts were useless. This wasn't the case – Liège's forts had been poorly constructed due to technical issues pouring the concrete. Even so, the French stripped valuable artillery pieces from their forts around Verdun to use elsewhere in the line, a decision that would cost them so dearly at the Battle of Verdun in 1916.

Some of the Belgian riders must have looked in astonishment at the remains of Loncin. In 1914 many of them would have fled south and west (or north into Holland) and they would not have been back to Belgium since the war ended. They would have had little idea of what exactly had happened to their homeland. Loncin was to be the first of many shocking surprises over the next few days.

Lucien Buysse left Liège with an 11-minute lead over Heusghem, Dejonghe, Nempon and Anseeuw, with Duboc, Van Hevel and Deruyter another few minutes behind. There now followed a tough pursuit along the long, straight road to Brussels, the two chasing groups joining forces to reel in Buysse. The temperatures were still only a couple of degrees above freezing, the sleet and rain continued to fall, and the wind continued to blow in their faces. Riding into a strong headwind, a rider sheltering behind the rider in front of him can save around 40 per cent of his energy, so when riders take turns on the front a group can ride faster than a solo rider. There were now ten riders in the chasing group and the gap to a tiring Buysse closed quickly.

The catch was made somewhere near Tienen, and for a while the pace let up as everyone drew breath. Then they began plotting their race strategies. Those like Van Hevel, who were quick sprinters, hoped the group would stay together, rest up, and then sprint for victory in the last few hundred metres. But riders who weren't fast finishers needed to break away from the group and build up a time gap. They watched, and waited.

Then, on a slight hill in the village of Kumtich, 40km from the finish, Dejonghe suddenly attacked, sprinting out of the saddle to pull out a small lead. Buysse and Heusghem tried to go with him, but couldn't hold his wheel. Behind them the others tried, too, but with 250km in their legs they had nothing left.

They had split into several small groups as they reached Leuven, a small but picturesque university town. At least it used to be. In late August 1914 the German occupiers set fire to the town, murdered nearly 300 civilians, and expelled the rest. One of the buildings burned to the ground was the university library, which contained 200,000 rare and valuable books, as well as hundreds of medieval manuscripts. Fortunately, the majority of the library's most valuable manuscripts had been removed to Brussels at the outbreak of war. As an act of wanton vandalism it was hard to beat, and it shocked the rest of the world.

But this was just one act in a brutal and merciless occupation by the Germans. After they invaded, the occupying forces set about subduing the Belgians. The Germans had encountered problems in their occupation of France in 1870–1 with *francs-tireurs*, armed resistance fighters who would take pot-shots at German soldiers. So when they invaded Belgium they came down very heavily on acts of resistance, took and executed hostages, burned houses, and deported families of suspected *francs-tireurs* for forced labour in Germany.

The Rape of Belgium, as the occupation became known, was reported by the British and American press in lurid, prurient detail, with tales of crucified babies, raped nuns and executed nurses. Sadly, this blatant propaganda obfuscated the real truth and offered the Germans plausible deniability, as we'd call it these days. But the fact was that the occupying regime was appallingly brutal. The Germans murdered more than 23,000 civilians, forcibly deported more than 120,000 more as labourers, left 500,000 people homeless, and then set about requisitioning anything of any use, from food and clothing to farm machinery and livestock. The population ended up living in rags, on the brink of starvation, and was reduced to living off hand-outs from the USA and sifting through slag-heaps looking for bits of coal to keep them warm.

It didn't stop there, either. Throughout the war the Germans systematically stripped Belgium of her industry, dismantling factories and transporting the equipment to Germany. Before the war Belgium was the fifth biggest economy in the world, but it would never be so again. What industry they couldn't steal (primarily the coal mines), the Germans pressed into service for their own war effort, or destroyed. There is speculation that whatever the outcome of the war, the Germans didn't want Belgium to regain her status as a competitive industrial power. And she didn't.

As the riders passed through Leuven, they would have looked in horror at the dilapidated state of this once-pretty town. Some rebuilding had been started, but the place was still a shambles of burned and collapsed buildings, with weeds growing everywhere.

It was now a four-way battle for the stage win, but Dejonghe was strong and the other three just couldn't pull him back. From now on it was every man for himself as each rider made a last push for the line (and warmth). The cold and hunger were having a terrible effect on the riders in the last miles, every man drawing on whatever reserves of mental and physical strength he could muster.

In Brussels, the crowds had been gathering for some time, eager to see the riders come across the line. The grandstand in the Park van Laeken was full of the great and the good of the Belgian sports world (including the winner of Le Petit Journal's cross-country race in Strasbourg), as well as the mayor and other civic dignitaries. It's estimated that a crowd of 20,000 gathered to see the race arrive. The riders were expected at around 3 p.m., but by 5 p.m. they still hadn't made it. However, the local philharmonic orchestra and the band of the Belgian 19th Infantry Regiment kept the spectators amused in the meantime, and there was also a 37-lap race round the Park van Laeken for local amateur bike racers.

At 5.18 p.m. Albert Dejonghe crossed the line and the Belgian crowd went mental. Thousands burst through the barriers and onto the course, eager to carry the victorious Belgian shoulder-high. Such was the pandemonium that it took the police and stewards nearly ten minutes to restore order, just in time for the crowd to cheer home five more Belgians. Dejonghe won with a time of 12 hours 18 minutes, averaging 22.2kmh, in what the paper described the next day as a 'triumph of the impossible'. It was to be one of the very few victories in his 14-year career as a bike racer. Dejonghe's finest hour came when he won the Paris–Roubaix in 1922, but apart from that and a stage win at the 1923 Tour, poor Dejonghe never quite lived up to expectations.

The rest of the riders came to the line in dribs and drabs. Buysse was second, 11 minutes down, and complained bitterly about how Dejonghe had managed to take so much time out of him, and praising Dejonghe's 'driver'. Buysse may have had a point . . . gaining 11 minutes in 100km as a lone rider on a flat stage is pretty unusual. Anyway, Anseeuw was third, 19 minutes down, and Duboc and Heusghem arrived together 40 minutes behind the leader. Then the crowd was treated to the extraordinary sight of Charles Deruyter crossing the line in ninth place, wearing a full-length woman's fur coat to keep out the cold. Where he got the coat we don't know, and clearly this was in total contravention of race rules, but the organisers were more concerned with keeping riders in the race than throwing them out.

In total, 51 riders finished the stage, out of 67 starters. It had been an unbelievably hard day's racing and the riders had suffered terribly. The roads had been muddy, the weather had been a mix of sleet, snow and rain, the headwind had been relentless, and the temperatures had barely got above freezing. Joseph Verdickt lost a shoe in the mud and finished the stage with frostbite in several toes, riders took an eternity to mend punctures with wooden, frozen fingers, and many resorted to peeing on their hands to try and warm them up. At just after 2 a.m., when the control point at the finish line was packing up and getting ready to head home, the lone figure of Louis Ellner rolled over the line.

Ellner had been on the road for 21 hours, 2 minutes and 15 seconds. He was covered from head to foot in mud, he was soaked to the skin, and he had lost all feeling in his hands and feet. His face was so cold he couldn't actually speak. It was only by looking at the numbers on his bike that the commissaires were able to work out who he was. One of them placed Ellner gently in his car and drove him to his home, where his wife set about trying to revive the poor man with hot soup and a bath in front of the fire in the kitchen.

★

It was probably just as well that Fort de Loncin was closed, otherwise I would have fallen even further behind schedule. I shoved a croissant and an energy bar down my gob by way of a late lunch, and then pressed on westwards as the drizzle turned to proper rain.

The road was long and straight and flat and boring, lined with the usual stuff – tyre centres and unattractive houses with hideous concrete statues in the front gardens (the Belgians absolutely *love* these things), and so on and so on. It was an endless, cold and soul-destroying ride. *Splish-splosh-ther-dunk-ther-dunk*, I went, along the crappy bike lanes. For hour after hour.

I was briefly cheered up by Belgium's resolute refusal to join the twenty-first century, or even the latter part of the twentieth century. No, I'm not talking about their 1970s dress-sense, I'm talking about their overt and unrepentant sexism. Specifically, I passed a huge, garish billboard advert for a local second-hand car emporium called Bart's Bangers, or something of that ilk. To illustrate the wonderfulness of this establishment the billboard portrayed a nearly-naked lady sitting at 45 degrees to the camera, with her knees up, as she apparently fired highly desirable second-hand cars from her nether regions. It was an extraordinary image and I was genuinely shocked. Really? In this day and age? Apparently so.

I knew I wasn't going to be able to ride all the way to Brussels in time to meet Joe off the Eurostar, so it was now just a matter of how far I got before hopping on a train. I got as far as Sint-Truiden and then threw in the towel. Even though I'd only done a fraction of what the racers had to endure, I'd had enough of today. Seriously. Enough. Louis Ellner, I am not.

The train was warm, and busy, and I managed to choose the only carriage that also contained a double-bass. At every stop there was an elaborate dance that involved me, my bike, a small lady, and her double bass, trying to create enough space for other passengers to get on or off the train. It was probably fairly comical, but I was too tired and wet to appreciate the funny side.

I cheered up a lot when Joe arrived at the hotel in Brussels. I'd had a shower and warmed up a bit, and now I was sitting in the bar with a beer when my boy arrived. He produced, out of his bag, two new clips for my Apidura saddle-bag . . . result! Bless him, he'd gone down to Apidura's HQ in central London and picked up some spares before jumping on the Eurostar. No more coat-hanger and zip-ties for me.

The following morning: Oh, the unalloyed joy of a lie-in! Ah, the relief of realising that I won't have to spend 20 minutes struggling to get all my kit into my bags! Mmmm . . . a leisurely breakfast of eggs and bacon. After five days and 530km, mostly in the rain and snow, it was nice just to kick back and loaf for a bit. My first rest day had been planned to allow Joe and me to ride what are traditionally the final two cobbled climbs of the Ronde (the Tour of Flanders), something we missed out on last time we were riding in Belgium.

I have a bit of a thing about cobbles, or *pavé*, or setts. I love the history of them, the timelessness, and I love riding on them on my bike (although I'm not sure I'd have liked to ride them for hundreds of kilometres, as they did in the Circuit des Champs de Bataille). What I particularly like about cobbles, especially those of the Paris–Roubaix and the Tour of Flanders, is that they are a direct connection between me and people like Eddy Merckx, Roger de Vlaeminck, Johan Museeuw and Tom Boonen. These roads have not changed in several hundred years, and as you grovel up the Koppenberg or the Kapelmuur you are riding directly in the wheel-tracks of cycling legends. This is pure,

unadulterated cycling history in all its mud and pain and glory.
And I love it.

Over the past few years Joe and I had 'bagged' quite a few *sec-*
teurs of *pavé*. A couple of years back we rode the last 110km of
the Paris–Roubaix route, which included 45km of *pavé*. At the
end of the Arenberg Trench (a 2.4km stretch of the roughest,
hardest, most irregular *pavé* you'll ever find) I genuinely thought
I was going to have some kind of seizure and die. My brain
had been shaken into a frothy smoothie which slid thickly out
of my nose and down my chin, where it joined some kind of
green stuff coming out of my lungs. My arms and hands were so
pumped up from desperately hanging onto the wildly bucking
handlebars that I struggled to let go when I got to the end. Riding
the Paris–Roubaix cobbles is like hanging onto an out-of-control
pneumatic road drill, while having your genitals kicked by a gang
of skinheads. It's great!

Having enjoyed that so much, the following year Joe and I
went to Belgium to tackle the cobbled *bergs* of the Ronde. And
it was truly excellent – heaving my whimpering, sweating bulk
over the Oude Kwaremont, Koppenberg, Molenberg, Paterberg
and Taaienberg was hugely emotional. Yes, I nearly cried at the
top of the Koppenberg, not because I was about to throw up
one of my internal organs but because . . . because . . . it's the
Koppenberg! And I made it!

So after our leisurely breakfast we made our leisurely way to
the station and caught a leisurely train to Geraardsbergen, 20 or
so miles south-west. Here we climbed the Muur van Geraardsbergen (aka the Kapelmuur). There was nothing leisurely about
that . . . it's a short, tough, cobbled climb, but the sight of the
chapel at the top, something I've seen in a thousand photos, is
something special. So special that we went back down and did
it again. Then, with photos duly taken, we headed for the traditional final climb of the Ronde, the Bosberg, a few miles distant.

BANG . . . pshhhhhhh! *Well that's odd*, I thought, looking
around. *What was that?* After the bang-pshhhhh came a horrible,

harsh shuddering from the front end of my bike that rattled my dental work and blurred my vision. *Ah, that'll be a sudden and potentially catastrophic failure of my front tyre,* I thought to myself, expecting to be pitched face-first onto the Kapelmuur's *pavé* descent.

Despite the cobbles and the steep descent, I managed to bring the bike to a nerve-shredding halt, rubber-side-down. I was crouching by the side of the road inspecting a 3cm tear in my front tyre when Joe rode back up to me. I set about sticking in a tyre boot (a thin, flexible piece of rectangular plastic that prevents the inner tube from poking through the gash in the tyre under pressure) and replacing the inner tube. A quick squirt of CO_2 to pump it up and we were on our way again. The Bosberg was surprisingly easy and we breezed up it in the company of a sportive (a mass-participation ride that many participants fondly imagine is a race, but isn't).

Then we had a pleasant lunch outside the café at the top of the Bosberg and watched the wheezing remnants of the sportive wobble past while we discussed cobbled climbs, which of the Lions of Flanders was the greatest, and how to deftly handle a front-tyre blow-out on cobbles. My barely disguised smugness at having evaded the clutches of the grim reaper on our descent of the Kapelmuur, thanks mainly to my exemplary bike-handling skills, was wiped off my face shortly after lunch. And then some.

'Are you OK?' asked Joe, who seemed to be peering down at me with a slightly worried frown.

'Um . . . I think so. It's all a bit starry,' I heard myself mumble.

'OK, you stay there, I'll direct the traffic.'

Then he disappeared, leaving me to contemplate the multitude of dots, sparkles and specks of bright light that were whirling slowly around my field of vision. It was pretty, but confusing. What did he mean, 'direct the traffic'? And why was he up there, when I'm down here? I tried to make sense of the last hour or so. There was the Bosberg. There was lunch. There was a lovely bike path. Then the bike path turned into some rather ugly cobbles. I remembered riding onto them at a fair speed and I remembered attempting . . . oh crap. The bunny-hop. That was it, the sideways bunny-hop.

A bunny-hop, for the uninitiated, is a technique for jumping over small obstacles on your bike that can be used to clear pot-holes, speed-bumps, kerbs and so on. When you get it right it's quite gratifying; when you get it wrong it's quite painful, or embarrassing. Or both. Mainly both. I closed my eyes and groaned.

Then I sat up and looked around. Joe was indeed directing traffic around my prone figure. I dragged myself and my bike to the side of the road and inspected the damage. The bike was fine, you'll be glad to hear. A few scuffs but nothing serious. I, on the other hand, was not so good. I'd banged my head very hard when I landed on my left side (the front wheel had cleared the lip between cobbled cycle path and raised tarmac road, the back wheel hadn't) and felt mildly concussed. More annoyingly, I'd shredded my expensive Gabba jacket, my base-layer and my leg-warmers, and put a ding in my helmet. Bollocks bollocks bollocks!

Further examination revealed a bleeding shoulder, a bleeding knee, a sore hip and a searing pain in my ribs on the left-hand side. Hmmm. I poked my ribs tentatively and the little stars and specks of light reappeared, along with a wave of nausea. OK, that's not good. With only around 15 miles back to the hotel in Brussels, we set off gingerly, only for the sat-nav to give up the ghost because some idiot (me) forgot to charge it the previous night. The rest of the journey was spent following Joe while he juggled with his phone, trying to navigate on the move using Google Maps while I wheezed slowly along behind.

At the hotel Joe patched me up using my medical kit. My eldest son is a junior doctor, and he'd prepared this small but useful kit for me. The road-rash wasn't good, but was bearable, the hip ached quite a lot, but the ribs were another matter. Having spent much of my working life testing motorbikes, cars, bicycles and powerboats, I'm no stranger to broken bones and

A&E departments. It's an occupational hazard. I've cracked or broken 14 bones in all (I think), including quite a few ribs, so I know the feeling. The ribs didn't feel too badly damaged, and I wasn't coughing up blood (something I've done before when one of them poked into my lung), so with any luck they were just bruised. I popped a handful of painkillers and then Joe and I went down to the bar to drink strong Belgian beer and wait for Phil to arrive.

Phil is an old friend and colleague from my motorcycle magazine days, an excellent photographer and an avid lifelong cyclist. He was coming out to ride with us for a few days – Joe would head back to university from Amiens, and Phil would stay with me as far as Paris. Phil is a club cyclist, a distance runner, and probably the fittest person I know. I was looking forward to wheel-sucking my way to Paris, assuming I could keep up with him.

When Phil arrived we jumped in a taxi and went into the centre of Brussels to carb load and drink more strong beer. Despite my aches and pains, it was a very pleasant evening and I was enchanted by central Brussels . . . much prettier than I'd expected. I went to bed gingerly, trying to avoid lying on my wounds. It would not be a good night.

General Classification after Stage 2

	Rider	Time	Time gap
1	Albert Dejonghe (B)	23hr 23min	0hr 0min
2	Lucien Buysse (B)	23hr 34min	+11min
3	Urbain Anseeuw (B)	23hr 43min	+20min
4	Jules Van Hevel (B)	24hr 04min	+41min
5	Hector Heusghem (F)	24hr 04min	+41min
6	Paul Duboc (F)	24hr 11min	+48min
7	José Pelletier (F)	24hr 18min	+55min
8	André Huret (F)	24hr 21min	+58min
9	Henri Hanlet (B)	24hr 30min	+1hr 07min
10	Charles Deruyter (B)	24hr 40min	+1hr 17min
11	Albert Desmedt (F)	24hr 45min	+1hr 22min
12	Jean Alavoine (F)	24hr 53min	+1hr 30min
13	Henri Van Lerberghe (B)	24hr 54min	+1hr 31min
14	Aloysius Verstraeten (B)	24hr 57min	+1hr 34min
15	Charles Haidon (B)	25hr 02min	+1hr 39min
51	Louis Ellner (F)	38hr 52min	+16hr 29min

STAGE 3

Brussels to Amiens

323km

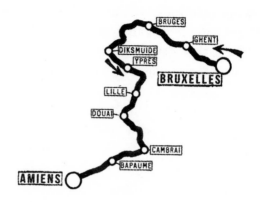

2 May 1919

Barely 24 hours after Louis Ellner struggled across the finish line in Brussels, after a 301km, 21-hour slog through the Ardennes, he was back on the start line for Stage 3. A mammoth 323km lay ahead, much of it over the battlefields of Flanders and the Somme. For most riders, the rest day was spent fettling their bikes and quizzing the survivors of the previous month's Paris–Roubaix race about conditions on the roads of northern France. They were not encouraged by what they heard. Ellner, however, had spent most of his rest day asleep, or gratefully wolfing down whatever food was put in front of him.

As *Lanterne Rouge*, Ellner had acquired minor celebrity status within the peloton. The rest-day chat had been all about his 2 a.m. finish and his 16-hour deficit on GC, and many of the riders thought he was mad, or brave, to continue. This strange, quiet man from Épernay was a mystery to them. No one had even seen him in a race before, he had no *palmarès* as far as anyone knew, he was the epitome of an *isolé*, and yet here he was. He didn't even have a proper racing bike! He was a figure of fun to some of the professionals, but also a figure of grudging respect.

But for some the rest day was also spent having a bit of fun – May Day in Brussels offered many diversions of interest to young men and ex-soldiers. And while some of them were enjoying what Brussels had to offer, others were closeted away with team owners and race organisers. According to *Sportwereld*, Jules Van Hevel and Henri Van Lerberghe signed a two-year contract with Bianchi that day, and committed to riding the Giro d'Italia a month later, along with Marcel and Lucien Buysse.

'Still with us, Louis?' enquired Duboc as the riders assembled at the Taverne des Augustins on the Boulevard Anspatch before the 4.30 a.m. start.

Ellner smiled, surprised that the great man even knew his name. 'Yes, just about, Monsieur Duboc. How are you getting on?'

'Sixth, 48 minutes down. Could be worse. Can't say I'm looking forward to today, though. I think it's going to be tough.'

'I'm sure it is,' said Ellner with a bitter laugh. 'Well, good luck, see you in Amiens.'

Duboc was surprised there were this many riders still left in the race. The first two stages had been desperately hard, and for 51 riders to make it this far was an impressive achievement. He thought back to the pre-war Tour stages he'd ridden, but couldn't think of any which compared to this in terms of physical discomfort. Yes, the Alpine stage over the Galibier in 1911 had been incredibly difficult, and being poisoned on the descent of the Aubisque the same year had been horrific, but somehow there'd always been light at the end of the tunnel. Here, this race, just seemed a relentless grind, something to be endured. *I suppose,* he thought to himself, *the war has made us all more accustomed to discomfort, cold and hunger.*

Also huddled together in the café were Ernest Paul, Maurice Brocco and Jean Alavoine. None of them had raced the Paris–Roubaix two weeks earlier, but they'd heard enough about the condition of the roads to make them worried.

'Van Mol says the roads around Lille are in a terrible state,' said Brocco. 'And Paris–Roubaix didn't even go through the worst areas, apparently.'

'I'm not so concerned about the roads, it's this damn headwind that worries me. It must be blowing at 30 or 40kmh out there,' replied

Paul. 'And I can't afford to fall any further behind . . . I lost three and a half hours on Wednesday!'

Ali Neffati, the Tunisian rider, came over to join them. 'Good morning, gentlemen,' he said, doffing his red fez and bowing in his rather exaggerated fashion. Neffati often rode wearing a red fez. It underscored his exoticness and made him instantly recognisable in the peloton.

'Morning, Ali,' said Alavoine. They were old friends, having ridden at the 1913 and 1914 Tours together. 'Enjoying the weather?' he continued, with a grin. Alavoine was referring obliquely to the time when, on a blisteringly hot 35°C day at the 1914 Tour, Desgrange had driven up alongside Neffati and asked him if he was all right. Neffati's response was to complain bitterly about the cold, delivered with a completely dead-pan expression. Desgrange didn't know if he was joking then, but the Tunisian was possibly feeling the cold more than most on this race.

Neffati was an interesting character. He showed great promise as a young bike rider back in Tunisia, winning the Tunis-to-Sousse race in 1912 at the age of 17, such that members of the Tunisian athletics associations had a whip-round to send him to the 1913 Tour de France. He rode in the 1913 Tour, abandoning on Stage 4, and in 1914, when he was knocked off his bike by an organiser's car ('twas ever thus) and abandoned on Stage 8. He was 'adopted' by Henri Pélissier, who became his mentor (possibly not the perfect mentor, considering Pélissier's belligerent nature and untimely death at the hands of his mistress), and he also became a firm favourite of Henri Desgrange. After Neffati retired from racing he worked as a driver for Desgrange at *L'Auto*, and married an opera singer from Paris.

Given Neffati's blank *palmarès* from late 1914 to early 1919, it would seem likely that he enlisted to fight for France, probably in one of the Moroccan regiments (which included battalions of Tunisian *tirailleurs*) that served with great distinction throughout the First World War. He may well have fought alongside

François Faber at Vimy Ridge in 1915, and the Moroccans saw active service on the Marne, Aisne, Champagne, Somme and Verdun fronts.

'No, I bloody hate it,' replied Neffati with a grimace. 'I wish I'd stayed in Paris and ridden the Grand Prix de l'Heure.'

The others nodded in agreement. Track racing was where the money was, and conditions were far easier, but the publicity and prestige from stage races was invaluable, and the team managers wanted them out there flying the flag for their sponsors.

'It doesn't help that my bike's an old heap and my tyres are made of cheese.' He eyed Alavoine's team-issue Pirellis enviously. 'But at least I still have my looks, which is more than you can say for poor Brocco here.' The others laughed uproariously.

'You wait,' replied Brocco with mock indignation. 'I'll kick your sandy Berber arse from here to Strasbourg!'

'Maghreb! My sandy Maghreb arse!'

'Berber, Maghreb . . . you're all a bunch of heathens to me.'

At that moment a rather stout, red-faced man barged his way through the thronged café and confronted Ernest Paul.

'You have not paid your hotel bill, Monsieur,' said the angry hotelier. 'You must give to me three Francs.' He waved the hotel bill in Paul's face.

'No, no,' protested Paul. *Le Petit Journal* is paying the bill. You must take it up with them.'

According to the report in *L'Auto*, there followed an increasingly heated exchange during which several other riders got involved, one of the commissaires was summoned, and it all degenerated into a rather Gallic display of arm-waving and shouting. Amidst the mayhem, Ernest Paul quietly slipped out of the bar and disappeared into the dark outside.

★

If the riders were apprehensive about the weather and the road conditions, I was pretty apprehensive, too, although my day would be spent riding barely 110km between Brussels and Bruges on tarmac roads and concrete bike paths. The night had been spent trying not to roll onto my left side, failing, then waking up wincing. The shoulder and knee were bandaged and not too bad, but my left hip ached like hell and the ribs were pretty sore. It was a long and not particularly restful night.

But the good news was that it wasn't raining when I finally gave up trying to sleep. In fact there was blue sky, sunshine, and a temperature of 9°C. After the usual massive breakfast, and a moment or two spent checking over my bike, we were off. The Sunday morning traffic was light, and Joe, Phil and I made our way out of Brussels and into the teeth of a stiff westerly wind. The roads were flat and straight, the scenery was basically flat farmland interspersed with the usual car showrooms and bathroom superstores, and we were obliged to use the crappy cycle paths.

I appear to be alone in this, but I generally don't want to use cycle paths. Cycle paths are almost always worse than the roads – inconvenient, badly surfaced, covered in broken glass, and with horrible bumps caused by tree-roots. They're probably fine for the heavy, upright, do-it-all bikes they ride in the Low Countries, but on a race bike with relatively narrow, high-pressure tyres they're a pain in the arse. Literally. At least in Belgium they give you right-of-way over cars emerging from side-roads, but even so I'd rather be on the road.

But we were condemned to the cycle paths, so on the cycle paths we rode. Amazingly, we only had one puncture that day. To be honest, I don't remember too much about that Sunday. I remember stopping for coffee in a pretty place called Aalst, but apart from that there wasn't much to look at, I hurt all over, and all I did was follow Phil and Joe as they took turns on the front. Phil is a proper club cyclist, so he's all about high average speeds, through-and-off pacing, free and thorough expectoration, and mystifying hand signals.

I do remember being particularly impressed with Phil's ability to spit with incredible power and precision. I genuinely am in awe of this, because for me spitting never goes well. Every club cyclist is an expert in this field, footballers seem pretty good at it – hell, even Leonardo di Caprio and Kate Winslet can do it. Me? Not so much. To be honest, I don't really do the spitting thing unless absolutely necessary (ingested flying insects, accidental mouthful of aubergine, claggy gob after eating an energy gel, that type of thing). And what invariably happens is that I turn my head sideways and spit as hard as I can . . . into my own ear. For some reason I just can't seem to spit far enough to prevent the wind from blowing it into my ear, or onto my shoulder.

Having transferred the drowning insect from my mouth to my ear, I then have to shake my head manically while trying to scoop the disgusting buzzing mess from the side of my face and wipe it on my clothing. So generally speaking, I prefer a slightly claggy gob to having a thick layer of carb-mucus on my face, ear, shoulder and gloves. And don't get me started on snot-rockets. How (and, more importantly, why) can anyone do that without getting absolutely covered?

Anyway, we ploughed on through the cross/headwind, stopping for a pleasant lunch in Ghent. I spent most of the time trying not to think about the pain in my ribs. On and on we rode. Occasionally there would be a house with a particularly hideous life-size concrete Venus de Milo on its front lawn, or a nightclub with an aeroplane parked outside, or a T34 tank by a roundabout, but mostly it was rather dull. Back in 1914 this road carried a tide of miserable, frightened humanity, with nearly 1 million refugees fleeing west from the German advance, dragging their meagre possessions with them. Now it was just a busy A-road from Brussels to Ghent to Bruges. The bloody cross/headwind was awful, every breath was painful, and the gaps between the concrete slabs of the bloody cycle path became a fiendish torture. *Thurdunk, thur-dunk, thur-dunk, thur-dunk.*

By late afternoon we'd made it to Bruges, home to Belgian chocolate and strong beer. We headed straight for the nearest bar and drank Leffe, feeling pretty beaten-up by the day's ride despite the modest 65 miles we'd covered. Then we drank more beer, dumped our stuff at the hotel, and headed out for *moules* and *frites*. Over dinner we made an astonishing discovery. Phil, who has kids of a similar age to mine, and who I always assumed was around my age (mid 50s), is actually 69 years old. Really? The man who had effectively towed Joe and me for 65 miles into a stiff headwind at an average speed of 14mph (according to the sat-nav), was nearly 70 years of age. Bloody hell! It's not surprising he fell fast asleep during dinner.

I'd hoped that large amounts of Leffe would make sleep a bit easier to come by, but it wasn't to be. The road-rash, the bruises, and the aching ribs meant another uncomfortable night, but at least the relative warmth and sunshine during the day had been a pleasant change.

★

The riders on the Circuit des Champs de Bataille would have given anything for double-digit temperatures and clear skies. As it was, they left Brussels at 4.30 a.m. in near-freezing temperatures and with rain borne on a biting westerly. Ten of the finishers of Stage 2 didn't make it to the start line that morning, and Theo Wynsdau arrived at the start line five minutes after the race had started. Duboc clapped a friendly hand on Ellner's back as he passed and wished him luck, before making his way to the head of the peloton where the Belgians were massing for the first attack of the day.

The roads were tough, a mixture of *pavé* and macadam, but were still a long way behind the front line so were unaffected by the direct consequences of the war. But the roads had been used extensively by heavy German trucks going to and from the front, and as a result had become appallingly rutted and potholed in places. The Germans used Belgian forced labour to make repairs, but the Belgians weren't too interested in making things easier for the German war effort, and the repairs were generally pretty shoddy. Besides, the Belgians weren't allowed to travel anywhere without a fistful of expensively gained permits, so what did they care about the roads?

Ernest Paul cared. He, like many others, was having a torrid time with punctures, the weather, and the roads. He wasn't feeling strong, and he was dropped quickly when the Belgians pushed on. The race had split up, and Paul had teamed up with a handful of the slower Belgians, just trying to hang on. As they turned south-west from Bruges, the full force of the wind hit them head-on. Van Hevel, lying fourth on GC, slipped on some wet *pavé* and 'made a bottlenose dolphin', damaging his front wheel and forks. That's a rather clunky translation of a report in *Sportwereld* by Google, but the image of Van Hevel flying over the handlebars like a bottlenose dolphin is rather wonderful. While he was trying to fix his forks a car stopped and out got Karel Van Wijnendaele, pre-eminent Belgian journalist for *Sportwereld* and organiser of the Tour of Flanders, tool-kit in hand. Despite this outrageous piece of cheating, not to mention the complete dereliction of journalistic integrity on the part of Van Wijnendaele, Van Hevel was unable to repair his forks and was forced to retire from the race. Another of the pre-race favourites, and a hugely popular local rider, was out.

The pan-flat landscape allowed the wind and rain to batter the peloton unchecked, and they were now nearing the front line, so the roads became worse and worse. What had previously been hard work now became an horrendous ordeal. Apart from Leuven, Bruges, and the destroyed forts around Liège, the race had encountered relatively little evidence of the war so far, but at Diksmuide that changed. Diksmuide was, effectively, the northern-most point of the Western Front. Although 15km from the coast, the area to the north-west had been deliberately flooded by the Belgians in October 1914, creating a natural barrier the Germans were unable to cross. It was an incredibly brave and complicated operation, masterminded by two civilian engineers, Henri Geeraert and Karel Cogge, who were pretty much the only people who understood the system of sluices, dykes, locks and culverts that kept the sea at bay in this area.

Geeraert and Cogge worked out that if they blocked the 22 culverts through the Diksmuide-to-Nieuwport railway embankment (which was within sight and range of the Germans), and then opened various locks and sluices in a particular sequence, they could flood the low-lying area with enough sea water to halt the German advance. It worked perfectly, and the Germans didn't even realise the flooding was deliberate until it was too late.

Somewhere near Torhout an old man stepped into the road and flagged down one of the journalists' cars.

'What news of Van Hevel?' he asked.

'Van Hevel? He crashed out just after Bruges and could not continue,' came the reply. 'He has withdrawn from the race.'

The old man's face crumpled, and tears joined the rain that was running down his cheeks. His son's fledgling racing career had been halted by the war, and the wounds he sustained as a despatch rider for his artillery regiment had made his return to racing even harder. For Jules to suffer another misfortune was too much for his father to bear. He sobbed quietly as the car disappeared off through the tempest towards Diksmuide.

Urbain Anseeuw had endured a tough war, too. Mobilised into the Belgian army in 1914, he fought at Antwerp and then somehow ended up in an internment camp in Holland for the rest of the war, along with 30,000 other Belgian soldiers. Now, as he approached Diksmuide, not far from his home town of Wingene, he was struggling to believe what he saw. Away to his right, where once there had been kilometre after kilometre of flat farmland, there was now only a stagnant, sludgy, brown swamp interspersed with a few dead trees. After four years under salt water the land was saturated and poisoned, a lifeless morass of mud as far as the eye could see. Not even the willows had survived 'the inundations'.

The wind whipped rain in his face, and in the distance the leaden skies merged with the endless mud to create a monochrome, watery, grey landscape without feature or horizon. A more lifeless scene was hard to imagine. Anseeuw wiped the rain from his face and pressed on along the muddy embanked road.

Ahead of him, out of the marshy greyness, emerged the sprawl of collapsed buildings, charred wood, and mounds of masonry that was Diksmuide after four years on the front line. The scorched red bricks and sodden weeds were the only hint of colour in this sad, desolate place, and the only things recognisable were a couple of arches that were all that remained of the church, and the severely damaged railway station. Everything else was in ruins, dank and forlorn. The main road through the town had been cleared of rubble and hastily repaired, but all around was a confused mess of bricks, wood, weeds and tiles.

These two returning refugees found their home near the front line almost completely destroyed. So they moved into their cellar

Through the rain Anseeuw noticed a wisp of smoke rising from some kind of corrugated-iron shelter set back from the main road, against one of the few low walls that still stood. Surely people weren't living here, were they? Amongst this? Anseeuw shuddered, and pressed on, glad to put this sad ruin behind him.

Ahead of him, the leading group was approaching Ypres. The report in *Le Petit Journal* describes the riders as 'pinned to the road by the wind and rain', so harsh were the conditions they had to endure. Karel Van Wijnendaele had this to say: 'They are cold. They tremble. They are despondent. But they ride on, straight-ahead-facing corpse people who do not know or see results.' 'Straight-ahead-facing corpse people' is an image that will be familiar to many long-distance cyclists.

Although the riders had seen photographs of Ypres in the newspapers, nothing could have prepared them for what they encountered. If they were shocked by Diksmuide, the sight of Ypres must have been almost beyond belief. Four years of shelling had reduced this jewel of medieval architecture to rubble. The exquisite cathedral and Cloth Hall were skeletal ruins, shored up with bits of timber, and the only building to survive intact was Chateau Goldfish, a large, fancy house on the western outskirts. Apparently General von Bissing (the German commander in this sector) had taken a shine to it and wanted it for himself after the war. He forbade his gunners to shell it, and it was still standing in 1919. But not for much longer.

Next to Chateau Goldfish was an enormous dump of un-exploded ordnance, collected from all over the Ypres Salient. By 1920 over 1,000 tonnes of shells had been collected and stored there, awaiting disposal. Returning civilians – cold, starving and penniless – used to sneak into the munitions dump after dark in search of scrap metal to sell. Specifically, they were after the driving bands from unexploded shells, which were made of valuable copper, and the aluminium nose-caps which fetched two Francs each on the souvenir market. With hammer and chisel these poor, desperate people would carefully knock off the bands and nose-caps, praying that the shell between their knees didn't go off (as happened to hundreds of people in those post-war years). One night in 1920 someone got careless, or unlucky, and the whole dump went up, blowing Chateau Goldfish off the face of the earth.

Deruyter, Verstraeten, Van Lerberghe and Dejonghe, all Belgians, made their way through the remains of Ypres, slowing to a touring pace as they surveyed what was left of this once prosperous city. For Verstraeten, the old man of the group, the sight of this beautiful old town reduced to rubble must have been heartbreaking. He had lived only 20 miles from here before the war and had known Ypres as a young boy. The others, too, must have been dumb-struck by the devastation.

Through the remains of the old Menin Gate they rode, out to Hellfire Corner, once said to be the most dangerous place on the Ypres Salient. As they picked their way over the broken *pavé* and across the logs that spanned the numerous shell-holes, the wind blew sleet and rain straight in their faces. Already soaked to the skin and freezing cold, they looked up towards the Gheluvelt plateau (all of 60m above sea-level) and wondered what else the organisers could do to add to their suffering.

They weren't to know, but their suffering was only just beginning.

As the Menin Road climbed gently south-east, past Hooge and Gheluvelt, all around the racers was churned-up chaos. To the right of the road, a tank cemetery where 14 rusting hulks were slowly sinking into the mud, to their left the remains of Hooge and Glencorse Wood, now just a tangle of blasted tree stumps, isolated graves and rusting belts of wire, populated by the ghosts of the ill-fated 53rd Brigade which had been all but annihilated here two years earlier.

'As far as the eye can reach,' reads a Michelin guidebook to Ypres published in 1919, 'nothing is seen but a chaotic waste patched here and there with weeds and barbed-wire entanglements . . .

In 1919 the Menin Road ran through the hellish wasteland of the Ypres Salient

the woods, turned into fortresses, have vanished, only shapeless tree-stumps being left . . . the road, although in bad condition, is passable with careful driving. It crosses a devastated, shell-torn region in which are numerous graves, shelters and gun emplacements . . . bits of road being connected up by little bridges thrown across the shell-holes.'

In the wind and the rain these log bridges were so slippery that they had to be negotiated on foot. The rest of the road was just mud and smaller potholes, filled with whatever came to hand . . . smashed weapons, discarded haversacks, rags, rocks and mud. The riders slipped and cursed their way towards Menin, unaware of the significance of the strange road-side signs that read *Clapham Junction, Tower Hamlets, Surbiton Villas* and *Stirling Castle.* Apart from a few months at the beginning of the war, this sector had been entirely British and so the strongpoints, trenches and crossroads were all given British names that made no sense to the French and Belgian riders.

Before the war this area had been dotted with woods and farms, hedgerows and avenues of trees. Now there was nothing but the stark skeletons of trees eviscerated by shell-fire and an endless jumble of earth slowly being colonised by brambles, weeds and a few wild flowers.

Pre-war, many of the racers had spent their off-seasons riding cyclocross (an off-road discipline using road bikes). Octave Lapize credited his 1910 Tour win to spending his off-season racing cyclocross, and the corpse-like Maurice Dewaele (winner of the 1929 Tour) won the Belgian National Cyclocross Championship in 1922. They were skilled at riding in the mud, and accustomed to jumping on and off their bikes, running across the parts that weren't rideable. But they still made painfully slow progress in the wind and the rain from Ypres to Lille, where their refreshment stop awaited them. To make matters worse, the road from Menin to Bapaume, via Lille, Douai and Cambrai, was entirely *pavé*. Yes, 120km of relentless, broken, subsiding, shell-torn *pavé* from which there was no escape.

*

Our progress from Bruges to Lille was heavenly compared to that of the Circuit des Champs de Bataille. The sun was shining, the temperature was a pleasant 14°C, and the headwind had dropped to a 'modest' 195kmh. Maybe slightly less. Again Phil and Joe took turns to shelter me, wheezing and panting, from the worst of the wind. Deep breaths were like having someone slide a sharp, hot knife between my ribs, and coughing/sneezing were an absolute no-no. Joe kindly took most of the weight out of my backpack, so at least that wasn't putting too much pressure on my ribs. I felt like a straight-ahead-facing-corpse person.

Still the land was flat and featureless, but at least the weather was dry and we were finally nearing the battlefields. Diksmuide, where we stopped for mid-morning coffee and croissants, was buzzing with life. It was the early May bank holiday and all the old biddies were sitting outside the cafés on the *Grote Markt* (main square) catching up with the gossip and enjoying the sunshine.

A few miles further south we turned onto the tow-path of the Yser Canal and headed towards Ypres. Protected from the relentless wind by the trees along the canal, we bimbled along looking at the herons, the willows and the canal boats in the dappled spring sunshine. It was a tranquil, idyllic scene, a million miles away from what had been happening here 100 years earlier, when German artillery rained down on the Allied troops dug into the west bank of the canal. We stopped to look at Essex Farm, a First World War first-aid station where John McCrae wrote the famous 'In Flanders Fields' poem. It's a strangely moving place, and that poem resonates deeply with me for reasons I don't really understand.

We are the Dead. Short days ago
We lived, felt dawn, saw sunset glow . . .

Ypres. Ieper. Wipers, as it was known by a generation of Tommies unable or unwilling to give it its correct pronunciation. I always feel the need to take my metaphorical hat off and bow my head when I come here. Both my maternal Grandfather and my paternal Great Uncle fought here in 1917, during the Third Battle of Ypres. My Grandfather (Royal Field Artillery) survived it, Great Uncle Jack (2nd South Wales Borderers) died of wounds sustained near Passchendaele. He had just turned 20 years of age.

Churchill said of Ypres: 'A more sacred place for the British race does not exist.' He wanted it preserved in its post-war state as a memorial to the fallen. The locals were understandably unimpressed by that idea and wanted it to be rebuilt, and there was a lot of debate about the form the reconstruction should take. Some wanted Ypres restored to its pre-war glory, others wanted a brand-new, modern (art deco) town. I've often wondered what an art deco version of the Cloth Hall would look like . . . pretty cool, I reckon. But the traditionalists won, and in 1919 the first steps of rebuilding were just getting under way. Small, prefabricated wooden houses, supplied by the USA, were being erected amidst the rubble as people slowly returned to their home towns. Amazingly, there's still one of these prefab houses in Ypres, just off Slachthuistraat, and it's still inhabited.

The beautiful mediaeval town of Ypres, reduced to ruins after four years of shelling. This is how the riders found it when they got there

The Salient probably typifies most people's view of the Western Front – mud, blood, suffering, and death on an unimaginable scale. The British forces were overlooked by the Germans on 'high ground' on three sides, and the ceaseless artillery barrages, the very heavy rains and the high water-table, turned this land into an incomprehensible jumble of trenches, craters and fortifications, all awash with mud and blood.

During the Third Battle of Ypres (also known as Passchendaele)

initial successes at Messines in June 1917 were followed by desperately slow progress as the British and Commonwealth forces
fought their way, inch by murderous inch, up the gentle slopes
towards Passchendaele and Gheluvelt, a distance of barely five
miles. The Canadians took Passchendaele on 6 November 1917,
and although all the ground won was lost again the next year,
the pressure had been taken off the beleaguered (and mutinous)
French army for a crucial period of time. The cost was 35 British
soldiers killed or wounded for every metre of ground won; more
than 570,000 men were killed or wounded in a battle that raged
for five months.

After a quick lunch in Ypres we stopped at the Menin Gate.
Around us were carved the names of more than 54,000 men who
died here in Flanders' fields during the First World War, and who
have no known grave. And it's here that you're faced with the
stark reality of this conflict – the statistics, the facts and figures,
are made flesh and blood by name upon name upon name. The
weight of all those names is unbearable. Ordinary people, from
the back-to-backs of Manchester, the shipyards of the Clyde, and
the far-flung corners of the empire, obliterated by the machinery
of war. Each and every one of those names on this imposing
memorial is a story of unfulfilled dreams and devastated families.
It's absolutely heartbreaking.

On the outskirts of Ypres we negotiated an ordinary-looking
roundabout on the ordinary-looking ring-road. This is Hellfire
Corner, a vital intersection for the Allied forces. It was under constant German observation and bombardment, their guns ranged
perfectly to catch Allied troops and supplies on their way up to
the front line. It was once the scene of daily carnage, strewn
with the bodies of men and horses, smashed gun carriages and
burned-out wagons. This was a very unhealthy place during the
war.

But it's surprisingly healthy for cyclists these days. As we negotiated this busy roundabout I still couldn't quite get used to
the respect afforded to cyclists in Belgium. A manoeuvre that, at

home, would be fraught with danger and anxiety was disconcertingly pleasant . . . a huge truck stopped mid-roundabout to let us pass safely and cars waited patiently rather than edging forward into our bike lane. With a cheery wave of appreciation we were on our way, thankful to a culture that puts pedestrians and vulnerable road-users at the top of the pecking order.

Before heading for Lille we took a few hours to explore the Ypres Salient, and it's an interesting experience exploring the battlefield by bike. In a car you don't really appreciate the topography in the same way . . . it's ironed out by the comfort of four wheels and the power of the engine. But on a bike, even the most gentle rise and fall of the terrain is noticeable, and I began to appreciate how these shallow slopes must have seemed to the soldiers as they slogged knee-deep in mud and corpses towards Langemarck, Passchendaele and Gheluvelt in a hail of fire and lead. This apparently flat and featureless agricultural landscape is actually a series of almost imperceptible folds in the land, noticeable only when we were able to freewheel from time to time.

Tyne Cot, situated on a gentle slope leading up to Passchendaele village, is extraordinary – a Commonwealth War Graves Commission cemetery with 12,000 headstones and the names of a further 34,000 soldiers with no known grave. The names of the dead are broadcast over a discreet loudspeaker system, read by a lady with an achingly beautiful, soulful voice. The scale of this place is chilling, but the view down to Ypres gives a perfect illustration of the field of fire commanded by the Germans. How anyone made it up these slopes under fire from German machine-guns defies belief.

At the Sanctuary Wood Museum shocking three-dimensional photographs show the full horror of this war – the decaying remains of a horse in a tree, jumbled bodies in trenches, dismembered torsos, severed limbs, the chaos and mess of war. These are images you rarely see in the history books, but it feels important to look, to remember, to understand the unspeakable horror.

Outside, the preserved trenches amongst the trees were awash with muddy water, just as they had been 100 years ago. The dank smell of mud, rust and decay adds to the sombre atmosphere.

Middle son Joe exploring the trenches at Sanctuary Wood on the Salient

As we rode, I was constantly (with every breath) aware of my injuries. But the suffering and privations of the soldiers a hundred years ago put my minor discomforts firmly into perspective. I was aching a bit, but no one was shooting at me, and I wasn't going to be killed by shrapnel or poison gas. In a few hours' time I'd be relaxing in a warm bath in a warm hotel, rather than sharing a muddy shell-hole with the dead and the dying while the incessant roar of artillery drove me to breaking point.

Back on the Menin Road, in the wheel-tracks of Deruyter, Anseeuw et al., we paused near Clapham Junction and Surbiton Villas. In a shell-hole, hereabouts, during the Battle of Broodseinde in October 1917, Private Thomas Sage of the Somerset

Light Infantry was sheltering, along with eight other soldiers. One of them stood up to hurl a grenade, was hit, and fell back into the shell-hole, dropping the primed grenade. In one of those astonishing, selfless acts that defy belief, Tom Sage threw himself on top of the live grenade just before it exploded. He was very seriously injured, but amazingly survived. And so did the other eight men. He was subsequently awarded the Victoria Cross.

And Tom Sage wasn't the only one to do this. Billy McFadzean, of the Royal Irish Rifles, did the same thing in a trench near Thiepval Wood on the first day of the Somme, although he died as a result of his actions and was awarded a posthumous VC.

Part of my interest in the First World War comes from the stories of people like Tom and Billy. What was it that made them act instinctively to save their friends and comrades? There was no time for rational thought, to think through the consequences . . . they just did something extraordinary. What was it inside them that allowed them to act in this way?

As one of the few generations that has never had to go to war, I can't imagine how I would cope under conditions such as they faced. I suspect myself of being an abject coward, and I suspect that ten minutes under an artillery barrage would cause me to lose my mind completely. But I also have an alarming disregard for my own safety and well-being, a misplaced sense of invulnerability, and a liking for an adrenalin-rush. Would I have run away crying, or plunged headlong into a blizzard of shell-fire and machine-gun bullets?

Then again, would I even have joined up in the first place? The twenty-first-century middle-aged version of me would not have done, but an early twentieth-century, 18-year-old version of me might well have answered the call. Most of the men in my family tree who were of fighting age in 1914 joined the army (three great-uncles and a grandfather), and maybe I would have gone with them. Straight out of school, eager for adventure, with no idea of the realities of what was to come. That sounds like the 18-year-old me. And I think many of us wonder what we would have done, and how we would have coped. I have no idea, but I do know I'm glad I'll never have to find out.

The road back down to Ypres seems so ordinary these days, a dead straight, tree-lined single carriageway that descends gently to Ypres 3km away. It's hard to imagine what this place was like in 1919, let alone in 1917 when it was the scene of some of the worst fighting on the Western Front. On either side the land was churned-up mud for miles in every direction, the only buildings were squat, pock-marked concrete gun positions, and the woods were just a tangle of felled trees and dead branches. Forlorn crosses marked the thousands of battlefield burials and rusting wire was strewn everywhere.

I'm reminded of another poem, this one by Siegfried Sassoon:

I died in Hell (they called it Passchendaele);
my wound was slight
and I was hobbling back; and then a shell
burst slick upon the duckboards; so I fell
into the bottomless mud, and lost the light.

Beneath our feet, underneath the Menin Road, the Germans dug a tunnel over 1,500m in length that allowed their troops to move up to the front line in safety; the road above was too exposed and too dangerous. Amazingly, this tunnel was entirely forgotten after the war until one day in 1931, when a large part of the Menin Road collapsed into it. Even now, buildings in this area subside and craters appear overnight thanks to the forgotten underground First World War workings.

It was near here, during the Third Battle of Ypres, that one of those awful twists of fate occurred that were all too common during the First World War. The 90th Brigade (of the 18th Division), made up of Manchester Pals battalions, attacked German lines on the north-east edge of Sanctuary Wood, en route to take Glencorse Wood beyond. It took an hour of bitter fighting, eventually hand-to-hand in the German trenches, to take the German front line. Without pausing for breath, they pushed on, occupying the wood beyond and flashing a message back that their objective had been achieved. It was now time for the waiting 53rd Brigade to leapfrog the 90th Brigade and advance on to Polygon Wood.

There was only one problem. Having fought so hard to break the German front line, the Manchesters had become disoriented and advanced on Chateau Wood, slightly to their left, thinking it was Glencorse Wood. Chateau Wood had mostly been cleared by the neighbouring 8th Division, so they met with little resistance from the remaining Germans. But their mistake opened up a gap in the British front line into which the 53rd Brigade advanced, assuming that the Manchesters were holding the wood in front of them.

The term 'wood' is something of a misnomer . . . the woods had long since been smashed to pieces by shelling and had become an impenetrable tangle of felled tree-trunks, branches and undergrowth which the Germans had reinforced with concrete bunkers and machine-gun nests. The 53rd had an additional misfortune. Not only was Glencorse Wood still full of Germans, they were fresh *Eingreif* battalions, specialist second-line counter-attack troops brought up in anticipation of a British attack.

The 53rd advanced almost casually towards Glencorse Wood, led by an officer with a yellow flag looking for all the world like a tour guide. They were met with murderous machine-gun fire from strong-points at Stirling Castle and Glencorse Wood, and enfilade fire from Inverness Copse to their right. The British artillery barrage had long since moved on, so the 53rd were sitting ducks. Realising that something had gone seriously wrong, they set about trying to take Glencorse Wood themselves. They made it to the far side of the Menin Road, where we had stopped on our bikes, but got no further.

Further north, near Kitchener's Wood, my grandfather's gun battery was moving forward, but four days of rain had turned this area into an impossible slough of mud and debris. It took them 7 hours to manhandle his 18-pounder (weighing just over a ton) 250 yards forward.

Reluctantly we turned our backs on the Salient and headed towards Menin and the French border. After several days of Belgian drivers I'd become a bit complacent, but my wake-up call came within 300 metres of the border, when a French white van man came within inches of wiping me out. Ah, *la belle France*. Although in fairness, white van men everywhere seem to be the same. Even so, the cultural differences between the two countries are startling when it comes to their driving.

There followed a fairly unpleasant ride through the post-industrial grot of Tourcoing (home town of Charles Deruyter) to Roubaix. We were off the race route, but we wanted to visit the outdoor velodrome in Roubaix and ride a couple of laps of this iconic venue. It's not the historic velodrome of the pre-war era, though – the Germans demolished that and reused whatever they could for their war effort. Even so, this is the place where Boonen, De Vlaeminck, Museeuw, Merckx and others have won famous victories in the Paris–Roubaix race, one of the toughest one-day races on the calendar. And you can just rock up and ride your bike on it (assuming the Roubaix rugby team isn't using the infield for training) for free. So we did. We rode our bikes round and round. And round again. It was magical.

These things move me. I feel a connection, an inspiration, a sense of excitement and joy. It's the same on the Koppenberg, or the Tourmalet, or the Alpe. Extraordinary things happened here, legends were created, heroes rose and fell. This place is like Lord's for cricket fans, or Wembley for football fans. So we basked in the historic ambience until the gathering clouds threatened rain, then made our way to our hotel in Lille. After an 82-mile day I was looking forward to *steak-frites* and a *pichet* of cheap plonk, and maybe even a decent night's sleep.

★

Charles Deruyter had covered 200km, and ridden for 9½ hours, by the time he reached the checkpoint in Lille on Stage 3. It was just after 2 p.m., he was soaked to the skin, covered in mud, and absolutely frozen. The rain and sleet had not let up for one moment, and now the wind was blowing even harder. Some-one handed him a towel and he dried off as much as possible while shoving eggs and pieces of chicken down his throat, and drinking hot, sweet coffee. Five minutes wasn't long enough to warm up, it was barely long enough to eat his allowance of food. Thirty seconds after Deruyter came Verstraeten, and 30 seconds behind him came Anseeuw. It would be another 20 minutes before the French pair of Duboc and Chassot arrived, both in a terrible state, spattered with mud and shaking from the cold.

The leading riders in the race had reached Lille 3 hours behind the hopelessly optimistic schedule laid down by the organisers. When the newspaper went to the presses that evening, only 28 of the 42 riders had got to Lille, and no one had yet made it to the finish in Amiens. Things were not looking good for the organisers, and they looked even worse for the riders who still had 120km to go, mostly across battlefields that had seen fighting right up until the last days of the war, six months earlier.

Deruyter climbed reluctantly back on his bike and set off south. Lille was relatively undamaged, despite initial German shelling in 1914, having been behind the German lines for four years. But when the Germans pulled out in October 1918 they blew all the bridges and destroyed what industry they hadn't already shipped back to Germany. As Deruyter approached the Port de Douai on the southern outskirts of the town he was astonished to see a huge area of utter devastation. A massive German ammunition dump at Dix-Huit Ponts blew up in 1916, creating a crater 100 feet deep and 500 feet across (bigger than the Lochnagar crater at La Boisselle on the Somme), and wiping out 738 houses, 21 factories and at least 108 civilians. One huge stone, weighing more than a tonne, crashed through the studio roof of famous sculptor

Valentin Deplechin. On it he carved a bas-relief of a woman in mourning called *Lille in Tears*, and displayed it in the École des Beaux-Arts.

Lille's industrial centre was devastated by a huge exoplosion in 1916 when an ammunition dump at Dix-Huit Ponts mysteriously exploded

Verstraeten and Anseeuw caught up with Deruyter briefly as he slowed to take in the devastation. They looked at one another – no words were necessary – then pressed on towards Douai. The road was terrible, having been used as a major supply route by the German army. The *pavé* had been severely damaged by the endless stream of trucks and artillery being moved around behind the German lines, and the riders made agonisingly slow progress. The three leaders pushed on, gritting their teeth against the howling wind and rain. Behind them, Albert Dejonghe, leader of the race on GC, came down hard on the *pavé* near Pont-a-Marcq and damaged his bike so badly that he could not continue. Another of the favourites had fallen by the wayside.

Back at the checkpoint in Lille, riders were still appearing in dribs and drabs. Alavoine was 75 minutes adrift of the leaders, there was no sign of Brocco or Neffati, and Ernest Paul rolled in at 5.17 p.m. looking like he'd just emerged from a dug-out near Verdun. He was one of the lucky few who had a waxed-cotton jacket, but even that only kept the rain out for an hour or two. He was hungry, tired, shaking with cold, and completely sick of the whole thing. He eyed the train station opposite. In 3 hours he could be home in Colombes, in a warm, dry bed. Instead he took a pill from the tin box in his bag, washed it down with some coffee, and set off once more.

The wind had been picking up all afternoon, and now it blew with such ferocity that direction signs were blown away and the telegraph poles across the region came crashing down. Now the riders had little idea where they were or where they were supposed to go, and the organisers had no way of contacting each other. And it was beginning to get dark.

With the telegraph system down, the last report that day was from Lille to say that Ernest Paul had just left at 5.22 p.m. Then there was nothing. The control points at Douai, Cambrai and Bapaume continued to log the riders as they appeared, but had no means of communicating their progress to the commissaires in Amiens or the newspaper in Paris. The official race convoy was faring no better than the riders, with cars and trucks getting stuck, sliding into ditches and breaking down in the biblical storm raging around them.

With the roads in such a state, and the average speed so slow, Deruyter decided there was no advantage in riding as a group, so he pushed on as hard as he could on his own. Arriving in the small village of Aubigny-au-Bac, he discovered that the temporary bridge built over the Canal de la Sensée six months earlier had recently collapsed under the weight of an overloaded truck, which was now in the canal along with the remains of the bridge.

He stared in horror. Now what? There were no signs, and no officials to tell him where he was supposed to go, so he set off along the canal bank in search of another crossing point. When Heusghem and Hanlet arrived a couple of hours later they faced the same problem, but made a catastrophic miscalculation which led to them getting hopelessly lost. There were no signposts, no houses, no one to give them directions. On and on they rode, lashed by wind and rain, hoping they were going in roughly the right direction. They weren't. By 10 p.m. they were back in Douai, where they had come from 6 hours earlier, having covered an extra 60km on terrible roads for nothing.

At Cambrai Deruyter paused briefly at the checkpoint. The town was another bleak and miserable ruin, torched by the Germans in October 1918 as they retreated. Around 1,500 of Cambrai's 3,500 buildings were gutted by fire, including the town hall that contained records going back to the middle ages. In amongst the ruins a few returning civilians were living in damp cellars and corrugated-iron shacks, trying to salvage what they could from the devastation.

A little while later Duboc and Chassot, followed by Van Lerberghe and Anseeuw, turned south-west from Cambrai and picked their way carefully through the gathering gloom that was descending on the 1917 battlefield. One of the organisers' cars passed the two Belgians, slowing to enquire as to their well-being. They shrugged, and watched it disappear in the direction of Bapaume. Either side of the road, the wreckage of war was everywhere. And still the sleet and rain fell. And still the wind blew, unchecked by trees or hedgerows, which had long since been shelled out of existence. The landscape was an horizonless, turbulent sea of grey-brown mud over which sickly grey-green weeds and brambles were attempting to gain a foothold.

Anseeuw and Van Lerberghe struggled past Bourlon Wood, scene of unbelievable carnage in November 1917, and then crossed the temporary bridge over the Canal du Nord. All around were shattered bunkers, broken weapons, burned-out tanks, discarded helmets and scraps of rotting clothing. They didn't know it, but this was the Hindenburg Line, Germany's last hope.

On and on they pedalled, the battle-scarred, dead-straight road rising almost imperceptibly towards the remains of Bapaume, where Deruyter had collapsed at the checkpoint. Perched on an old wooden chair, he wiped his face with a towel and informed the time-keepers that he'd had enough and was quitting. They tried desperately to persuade him to carry on, but Deruyter was physically and mentally finished.

Some soldiers, who'd stopped to see what was going on, took pity on Deruyter and set about trying to revive him. Someone fetched a blanket, another scrounged a hot drink and some bread, while another started to rub some circulation back into Deruyter's aching limbs. It was all against the rules, but competitors and organisers alike had long since given up worrying about the regulations and were just focused on surviving.

After a while Deruyter began to recover, and sufficiently revived by the soldiers he remounted his bike and set off on the final 50km to Amiens, where he could finally get some warmth and rest. But the landscape he now crossed was a Dantean vision of hell. Before the war there were rolling hills and streams, with woodlands dotted amongst the fields and farms. An idyllic vision of pastoral France. When the First World War lapsed into a static form of trench warfare, the front line ran straight through the middle of this picturesque area and the shelling started. Anything that afforded cover, or the potential to be used as a look-out, was targeted by the guns and pounded to dust. Month upon month of shelling, and terrible weather, turned the Somme into a featureless morass of chalky mud and water-filled shell-holes as far as the eye could see.

The rain had abated slightly as Deruyter climbed passed the Butte de Walencourt, turning from a deluge into occasional wind-swept showers. From time to time the clouds even parted for long enough to afford him moonlit glimpses of scattered graves in the 'fields' around him. The previously charming countryside had been replaced with a stinking primordial swamp of mud, corpses and twisted, rusty metal. There was no colour, no respite, no comfort, and the names of the tiny villages and woods had become the stuff of legend, and nightmare – Contalmaison,

The roads across the battlefields in 1919 were in a shocking state, often lined with collapsed buildings and piles of unexploded ordnance

High Wood, La Boiselle, Delville Wood, Mametz, and Beaumont Hamel – all synonymous with suffering and slaughter. In 1919 these fields were still peopled by ghastly shattered corpses, and a dank, rotting smell of death and mud and rust oozed from the lifeless soil. Van Wijnendaele reported:

> When it turned dark, there was no one to cheer them on and there were no houses in sight, besides the wooden barracks and coloured people from the French colonies who aided the reconstructions. Cyclists had to climb poles to see what was written on the traffic signs. It was inhuman.

The wind blew with relentless ferocity across the tortured battlefields, whistling and howling amongst the crosses and wire. In Deruyter's numb, addled mind he was surrounded by the ghosts of the thousands of men who fought and died in this abysmal landscape. He desperately wanted this terrible day to end.

*

I desperately wanted this terrible night to end. Lying in my hotel bed in Lille, I had managed only a couple of hours of fitful sleep, constantly disturbed by the hot knife between my ribs. The pain was annoying, but it was the lack of sleep that was beginning to get to me. I got up and changed the dressing on my knee (scabbing nicely), inspected the trench-foot (almost gone after three days without rain or snow), checked out the undercarriage for signs of wear and tear (none), and then read a couple of chapters of *The Hell They Called High Wood* on my Kindle while I waited for dawn.

We had another 80-mile day ahead of us, including a fair amount of sightseeing on the Somme, so we were up and out early. It was a glorious day – the wind had dropped a fair bit, the sun was shining, and the temp was a pleasant 16°C. Lille is a hellish place to cycle in, a confusion of one-way systems, multi-lane cobbled roads, tram-lines, and impatient men in big trucks. To add to the early-morning excitement, my sat-nav had another melt-down. 'WHAT THE HELL IS WRONG WITH THIS USELESS PIECE OF JUNK,' I yelled. I then had a coughing fit and had to sit down by the side of the road, clutching my chest and trying not to pass out. Phil and Joe tried quite hard not to laugh.

A few miles south of Lille we took a small diversion to ride some Paris–Roubaix *pavé* – Pont Thibault, 1,400m of *pavé* rated as 3 out of 5 on the difficulty scale. We wanted to experience exactly what road conditions had been like in 1919, and this is as near as it gets these days. And yes, I loved it, even though bouncing over cobbles for 1,400m was hard on the ribs. Again, it's that sense of history, and place, that makes this special for me. Somewhere not far from here, on a road just like this one, Albert Dejonghe crashed out of the Circuit des Champs de Bataille.

One of the pavé sections south of Lille, giving a very authentic (and uncomfortable) experience of the Circuit des Champs de Bataille

Our *pavé* excursion also brought home just how tough Stage 3 of the Circuit des Champs de Bataille must have been for the riders. We had ridden a measly 1,400m of reasonably undamaged *pavé* in dry, sunny conditions, and it wasn't easy. The riders in 1919 had to negotiate 120km of *pavé* that was wet, muddy and in terrible repair. In a howling gale. In near-freezing conditions. Across deserted battlefields. In the dark. When Van Wijnendaele described the conditions as inhuman, he really wasn't kidding.

The remainder of our morning was spent riding south, across terrain that got more interesting with each passing mile. The flatlands gave way to rolling countryside, farms and woods speckled the landscape, and the warm spring sunshine (and lack of wind) cheered all of us up. It was here that Joe and I discovered Phil's cycling Achilles heel. On the flat, Phil keeps up a punishing pace, powering along with us tucked in behind him, and he seems to be able to do it all day. But come to a hill, and Phil starts to slow down. The 69-year-old legs just don't have the raw power they used to, or the power of my spritely 55-year-old legs (yeah, right!). For the first time in my life (almost) I actually rode someone off my wheel. I was secretly delighted. Of course, the minute the road flattened out Phil was back on the front, churning away like a diesel engine.

After a quick lunch stop in Bapaume (stodgy pizza which weighed heavily on all of us for the rest of the afternoon) we were on the Somme. For the British, and many Commonwealth forces, the Somme represents our darkest hour. On the morning of 1 July 1916 around 100,000 men went over the top. By nightfall 60,000 of them had been killed or seriously wounded. There followed a 141-day battle to drive the Germans out of their expertly constructed defences, a battle which resulted in over 1 million casualties.

Henry Williamson, later to become author of *Tarka The Otter*, was a Lieutenant in the Machine Gun Corps who fought on the Western Front. He returned to the battlefields shortly after the war in an attempt to lay his ghosts. Describing his return in his extraordinary book, *The Wet Flanders Plain*, he writes:

> The wraith of the War bears me to the wide and shattered country of the Somme, to every broken wood, and trench and sunken lane, among the broad straggling belts of rusty wire smashed and twisted in the chalky loam ... Again I crouch while the steel glacier, rushing overhead, scrapes away every syllable, every fragment of a message bawled in my ear, while the gaping, smoking parapet above the rim of my helmet spurts and lashes with machine gun bullets.

The book is an astonishing insight not only into the minds of men deeply affected by what they experienced, but also a rare glimpse into how the battlefields appeared to the riders racing in the Circuit des Champs de Bataille.

Approaching from Bapaume, you cross the Somme battlefield

in reverse chronological order, working back in time from 18 November 1916 near Bapaume to 1 July 1916 near Albert. Every mile or so along this road there are signs which mark the position of the front line and the painfully slow progress made in pushing back the Germans. We turned off the race route near Martinpuich and made our way along Longueval Ridge to High Wood. The first time I came here, in foul March weather a few years previously, I experienced an actual physical reaction to the place. As I approached this dark, brooding presence on the horizon I was gripped by a palpable sense of fear. My heart raced and I felt a strange sense of urgency and dread. I peered into the impenetrable tangle of woodland as the wind seethed and shrieked through the trees. There was a sense of malevolence I found genuinely frightening – heightened, I'm sure, by the storm raging around me and the knowledge of the unspeakable two-month struggle that took place here 100 years earlier.

Today couldn't have been more different. On a beautiful May afternoon there were larks (still singing) above, and all around spring was bursting forth. Although it is private property, a gate into the wood was open and we sneaked in to have a look. It was stunning. The ground was carpeted with thousands of bluebells, the trees had just come into leaf, and sunshine dappled this beautiful, peaceful spot.

Among the trees and flowers of this small wood lie 8,000 unrecovered bodies.

After the war, when the battlefields were being cleared, the Graves Registration Units produced what was called a Body Density Map of the Somme. The area around High Wood is truly horrifying. A grid of squares (each 83 × 83 yards) shows the number of bodies found in each square. The squares incorporating High Wood are blank because it was too difficult and dangerous to clear, but the ones in the immediate vicinity are mind-boggling – 749, 234, 702, 808, 485, 829, 299. Over 800 bodies in a piece of land measuring less than 100 yards by 100 yards? These really were killing fields.

I stood amongst the bluebells, the smashed concrete bunkers and the old splintered tree-stumps, with my 22-year-old son by my side, and shed a tear for all the young men who never made it out of this wood. It wasn't until my own sons reached an age when they would, 100 years ago, have gone off to war, that I really got to grips with this conflict. And I'm still uncertain about what I really feel. A crushing sense of loss sometimes overwhelms me on these battlefields. So many dead. Sons, fathers, husbands, brothers – cut down by machine-gun fire, torn apart by shrapnel, choked by gas, blasted by artillery shells, their blood seeping into the mud, losing the light. The tears fell for the loved ones left behind, for the lives ripped apart, for the families devastated. And for the fear and pain these young men endured in conditions unimaginable to those of us who were not there.

I thought about my Great Uncle Jack, a 2nd lieutenant in the South Wales Borderers. At the age of 19 he was fighting on the Somme. Then in the snow and bitter cold at Monchy-Le-Preux, near Arras. And finally at Pilkem Ridge and Langemarck just after his 20th birthday. I tried to imagine my own sons advancing into the storm of bullets and shrapnel and mud that engulfed Jack that morning in August 1917, but it's too painful. How did Jack cope? What must he have thought? Did he become inured to the disgusting reality of pain and suffering and death? At the age of 19 he was flung into a world of blood and gore and screaming. How was it possible to get through it? God, family, country – could any of that have meant anything when living with the stink of the dead, the thirst, and the drumfire-roar of artillery?

For the riders struggling across these battlefields so soon after the war, the emotional turmoil must have been hard to bear. Even for those who hadn't seen front-line action, the sight of these devastated fields and villages must have been a horrible reminder of four hard years, and of friends and family who never came home. The French mobilised over 8 million men during the First World War, and 1 in 20 of the entire population was killed. There would not have been a single French rider who was not affected.

We made our way carefully out of this sad but beautiful place and rode a mile or two along the road to Delville Wood, which the South Africans fought in horrific conditions to capture. They managed it, but of the 3,000 men and 130 officers who went in, 750 men and 30 officers came out. It would have been nice to stroll through the peaceful wood, but this was a whistle-stop tour and time was short.

The Thiepval Memorial to the Missing on the Somme, where the names of 73,000 men, who have no known grave, are recorded

Instead we cycled over to Thiepval, past places whose names resonate with sad meaning – Caterpillar Valley, Mametz Wood, Contalmaison, Pozières, Mucky Farm. And again I'm reminded why visiting battlefields is best done by bike . . . you feel more, you see more, you smell more. It's a far more immersive experience than by coach or car, although it's not so great when it's pouring with rain. But today the weather was glorious, the roads were empty, and we had the battlefield almost to ourselves.

The Thiepval memorial to the missing is astonishing. On this huge Lutyens arch that dominates the Thiepval ridge are carved the names of 73,000 men who have no known grave – those who were blasted to pieces, their bodies buried and reburied with every new bombardment. Like the architecture of the Menin Gate, I find Thiepval just a touch triumphalist, but those were different times and it's so important to remember these men. The view from the memorial down to the River Ancre gives a sobering perspective on just how difficult it was to take this ridge from a well-dug-in enemy.

Next stop was the Ulster Tower and the exhilarating plummet down the ridge and across the Ancre. J. R. R. Tolkien fought here during the First World War and his description of the marsh full of bodies in *The Lord of the Rings* comes from his personal experiences here on the flooded Ancre marshes.

My bike registered its disapproval at being laden with a heavy bar-bag by flapping its handlebars furiously on the 40mph, 8 per cent descent, causing me to squeal like an 11-year-old girl. It had happened a couple of times in the Ardennes, so it wasn't completely unexpected, but still slightly nerve-racking.

The Newfoundland Memorial Park near Beaumont Hamel, where the lines of trenches and wire are still visible, is another very moving place. On 1 July 1916 my Great Uncle's battalion, the 2nd South Wales Borderers, went over the top in the first wave. Two-thirds of them, 399 men, were killed or seriously wounded in less than 20 minutes. By the time the Newfoundlanders went over in the third wave, the front line and support trenches were so full of the dead and dying that they had no option but to climb out of the trenches and advance across open ground. Most were cut down before they had even reached their own front line. At roll call the next morning, 68 of the 800 Newfoundlanders were able to report for duty. Sixty-eight.

Today the park is tranquil and calm, looked after by delightful volunteer Canadian students. In the late-afternoon sunshine, once the school parties had departed, this place was quiet, almost beautiful, as the low sun cast long shadows across these grassy fields, highlighting the lines of trenches and craters. A kestrel perched on a rusty iron picket in no-man's-land as the setting sun warmed the back of my neck. The scene was so peaceful, so pleasant, it was hard to reconcile it with what happened here 100 years earlier.

As we rode along the Ancre valley I thought about another relative of mine, my maternal grandfather, who fought with the 48th Division here in July 1916 as a lieutenant in the divisional field artillery. He was on the Somme from June to November 1916 and came through the war relatively unscathed, apart from being rendered stone deaf as a result of firing an 18-pounder for four years. Like many of that generation, he didn't talk much about his war experiences other than to remember the terrible suffering of the horses that were used to drag the guns forward. His battery was sited somewhere on the slopes of this valley, supporting infantry attacks at Ovillers, Mucky Farm and Thiepval.

The last stop on our lightning tour of the Somme was the huge crater at La Boisselle, where the British exploded a massive mine beneath the German front line. Apart from making a very large crater, and killing several hundred people, it made little difference to the events of 1 July. But as you stand beside it and look down, you can't help but be amazed by the result. Around 300ft across and 90ft deep, the Lochnagar Crater is testimony to the grit and determination of those poor sods in the tunnelling companies who spent months underground, sometimes fighting hand-to-hand in the pitch darkness with German tunnellers, to lay these enormous mines.

We arrived at our hotel in Albert as sunset glowed, just in time for an excellent dinner and a few drinks, tired after 80 miles and 11 hours on and off the saddle. I was pleased to have been able to show Joe and Phil a few of the sights, and I think we all felt physically and emotionally exhausted by the Somme.

★

In Amiens the commissaires were concerned. Very concerned. They'd expected the riders to start arriving around 5 p.m., but by 8 p.m. there was no sign of anyone, not even the other commissaires in their cars. The rain and wind continued to sweep across northern France, all communications had stopped, and there was genuine concern that the race might become a literal wash-out, a very public humiliation for the newspaper. Then, at 8.30 p.m., the leading car arrived at the finish line by the bridge over the River Somme on the Boulevard de Beauville. Finally, some news.

According to the exhausted commissaire, who had been on the road for 16 very hard hours, Deruyter was leading and was way ahead of the others. But he was still at least three hours away. There seemed little point in everyone waiting around in the freezing cold for another three hours, so the race organisers packed up their things and retired to the Café de L'Est a few hundred metres up the road where they could at least stay warm and dry.

On the road, the riders were battling on. Or at least some of them were. Many, exhausted by the overwhelming physical effort, the debilitating wet and cold, and mechanical problems with their bikes, had thrown in the towel and abandoned. It was just too hard for them. Even an athlete in peak physical condition using modern equipment would have struggled under these circumstances, let alone men who had suffured four years of deprivation and hardship. Enduring this sort of physical torment in wartime for the sake of one's country and mates was one thing, but doing it for a few hundred Francs was another thing entirely. The stations at Lille, Douai and Cambrai saw groups of riders huddled in waiting rooms, hoping to get a train out of this Godforsaken part of the world. Maurice Brocco was among them. Others had headed to guest-houses or hotels, or even private homes.

For those still racing that evening, the conditions were almost impossible. The riders had to stop every few kilometres to clear the mud from their chains and brakes, there was no let-up in the terrible weather, visibility was awful, and the roads were in a dreadful state. Every town and village was dark, in ruins, abandoned. Between Bapaume and Albert there was literally nothing, and no one, just an empty wasteland haunted by the ghosts of lost battalions. The average speed from Douai onwards dropped to less than 7kph for those riders still in the race.

In the gloom Séraphin Morel heaved his bike over his shoulder and gingerly picked his way across the churned-up ground towards the distant light, praying to God that he didn't fall in a trench or step on anything explosive in the dark. The clouds occasionally parted to allow Morel glimpses of the battlefields by moonlight, which made him shudder. A more desolate, haunted scene was hard to imagine.

The source of the light turned out to be some kind of wartime dugout, hacked into the side of an embankment. Probably a command post, thought Morel, judging by the size of it. One of the *sinistrés*, the returning civilian inhabitants, had obviously moved in and had made a few 'improvements', which included a chimney, a corrugated-iron door, and a small glass window. Morel knocked on the door, and called out for help: '*Bon soir, j'ai besoin d'aide, si vous plaît.*' After a few moments the door opened a few centimetres and a figure surveyed him suspiciously through the gap. 'Yes? What do you want?'

'Please, I need shelter,' explained Morel. 'I'm taking part in a bicycle race from Brussels to Amiens. I've been riding since dawn, I'm lost, I'm cold, and I'm tired. May I come in and rest for a while? I won't be any bother.'

'Who is it, Philippe?' called a woman's voice from inside.

'A guy on a bike. Says he's come from Belgium, this morning. He's lost.'

'What? Well, let him in.'

The dim figure stepped back and opened the door. Morel leaned his bike against the side of the shack and followed the man inside.

'*Mon Dieu!*' cried the woman when she saw Morel, wet, shivering, and covered in mud. 'Sit. Here, by the stove.' She motioned to a rickety, roughly repaired chair by the pot-bellied stove in the centre of the room. Philippe put down the pistol he'd been holding at his side (gangs of thieves were known to prey on the *sinistrés*, and it paid to be careful) and pulled up another chair. He quizzed Morel about the race, about his background and his home town in the Vosges, while Madame prepared some ersatz coffee and a chunk of bread. Then she brought him some khaki trousers and a khaki jacket, salvaged from the battlefield and patched extensively, to change into while his riding gear hung above the stove to dry. Morel knew he was wearing dead men's clothes, but he didn't care. They were warm and dry.

The coffee tasted terrible, but it was hot, and the relative warmth of the dug-out slowly restored Morel. Even the stale bread was welcome after 18 hours with very little to eat. The *sinistrés* talked about their return to their farm a month earlier, to find only a few bricks and pieces of wood. They had discovered this dug-out nearby and made it habitable, using whatever they could scavenge from the battlefields. Apparently there were dozens of families living in cellars and dug-outs all over these fields.

'The children are staying with my sister in Normandy,' explained Madame. 'We'll send for them when we have built something better than this.' She surveyed the dug-out gloomily. 'We've put in a claim at the town hall in Bapaume, but it'll be months before we can move out from here. In the meantime we clear our land of wire and shells, and Philippe is starting to fill in the craters and trenches. We may be able to plant something this year, if we can get some decent-quality seed from somewhere.' She lapsed into a sad silence, contemplating the tough times ahead. Morel's chin sank slowly onto his chest, and he was aware of his eyes beginning to close.

He stirred himself. 'Perhaps, Madame, I might sleep here for an hour or two?'

'Of course. I'll find you something to sleep on by the stove.'

She fetched a couple of greatcoats, doubtless retrieved from a trench or dug-out somewhere nearby, and laid them on the wooden floor. Morel curled up, pulled another coat over himself, and slept the sleep of the dead.

Séraphin Morel was an interesting character. Before the war he was a moderately successful track cyclist who was to be seen racing a tandem with his partner Paul Didier on the velodromes of Paris most weekends. He tried his hand at road-racing, but despite being born in the Vosges mountains, he was more of a sprinter than a climber. He entered the 1914 Tour de France as an *isolé*, but abandoned on the Pyrenees stage which involved climbs over the Aubisque, Tourmalet, Aspin and Peyresourde.

Morel was 31 when war broke out, but was excused military service because he was blind in one eye following an eye infection, probably due to getting dust and grit in his eye while bike racing (something that wasn't uncommon with cyclists in those days). In October 1918, less than a month before the armistice, Morel took part in a very high-profile contest against Georges Carpentier, the most famous boxer of his generation, at the Velodrome d'Hiver. The contest was a 100m sprint from a standing start, with Carpentier on foot and Morel on his bike. Morel won by a nose, in a time of 10.6 seconds.

After the war he took part in the Circuit des Champs de Bataille before heading back to the track, where he became a celebrated sprinter. In 1922 he decided to have a crack at the world 100m standing-start cycling record, which stood at 9.4 seconds and was set by Léon Barthiat in 1898. Morel set a new world record of 9.2 seconds at the Parc des Princes velodrome. Two weeks later he was back, and set two new world records for the standing-start 200m and Quarter Mile (402m). He was 41 years old.

In the Café de L'Est in Amiens the commissaires waited for the riders. Each time a car passed, it was flagged down and the driver quizzed about whether he had seen any of the riders. They hadn't. The commissaires were on the verge of giving up all hope when the door of the café burst open and someone yelled, '*En voilà un!*' At 10.58 in the evening, 18 hours and 28 minutes after he set off from Brussels, Charles Deruyter crossed the finish line in Amiens on two flat tyres, unable or unwilling to change them in the dark and cold. *L'Auto* described the scene:

> It was nearly 11 p.m. From the depths of the night an unspeakable mud-man appeared suddenly in the flickering light of the Café de L'Est, shivering with cold, he moans, he cries, he wails with the suffering he has had to endure. This is Deruyter, exhausted and almost unrecognisable.

A small but enthusiastic crowd carried him into the café, and Degrain helped Deruyter sign in. He was too cold to hold the pen. Deruyter's wife was one of those waiting in the café. She took her stricken husband in her arms and held him as sobs racked his broken body. 'Not since the dawn of cycling had riders been set so hard a course,' proclaimed *L'Auto*. For once, they weren't exaggerating.

Wrapped in blankets, Deruyter was laid on a banquette and one of the *soigneurs* set about massaging some life back into him, while his wife fed him coffee and eggs. He was a pitiable sight. The commissaires returned to their uneasy vigil, wondering if anyone else would make it.

A little over 90 minutes later, Paul Duboc arrived in a similarly filthy and distressed state after 20 hours on the road. 'This is ridiculous!' he raged when he'd regained some feeling in his face. 'How can we be expected to ride in this? It's insane!' Commissaire Perrine got him a blanket and Madame Deruyter poured him some coffee while the *soigneur* got to work. Duboc had experienced some bad times on a bike, but nothing compared to this. He cupped his coffee in both hands and glowered at the organisers across the café.

At 1 a.m. Van Lerberghe and Anseeuw stumbled into the café together. Colder and wetter than the riders before them, they had endured nearly 21 hours of exhausting physical effort. Van Lerberghe slumped in a chair, his gaunt, pallid face smeared with dirt, his eyes staring blankly ahead, his mouth hanging agape. He looked like one of the many corpses that the labour battalions were still removing from the battlefields.

*

I knelt on my hotel-room floor, sweat dripping from my pallid face, as the pain in my ribs slowly subsided. Who'd have thought that packing a saddle-bag could be such hard work? The motions of rolling, stuffing, compressing, and tightening, combined with another disturbed night, left me exhausted and in pain. *Gah! I'm properly sick of this,* I thought. The riding actually hadn't been too bad, it was the other stuff that hurt – packing, washing, getting dressed, doing shoes up.

However, on the up side, my trench-foot had cleared up, my undercarriage was in splendid fettle, the bike was running smoothly, and the weather outside looked lovely. As we set off to Amiens the wind had swung round in the last 24 hours and now a gentle easterly blew at our backs. Rather than take the main road to Amiens, which is a horror-show of impatient trucks and vans on a not-very-wide main road, we meandered south to the Somme River and then followed it towards Amiens. It was another lovely spring morning, albeit fairly chilly, and the rolling countryside of the south Somme battlefield was typically idyllic.

Near Corbie we stopped opposite the old brickworks and looked at a nondescript field. This was where the Red Baron, Germany's leading air ace, crash-landed in April 1918 after being mortally wounded by an Australian machine-gunner. It's strange to think that one of the greatest legends of air combat died somewhere here in this field. And even before his body had grown cold, the souvenir-hunters began stripping his Fokker tri-plane. By the time he was buried, the entire plane had disappeared, such were his fame and celebrity.

Baron Manfred von Richthofen was buried with full military honours by the Allies at Bertangles. Then he was dug up and moved to Fricourt. Then he was dug up and moved to Berlin. Then he was dug up and moved to Wiesbaden where, finally, the poor sod may have rested in peace.

By late morning we were rolling into Amiens, across the finish line at the bridge over the Somme. Opposite the station we sat outside a café in the sun and drank coffee. This was almost certainly the location of the Café de L'Est, scene of such drama all those years ago. We put Joe on a train to Lille, and then home, and then Phil and I turned east and prepared to make our way to Paris via Saint-Quentin and Soissons.

★

Outside the Café de L'Est, at 4.30 a.m., a large Atlas truck shuddered to a halt and Marcel Allain, editor of *Le Petit Journal*, climbed wearily down from the front passenger seat. He had on a thick woollen hat with earflaps, two coats, a thick pair of gloves, and some heavy boots. But he was chilled to the bone and exhausted. It had taken them 24 hours to drive the truck from Brussels to Amiens, and it had been a miserable experience. With its primitive leaf-spring suspension, the truck had bounced and lurched over the broken *pavé* and rutted roads, its occupants pounded this way and that. Allain had several bruises where he had been slammed against the dashboard or doorframe, and his mood was as dark as the night.

Inside the café, Degrain and Lecomte were dozing by the fire when Allain stomped in, shaking the rain from his coat.

'How many do we have in?' asked Allain.

'Four, Monsieur Allain,' replied Lecomte, jumping to his feet in the presence of the boss.

'What? Four? Only four?'

'*Oui*, Monsieur. Deruyter, Duboc, Van Lerberghe and Anseeuw.'

'Dear God,' groaned Allain, sitting down heavily. 'Only one Frenchman so far?'

'Yes, sir.'

'Dammit! What the hell was Steinès thinking?' he snarled. 'He said it was hard but possible . . . it's a bloody nightmare!' Allain was furious. His race was in serious jeopardy and he risked looking a complete idiot. Plus, this was costing the newspaper a fortune. 'I'm going to get some sleep. I'll be back in a few hours.'

Degrain and Lecomte exchanged a weary glance and settled back down to wait. Maybe some of the riders had stopped en route and would make their way in over the next few hours.

They had, and they did. Next to appear was Theo Wynsdau, at shortly after 8 a.m. The rain had cleared overnight, but the skies were grey and still a strong westerly wind was blowing, making riding a horrible ordeal. Alavoine arrived next, at around 9.40 a.m. He was almost as angry as Marcel Allain. As a full-time pro riding for an established team, and sporting an impressive *palmarès* (six Tour stage wins, and two third-place Tour finishes before the war), he was a big cheese at this race. And he was not happy. '*C'est stupide*,' he spat, as he signed in. He had stopped for a couple of hours that night on the Somme, huddled in a damp, cold dug-out beside the road. It had contained a rusty old bed and a bundle of disgusting-smelling rags. He got a few hours' rest, and as day was breaking he got back on his bike and pedalled onwards. In the cold dawn the churned-up fields around him looked bleak and monochrome, and he wondered just how anyone had managed to survive in this environment.

By early afternoon another 20 riders had found their way to Amiens, most having slept rough in dug-outs and trenches somewhere on the Cambrai and Somme battlefields. Ali Neffati made it in at around 11 a.m., Ernest Paul arrived just before 1 p.m., and Lucien Buysse came in half an hour after that.

Marcel Allain returned to the Café de L'Est after a few hours' sleep and convened a meeting of the commissaires to discuss what to do next. Given how long and arduous Stage 3 had been, the humane thing would have been to allow an extra rest day. Unfortunately 20,000 tickets had been sold at the Parc de Princes velodrome in Paris for the arrival of Stage 4 on the following day, and there was also a civic reception planned. They simply could not afford to give the riders the extra rest day they so badly needed.

The other problem they faced was the time-cut. If they applied the letter of the law they would only have a handful of riders left in the race. After only three stages of a seven-stage race, that might be a problem. Even if they extended the time-cut they didn't know if all the riders who had finished so far would actually start Stage 4. Henri Desgrange is said to have declared that the perfect Tour de France would be one in which only one rider made it to the finish line. The Circuit des Champs de Bataille was in danger of doing exactly that.

Taking into account weather and the road conditions, the organisers decided to extend the Stage 3 time-cut to 11 p.m. on Saturday 3 May, 42 hours and 30 minutes after the stage started. They also decided to fine Duboc 25FF for 'making incorrect proposals' at control points in Lille, Douai and Cambrai. We don't know what those proposals were, but it's safe to assume that some kind of bribe was offered in exchange for recording a faster time. Or maybe he just told the commissaires to shove their time-sheets where the sun doesn't shine.

As the organisers were discussing ways of salvaging their race, the door of the café opened and in stumbled Louis Ellner. It was just before 5 p.m., and the *Lanterne Rouge* had been racing for 36 hours 26 minutes (and 15 seconds). Like all the others, he was filthy, hungry and exhausted, a shambling shadow of a man pushed far beyond his physical limits. He now had just 13 hours to eat, sleep, and prepare for the departure of Stage 4. But for once, Ellner wasn't the last one to arrive. Although not mentioned in the newspaper reports (they arrived after the paper went to press), Camille Leroy and Arsène Pain arrived shortly after 7 p.m., having spent almost 39 hours racing. By the end of the 'rest day' it was clear that no more riders would be coming.

Needless to say, *Le Petit Journal* put a positive spin on the stage, with Marcel Allain himself writing a paean of praise to Deruyter, describing how he raced across 'deserted plains and chaotic land', how he beat the cars and trucks to Amiens, and how he was 'more than a champion . . . he was a proper man'. The race, wrote Allain, 'was a lesson of energy, a celebration of life after four years of death'.

Karel Van Wijnendaele was rather less effusive, describing the Circuit des Champs de Bataille as 'the most discredited race of all time'. Of course, he was no more impartial than was Marcel Allain, and had no desire to see this race survive and possibly threaten his hegemony in Flanders. Of Stage 3 he wrote:

> It was never properly explained how, and in what manner, he [Deruyter] reached Amiens. For the organisers it was a catastrophe. In the course of the day, there was now and then one rider who arrived; the organisers did not even ask how they got there. They were happy because they saw riders. The organisers were afraid to hear the truth, which most people knew, that most had come by train and had no intention of continuing the race 'because it was still too much'.
>
> But the organisers did not ask for explanations because they had to save their race at all costs. Afterward, the organisers held an investigation, but it was more for form, and to give the impression that sporting justice would be served.
>
> The truth is that the organisers had asked for an effort that did not have enough in common with the sport, and was beyond human capability. That is why their eyes were closed to many irregularities and they could not say with certainty whether Deruyter had made the whole distance by bike. But desperate times call for desperate measures!

Van Wijnendaele seems to have been particularly scathing and cynical (not to mention libellous), but it's quite possible that some of the riders cheated. However, L'Auto (which had no particular axe to grind regarding the race) had reported that the first commissaire's car to arrive in Amiens had passed Deruyter on the road a couple of hours previously. He'd also signed in at all the checkpoints. And when Deruyter arrived he was in a terrible state, and had clearly not just got off a train.

But Lucien Buysse was not a happy chap when he arrived at the finish. When he had signed in at the control in Bapaume, 50km from the finish, he'd been told he was fifth on the road, and no one had passed him between there and the finish. So how come he finished the stage in 24th place? 'It's a circus,' he muttered as he made his way to the public baths in town for a soak. Subsequently, Arsène Pain was penalised for getting a lift on a truck, so clearly some people were cheating. We'll never know the truth, but Van Wijnendaele was right about one thing . . . these were desperate times.

As a result of Stage 3 there was a huge shake-up in the General Classification, with Dejonghe and Van Hevel abandoning, and Alavoine, Heusghem and Buysse all losing significant chunks of time. Verdickt and Wynsdau appeared on the GC leader-board for the first time, and now it appeared to be a four-horse race between Deruyter, Duboc, Van Lerberghe and Anseeuw.

Most extraordinary of all, though, was the continuing presence of Louis Ellner, the mystery man from Épernay. While Deruyter was hailed for his athletic prowess, Ellner's dogged determination earned him the respect of his peers in the peloton. Who was he? They had no idea. But he was still there, didn't appear to be cheating, and was nothing if not determined.

General Classification after Stage 3

	Rider	Time	Time gap
1	Charles Deruyter (B)	43hr 09min	00hr 00min
2	Paul Duboc (F)	44hr 13min	+01hr 04min
3	Urbain Anseeuw (B)	44hr 29min	+01hr 20min
4	Henri Van Lerberghe (B)	45hr 40min	+02hr 31min
5	Theo Wynsdau (B)	53hr 38min	+10hr 29min
6	José Pelletier (F)	54hr 20min	+11hr 11min
7	Jean Alavoine (F)	55hr 02min	+11hr 57min
8	Joseph Verdickt (B)	55hr 20min	+12hr 11min
9	Aloysius Verstraeten (B)	56hr 09min	+13hr 00min
10	Lucien Buysse (B)	56hr 14min	+13hr 05min
28	Louis Ellner (F)	75hr 10min	+32hr 01min

STAGE 4

Amiens to Paris

277km

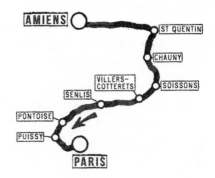

4 May 1919

There was a surprising level of cheeriness on the start line that morning. Duboc, as unofficial *patron* (leader) of the peloton, had been round chatting to the remaining riders that morning.

'Let's not make this too hard, eh?' he said to a group on the start line. 'We're all tired. Maybe ride *piano* for this stage? Keep it together, keep it steady. No need to go mad, eh?'

There were nods of agreement, and Duboc moved on to the next group. 'Nice and easy, eh lads? Let's take it steady today.'

'Sounds good,' smiled Ernest Paul. 'I'm completely done in.'

'Suits me,' shrugged Alavoine. 'Just make sure Deruyter understands, yeah? You know what he's like.'

Duboc nodded, and continued doing his rounds. The newspaper reported that the riders had rested well and were in good physical condition at the start. They really weren't. Particularly Verstraeten, who had a deep cut and serious damage to his knee. Before Stage 3 it had taken him 15 minutes to get down the stairs of his hotel, but once on the bike he seemed more comfortable (or maybe just doped to the eyeballs with a concoction of opiates and amphetamines).

Of the 30 finishers of Stage 3, an astonishing 29 took to the start for Stage 4. Only the Frenchman Alphonse Sarath was missing. How Marcel Allain managed to persuade everyone to keep going, after what they had already been through, is a mystery, but I'm guessing there may have been cash incentives involved. Why else would anyone get back on their bikes for another punishing 300km across the battlefields in freezing-cold, wet conditions? *Le Petit Journal* had invested far too much time, effort and money to allow the race to fizzle out.

So at 6 a.m. they set off through the ruins of Amiens, heading east along the dead-straight road to Saint-Quentin 68km away. Before the war this road was one of the best in France, laid with quality macadam and well maintained along its length. Now it was in the same state as the roads in Flanders and the Somme – potholed, rutted, muddy, pock-marked with shell-holes, and lined on either side with dead trees, destroyed vehicles, abandoned weapons, and the remains of dead horses. In the fields all around were isolated wooden crosses, often adorned with red, white and blue ribbons.

This part of the country was as smashed and pulverised as Albert and Ypres. This was the scene of the German Spring Offensive of 1918, and of the Allied counter-attack later that year. Less than 20km out from Amiens, the riders passed through what was left of Villers-Brettoneux, a once bustling market town, now reduced to mangled ruins. In March 1918 the German Spring Offensive had pushed the British back almost to the gates of Amiens before the line held and the Germans were stopped. From then on it was a hard slog to drive them back east, and as they withdrew the Germans destroyed everything in their wake. Literally everything. Every building was razed, every fruit tree felled, every well polluted, streams and rivers were dammed to cause flooding, every farm animal was stolen or slaughtered, and roads were mined. The desolation was horrifying.

This was the heart of the Zone Rouge, the Red Zone, land so damaged by the war that it was deemed by the French government to be no longer capable of cultivation or human habitation. The *regions dévastées* were surveyed by the French government in early 1919 and graded into three different-coloured zones

Nissen huts and prefabricated houses were used by returning sinistrés whose homes had been destroyed during the war. They often lived in these for years in very harsh conditions

denoting areas that simply needed clearance (blue), areas that needed considerable work (yellow), and areas that were too badly affected to bother with (red). Of the 33,000km² affected by the war, 15,000km² needed considerable work, and 1,160km² were designated as Zone Rouge (that's an area the size of Bedfordshire).

The extent of the damage left by the war is absolutely extraordinary, and it's something that has generally been overlooked by First World War historians more concerned with tactics and outcomes rather than what was left behind afterwards. In northern France in 1919, 333 million cubic metres of trenches needed to be filled in, 375 million square metres of barbed wire needed clearing, 442,000 buildings needed to be rebuilt or repaired, 200 million dud shells needed clearing, 21 million tonnes of unexploded ordnance needed to be disposed of, 3,500 square kilometres of woodland needed replanting, and 3.1 million farm animals needed to be replaced.

Those are astonishing numbers. The amount of earth required to fill in the trenches would fill 72 million builder's skips. And what do you do with 21 million tonnes of unexploded ordnance? Getting rid of 21 million tonnes of anything seems almost impossible, but live ordnance? These stats give an insight into just how bad things were in northern France immediately post-war. Even in areas not directly fought over or shelled, the land behind the front lines had been used by the armies for depots and camps, fields had been over-worked or left to the weeds, and woodlands had been felled for timber.

Barefoot children outside their thatched Nissen hut, a common sight for the riders in the race

As the race passed through these areas, only a few brave souls had made their way back to their homes. People were supposed to wait for permission from the local prefecture before returning, but many returned as soon as they could, desperate to bring their land and businesses back to life and start earning again. Most had lost everything, sometimes more than once. When the Germans withdrew to the Hindenburg Line in 1917, some intrepid locals returned to their farms and villages that were now well behind Allied lines. But during the 1918 Spring Offensive the Germans advanced back across those farms, forcing the population to flee for a second time, losing what little they had managed to scrape together in the meantime. It must have devastating for them.

Those that lived in the Zone Rouge were furious that their land had effectively been written off. Yes, they would get compensation (eventually), but farmers tend to be very attached to their land, and won't give it up without a fight. The local mayors were besieged by farmers (who were often friends or relatives) demanding that their land be reclassified. As a result, the size of the Zone Rouge shrank slowly over the years from 1,160km² in 1919 to a mere 170km² today. In Belgium they had no intention of abandoning land, no matter how badly damaged, and every square metre was pressed back into service as quickly as possible.

But life was unbelievably tough for those *sinistrés*. They lived in abject squalor and poverty, and risked their lives daily to clear their land. Hundreds were killed or maimed by ordnance they ploughed up, and the toll was particularly heavy on the children, who liked nothing better than to play among the dug-outs and trenches. Even today around 200 tonnes of unexploded ordnance is cleared from the Western Front battlefields each year. In 1919 alone, around 14 million tonnes of ordnance were destroyed in France during the clearances.

Living on rationed hand-outs, the *sinistrés* were malnourished and in poor health, a situation not helped by the complete lack of sanitation, damp living conditions, overflowing cess-pits, lack of clean drinking water, and non-existent health-care. Alongside them on the battlefields were labour battalions who had the unpleasant task of disposing of unexploded ordnance, clearing wire and weaponry, and filling trenches. Worse still was the work of the burial details, whose job it was to search for and identify

Children returning to the battlefields at the end of the war were at particular risk from unexploded ordnance

corpses, disinter battlefield burials, and transport bodies to the concentration cemeteries for reburial.

One of the 1919 Michelin battlefield guidebooks rather blithely reports: 'Thousands of shells, shell casings, rifles and machine guns lie scattered about. Corpses are occasionally seen.' The Michelin guide to Belleau Wood even has a photo of a partially decomposed German soldier. These Michelin battlefield guidebooks are an incredible record of the devastation wrought by the war, and some have recently been republished in facsimile form. Michelin had realised that thousands of grieving families would make their way to the battlefields after the war to visit the graves of their loved ones. So they sent photographers out in 1918 and 1919 to record the state of the battlefields immediately post-war. These pictures were included in guidebooks to the major battle areas in French and English.

Much of the clearance work was carried out by the Chinese labour battalions employed by the British army for the duration of the war plus six months, and by German PoWs. The Chinese had a reputation for bad behaviour. They seemed to like to drink heavily, and particularly enjoyed exploding ordnance *in situ* rather than taking it away for controlled destruction. These additional craters infuriated the *sinistrés*, and some campaigned vociferously for the removal of the Chinese labour force. The PoWs weren't much better, and the slap-dash filling of trenches and tunnels resulted in numerous instances of subsidence over the following years. In areas like the Somme, where the countryside had been fertile and valuable, the land was returned to agriculture as quickly as possible, but in other places the process was much slower.

In parts of north-eastern France where the land had been of poor quality before the war, with low agricultural yields, the French government refused to let the inhabitants return. Instead they gave these areas over to forestation or devoted them to the military for camps and exercise grounds similar to parts of Salisbury Plain. It was hard on the displaced population, but the ground was so severely damaged, often with bedrock churned up with the topsoil, that it would never be of any use for farming. There were also areas where there were too many unexploded shells and too many unrecovered bodies to make it worth clearing.

The authorities were still clearing bodies from the Champagne, Argonne and Verdun battlefields in 1921, and it was grisly work. After the armistice in 1918, when the business of clearing up had begun, burial details searched for battlefield burials, unmarked graves, mass graves, and corpses that had not been afforded a proper burial. These units then carefully exhumed the bodies and attempted identification from dog-tags, pay-books and personal belongings. If no name was available, they noted any insignia denoting regiment and rank.

The bodies were wrapped in blankets or tarpaulins, to which an identification tag was attached, and usually transported to what were called concentration cemeteries – cemeteries where individual burials were brought from miles around for reburial.

Burial details scouring the battlefields would have been a familiar sight to the riders as they raced through the zone rouge

One particularly good example of this is Tyne Cot near Ypres, which began as a small cemetery of 48 burials near a dressing-station, and grew into a cemetery of 12,000 burials collected from all over the Salient.

Dealing with decomposing corpses on a daily basis was horrendous work, but it had to be done. And the Graves Concentration Units took great pride in the respectful way they went about the task. They exhumed and reburied more than 200,000 bodies between November 1918 and September 1921, and they became experts at identifying insignia and uniforms. They also cross-checked regimental records and battalion diaries in an attempt to identify the dead.

Bodies are still being recovered to this day, and occasionally one can be identified. If you look closely at the memorials to the missing at the Menin Gate and Thiepval you can see examples of where a man's name has been removed because his body has been recovered, identified, and reburied in a named grave. Sadly, it was not uncommon in the years immediately post-war for farmers to plough up bodies but not report the discovery to the authorities. Reporting these finds meant delays before the authorities could come and attempt exhumation and identification, making the farmer's life even more difficult than it already was.

A huge amount of care was devoted to burying the dead, and in some ways this process helped to break down the Edwardian class structures that had existed pre-war. For the first time, officers were buried alongside their men, and their headstones were no different to those of their men. The Commonwealth War Graves Commission insisted that all headstones, regardless of rank, race or religion, be fundamentally the same. Prior to the First World War, enlisted men had usually been buried in unmarked mass graves, while the officers were afforded personal burials, or were shipped home to their families.

All these clearances and burials were going on as the riders raced across the battlefields, often accompanied by the sounds of munitions being detonated in the fields around them. It must have been a horrible reminder to those who had fought on the front line. All along the roads, as well as all the wrecked vehicles, there were belts and huge bundles of barbed wire awaiting collection, as well as vast piles of munitions and weapons, all of which were extremely dangerous and which sometimes went up with an enormous roar when a dud's fuse, reactivated when it was moved, finally achieved its purpose.

The weather was still very cold, and rain showers continued to plague the riders, but at least the wind was now behind them, making riding a little more bearable. The peloton rode as a group, soft-pedalling at a modest pace, led by Duboc. Crashes and punctures ensured that the peloton didn't stay together for very long, but the first couple of hours riding *piano* meant everyone was getting a bit of a rest. Even so, things weren't easy and immense concentration was required to pick a path through the craters and ruts on this terrible road.

Poor Henri Lobeau, in a moment of inattention, rode into

a partially filled shell crater and crashed heavily. His bike was wrecked and he was seriously injured. Some passers-by placed him in a car and drove him to the checkpoint in Soissons 100km away. It must have been an agonising journey for Lobeau over those bumpy roads, but he was made of pretty stern stuff.

As a front-line soldier in the First World War Lobeau had been wounded in April 1915. Once he'd recovered he was recruited as a cyclist into the Belgian secret service by the infamous Major Joseph Mage, and spent the rest of the war as a cycling spy, not unlike what Gino Bartali did in Italy during the Second World War. Except that Bartali didn't actually carry out any of the war-time exploits attributed to him (it was a myth, invented by a journalist, that Bartali never bothered to deny). Anyway, Lobeau declined to get out of the car at the checkpoint and instead went to get medical attention.

Then Deruyter attacked. Alavoine, ever attentive, sprinted after him, with Chassot in close pursuit. Alavoine couldn't afford to let Deruyter get away. By the time they reached Saint-Quentin they had a 3-minute lead over the peloton. Saint-Quentin was another ruin, its beautiful medieval basilica severely damaged and much of its housing destroyed. When the French liberated Saint-Quentin in October 1918 they captured a German army engineer in the process of trying to dynamite what was left of the basilica. They had drilled 93 holes in the pillars and walls of this beautiful old building, packed them with explosives, and were preparing to blow the whole thing to pieces.

For Chassot the sight of Saint-Quentin, where he had lived before the war, was heartbreaking. Tears fell as he cycled through the ruins, familiar streets reduced to scorched rubble, his old haunts now burned-out, collapsed buildings.

At the checkpoint in Saint-Quentin, Verstraeten and Neffati both climbed off and abandoned the race. Verstraeten's damaged knee was giving him serious trouble, and he was reluctant to continue in case he caused irreparable damage to it. He would be off to the Giro d'Italia in a month or so and needed to be fit and well for it. Neffati was cold and totally exhausted, and had also crashed. He'd had enough.

★

With Joe heading home on the train, Phil and I set off on the interminable 45-mile dead-straight road east to our hotel in Saint-Quentin. In 1919 this road was a shambolic scene of destruction, from one end to the other, but nowadays it's a smooth, well-surfaced, never-ending A-road. Riding in a straight line for hour after hour into a headwind is a fairly dreary experience. Mind-numbing, monotonous, tiring. So we took a short diversion off the route just before Villers-Brettoneux to ride via Cachy, the site of the very first tank-versus-tank battle, in 1918. If you have visions of massed armour, like at Kursk or El Alamein, think again. This was a British MkIV against a German A7V, which the MkIV won.

To be honest, it's barely worth the detour to see a field where this moment in history occurred, but it made a pleasant change from the endless main road. We paused in Villers-Brettoneux to eat a sandwich in the sun and pop some more painkillers. The Australians fought the advancing Germans to a standstill here in March 1918, and are still very fondly remembered by the French residents.

The road to Saint-Quentin dips and rises along its length, but always in a dead-straight line, and the gentle easterly wind was an annoyance more than an inconvenience, but Phil and I made reasonable progress, taking turns to pull on the front. The nice thing about this road was that it was fairly deserted, thanks to the nearby A29 motorway, and it had a hard shoulder / cycle path (this one full of road-kill rather than the usual broken glass and wheelie-bins) along much of its length. But it was a pretty boring ride.

Somewhere in the wide Somme valley to our left Phil's grandfather was awarded the Military Cross for his actions during the spring of 1918. He got his MC at the Battle of Saint-Quentin (part of the huge German Spring Offensive), where the 198th Brigade of the 66th Division fought a desperate rearguard action, being pushed back from Saint-Quentin almost to the outskirts of Amiens. After ten days' fighting, only 2,500 men remained in the 66th Division, from an initial strength of nearly 16,000.

On and on we rode, the farmland around us flat and unremarkable, the sun shining, and the larks ever-present. After a particularly wearisome slog up another long hill, Phil and I stopped in a lay-by and lay down on the grass for a rest. Out of the wind it was pleasantly warm and it was tempting to go for a full-on nap. I didn't. We got up again after ten minutes and carried on, pausing briefly to photograph a signpost on which was written two of my favourite things – *Ham* and *Brie*. A little further on we stopped at an impressive roadside memorial to two racing drivers killed in the 1933 Grand Prix de Picardie, which was held on public roads in those days at an average speed of 137kmh.

It was late afternoon when we rolled into Saint-Quentin. Our hotel was opposite the restored basilica which once again dominates the old town. The flying buttresses are sublime (I do like a flying buttress). After 70 miles of riding, we both felt surprisingly tired, and dinner (*steak-frites* again) in a nearby restaurant was taken mostly in silence, punctuated by the occasional 'Mmm . . . good' and 'More wine?'

I had another horrible, uncomfortable, frustrating, boring night trying to sleep without moving or breathing. Aaarrgh!

★

The remaining 26 riders turned south from Saint-Quentin, feeling the wind and occasional rain showers in their faces once more. The attrition continued with Lucien Buysse hitting a pothole, breaking his front wheel and forcing his withdrawal. By the time they reached Chauny, a group of the eight strongest riders had established a break (or everyone else had slowly disappeared off the back). Alavoine, Kippert, Desmedt, Chassot, Pelletier, Wynsdau, Huret and Van Lerberghe pushed on, probably smirking that Deruyter's irritating breakaway had been scuppered by a puncture. He now trailed them by six minutes but was pushing hard to catch back up. Any hope of riding *piano* all the way to Paris seemed to have disappeared.

Coucy-le-Château, a few miles further south, was another example of shocking vandalism on the part of the invaders. The Germans used 28 tonnes of explosives to blast this beautiful thirteenth-century castle to pieces when they abandoned it in 1917. A year later they were back, siting their long-range artillery in the forests around the town, and bombarding the civilian population of Paris.

Deruyter, who had got back to the leading group of riders, now put in another attack. And Alavoine and Chassot once again gave chase, dragging Kippert, Huret and Desmedt with them. 'Why can't the stupid bastard just take it easy for a bit?' snarled Desmedt as he pulled past Alavoine to head the chasing group. They were all thinking the same . . . there were still another 150km to go, and nobody needed this.

'Hey, Charles,' called Desmedt when they'd reeled Deruyter back in, 'just relax, will you? Let's just sort this out when we get to Paris, eh?'

Deruyter scowled and said nothing. He'd already earned 1,100FF prize money and had every intention of adding to that total. He'd rest up, and wait, he thought to himself. He was not a great sprinter, so if he were to win the stage he would need to attack before the last few kilometres.

All around the devastation was as bad as before, with places like Chauny and Coucy reduced to rubble and the roads as potholed and difficult as ever. Soissons was another medieval gem of a town, fought over constantly from 1914 to 1918 and suffering the inevitable consequences.

At the checkpoint in Soissons the lead group of six riders had a one-minute lead over the chasing group of Duboc, Anseeuw, Heusghem, Ménager, Van Lerberghe, Verdickt and Wynsdau. Deruyter's constant attacks, and the ensuing chases, put Chassot and Kippert into difficulties, and after Soissons they dropped back to the Duboc group.

Although dry, the weather was still very cold and the strong westerly continued to make riding along these damaged roads extremely hard. With Deruyter reined in, the lead group was soon caught by the chasers. The hostilities ceased, at least for the time being, as they made their way through the ruins of Longpont and Villers-Cotterêts.

The charming fields and wooded hills of this region had been blasted and churned during the final months of the war as the

Soissons was on the front line for four years, with the inevitable consequences

Germans made one last attempt to get to Paris. Then, as they retreated eastwards they looted, smashed and burned their way back towards the Belgian border, leaving utter devastation behind them.

The relatively sedate pace, and the shocking road conditions, meant that the leading group of riders arrived at the checkpoint in Senlis 2½ hours later than expected. The nine men ate, drank and rested for a few minutes, until the time-keeper told them it was time to leave. Five minutes after they'd left, Kippert and Heusghem arrived, followed five minutes later by Wynsdau and Leroy. Of Chassot, one of the early leaders of this stage, there was no sign. He eventually rolled in an hour later, bleeding heavily from a knee and an elbow, and propped his bike against a tree in the *parc fermé*.

'Enough. I'm done.'

Despite the best efforts of the commissaires to cajole him back onto his bike, he refused. As other riders came and went, Chassot remained where he was, dabbing his wounds with a piece of cloth. Eventually he got to his feet, took his bike, and hobbled towards the train station.

Beyond Senlis the route showed few signs of the war. This area had been briefly occupied by the Germans in 1914, but not since, so the roads were in reasonably good condition and places like Chantilly were untouched by the hostilities. The riders were on the home stretch now, skirting the north of Paris and approaching the finish from the west. The final checkpoint was at Pontoise, 37km from the finish. The same eight leading riders were still together, having dropped Ménager when he suffered a mechanical problem.

But a few miles later, on the Côte du Cœur-Volant in Marly-le-Roi, Deruyter saw an opportunity to break away from his companions and attacked again. Duboc and Alavoine tried to go with him, but they just couldn't reel him back in on this tough little climb. It was now every man for himself as they gave it everything they had, knowing they would get two rest days in Paris. As he neared the Parc des Princes velodrome just before 5 p.m. people came out onto the streets to wave and cheer Deruyter. Racing over the Pont de Saint-Cloud, he shot down the Route de la Reine and swung hard left to the Parc des Princes, where he had to complete one (timed) lap of the famous 666m velodrome before crossing the finish line.

The 20,000-strong crowd (which had been kept entertained by an afternoon of bike racing at the velodrome) rose and cheered Deruyter home, pleased to have a diversion from the hunger and shortages experienced even in Paris. There was a 100FF prize for the fastest lap of the velodrome, but Deruyter didn't care about that . . . he'd just pocketed 1,000FF for the stage win, taking his winnings to 2,100FF so far.

Four minutes later came Paul Duboc who, as the first

Frenchman home, got an even noisier reception. Every couple of minutes another rider appeared, until by 7 p.m., when everyone packed up and went home, there were 18 finishers. Kippert won the 100FF for the fastest lap, managing a 1-minute 3-second lap (38kmh) after 277km and 12 hours of racing on hellish roads.

Alavoine (left) and Duboc (right) at the finish of Stage 4 in the Parc des Princes velodrome

Six more riders finished Stage 4, arriving at the Night Control Point outside the offices of *Le Petit Journal* in central Paris throughout the evening. As ever, Louis Ellner was last, arriving just before 1 a.m., having been on the road for 19 hours. In those days the mantle of *Lanterne Rouge* (and its occasional prize money) was much sought-after, with riders who had no hope of winning a race often competing to see who could finish last without missing the time-cut. Ellner was streets ahead (or behind) his nearest competitor, the delightfully named Arsène Pain.

★

My own pain was present and correct as I crawled carefully out of bed and peered out of the window at Saint-Quentin. Excellent . . . blue skies, and sunshine. I'd even managed a couple of hours of fitful sleep, so Phil and I were in good spirits at breakfast. We had a longish day ahead, but the weather looked promising (although the 20mph easterly wind didn't look great) and we were taking a diversion to visit the battlefields of Chemin des Dames, an area of high ground above the River Aisne, east of Soissons, so named because it was a road frequently used by two royal princesses. We had 75 miles and 4,000ft of climbing ahead, so we ate our own weight in croissants at breakfast, did some routine bike maintenance in the hotel foyer under the approving eye of the guy on reception who clearly liked bikes more than carpets, and then got under way.

The road south to Chauny is another of those horrible dual carriageways with no bike path or hard shoulder, so we used the country D-roads further to the east, following the River Oise. Traffic was sparse, the villages were deserted, and the countryside was looking lovely in the spring sunshine. One of the things I enjoy most about riding a bike is the sounds and smells of the countryside, something you rarely experience in a car. In the villages the only sounds are those of distant tractors and the cheeping of sparrows (I miss sparrows ... London used to be full of them, but not any more), and the smells include the occasional waft of freshly baked bread as you pass a *boulangerie*. Out in the countryside the acrid smell of slurry and manure mixes with the scent of hedgerow flowers, newly turned earth or fields of oilseed rape. And everywhere, the sound of larks singing.

By lunchtime we had traversed the forest of Saint-Gobain, passed the astonishing abbey (which looks more like a royal palace than a place of worship) at Prémontré, and spent a frustrating 20 minutes cycling around Brancourt-en-Laonnais looking for somewhere to buy lunch. We found it in neighbouring Anizy-le-Château, at one of those lovely French *boulangerie/patisseries* that make you want to buy and eat everything in there. Mmmm ... macarons! Mmmm ... Florentines! Mmmm ... gateau! My saliva glands went into meltdown, followed shortly by my brain when I explained to the lady behind the counter that we were going to visit the *'champ de bataille de Chemises des Dames'* (the battlefield of the big girls' blouses).

From Anizy-le-Château we climbed steadily for three or four miles up to the high ground north of the Aisne River. The sat-nav, which had been playing silly buggers for the last couple of days, finally gave up the seemingly impossible task of navigating along a perfectly straight piece of road, and turned itself off, deleting the day's riding data. I looked at its stupid, blank little screen with hate and loathing. *You utter, utter, utter piece of crap. Three hundred quid? For this? Aaaaand relax.* Fortunately the Chemin des Dames is a 15-mile straight road, so the sat-nav was not required.

In 1919 the road along the top of this ridge no longer existed. Three major battles in four years meant the road had vanished, and it wouldn't be properly restored until the mid 1920s. When the German army was pushed back from the outskirts of Paris after the First Battle of the Marne in 1914, they retreated to the high ground of Chemin des Dames, an almost perfect defensible position on top of a 650ft-high plateau, overlooking the wide, flat river valleys of the Aisne to the south and the Ailette to the north, 450ft below. The high ground was riddled with caves and underground quarries, giving the Germans plenty of scope for deep shelters, and the slopes up from the Aisne valley floor were horribly steep, which made life almost impossible for assaulting troops.

After the First Battle of the Aisne in 1914, during which the French and British forces failed to dislodge the newly dug-in Germans, this part of the Western Front became a relatively quiet sector. Both sides knew that taking the ridge by frontal assault was impossibly hard, so they sat tight and waited. Battalions from both sides were sent here in 1915 and 1916 to rest and recuperate. It was a quiet, cushy billet.

Unfortunately, in early 1917, General Nivelle, the new commander-in-chief of the French armies on the Western Front, had a cunning plan. He had been commander at Verdun in late

1916, and now he wanted to use his successful tactics from Verdun to punch through the German lines on the Aisne. There were to be simultaneous diversionary attacks by the British at Arras, the Russians in the east, the Italians in the south, and by other French divisions around Reims on the Champagne front. But before the attacks could take place the Germans further north withdrew to the Hindenburg line, shortening their line and freeing up extra troops, the Russians sued for peace with Germany, and the Italians were in disarray. With his plans in tatters (and the details of it widely reported in the newspapers), Nivelle went ahead with the offensive anyway. On 16 April 1917 the French launched themselves up the slopes of Chemin des Dames, with wave after wave of infantry being mown down by German machine-guns. By the end of April the French had established a toe-hold on top of the ridge, at a cost of 120,000 casualties.

So horrifying was the slaughter that the French army, already exhausted by the blood-letting at Verdun in 1916, teetered on the brink of all-out mutiny. They were being sacrificed for little gain, and the army commanders had underestimated casualty figures so drastically that the medical services broke down altogether. There are stories of wounded men lying out on stretchers in the sleet and rain, waiting up to three days to be evacuated to a hospital. But still the attacks went on, and still the men died in horrendous numbers.

By early May some French regiments demanded an end to the futile attacks and were refusing to go back into the line. Around 40 per cent of French infantry regiments were affected by the mutinies, which were more like industrial strikes than active rebellion, and the French army was in crisis. They had lost nearly 1 million men since the beginning of the war, and the infantrymen were sick of what they saw as pointless bloodshed. There is a story that one regiment went back into the line bleating, like lambs to the slaughter, and more than 27,000 French soldiers deserted in 1917.

The British did their best to take the pressure off the reeling

French army by attacking at Arras and at Ypres. Nivelle was sacked, and Petain was brought in to restore morale and reorganise the army. It worked, but it was a very close-run thing, and the Chemin des Dames has always been viewed by the French as a shameful chapter in their military history. Even today there is a pride about the Marne and Verdun, but Chemin des Dames is only ever talked about as the shame, and the breaking point, of the French army.

Frankly, it's not surprising the French army was on its knees by this point. In the last five months of 1914 more than 2,200 Frenchmen were killed every single day. In total during the four years of the war the French army lost 1.4 million men (893 per day) and 4.3 million (2,745 per day) were wounded. The war created 700,000 widows and left 1 million children without fathers. Little wonder French morale was taking a battering.

The French finally forced the Germans off the Chemin des Dames in October 1917, by which time they had suffered 187,000 casualties and the Germans 163,000. The blood of 350,000 men was soaked into the churned-up, treeless earth of this small plateau, and just like at Ypres and the Somme, the whole lot would be retaken by the Germans in the spring of 1918.

Phil and I turned east at Vauxrains and started along the narrow plateau of the Chemin des Dames. Despite the blue skies it was still fairly cool thanks to the easterly wind, which was blowing with increased ferocity in our faces. Sigh. And the road surface was sucky. We stopped at Malmaison, the German-held fort that dominated this sector. The capture of this fort in late October 1917 forced the Germans to retreat north to the other side of the Ailette valley and effectively brought to an end the Second Battle of the Aisne. But you can't visit it (except by special arrangement). In fact you can't even see it because it's completely overgrown and looks like a wood. Even the vast German cemetery there isn't quite what it seems . . . it contains soldiers from the Second World War, killed when fighting once again descended on this part of the world.

Back on the Chemin, we ground our way eastwards along the top of the plateau, cursing the headwind and the lack of protection from it. All along the road are memorials to individuals and fighting formations that served here. It's noticeable that successive French governments have almost completely ignored Chemin des Dames, so bad are the negative emotions attached to it. There are significant French national memorials at Dormans and Meaux on the Marne, at Navarin Farm on the Champagne front, and at Douaumont near Verdun, but at Chemin des Dames there is nothing except for the cemeteries and a small commemorative church at Cerny.

Looking around at the gently undulating, bucolic landscape, with its fields of wheat and oilseed rape, dotted with woods and little villages, it's hard to believe that tens of thousands of men died up here in an inferno of lead and fire. And it's hard to believe that this brutalised landscape was ever returned to agriculture, particularly when you see post-war photos of an almost lunar-like landscape devoid of any vegetation.

We stopped for coffee and a rest in Cerny, exhausted by the painfully slow progress eastwards (we averaged a feeble 11mph along this stretch). The pretty French cemetery there is very moving, particularly so these days because Christian and Muslim soldiers are buried should-to-shoulder, just as they fought. A few miles further east we came to the Carverne du Dragon, one of the underground quarries that were occupied and fought over (and through) during the First World War. There is now a fantastic museum here, with wonderful 90-minute tours through the caves. At least that's what I'm told. When we got there we couldn't get a ticket until the 5.30 p.m. tour, finishing at 7 p.m. We would then have a 25-mile ride to our hotel in Soissons. Maybe next time.

A couple of miles further on, at the now-destroyed village of Craonne (a new Craonne was built just down the hill), we turned south towards the Aisne. Not far from here, in July 1919, a middle-aged English woman named Elizabeth Buckle came in search of

The French cemetery at Cerney-en-Laonnaise on the Chemin des Dames, where Christian and Muslim solders are buried as they fought, shoulder to shoulder

the grave of her dead son, wading waist-deep through the grass and weeds, crossing trenches and shell craters, easing through belts of rusting barbed wire, to where her son fell and was buried on the battlefield in May 1918. She wrote a remarkably moving little booklet about her visit, called *A Kingly Grave in France*. This is an extract from it:

> If one can forget the sadness of the waste land, and the desolate homes of the French villagers, one can see how extraordinarily beautiful the open country has become, for it is an absolute sea of blue cornflowers, scarlet poppies and white hemlock – mile after mile of red, white and blue blossom . . . there were helmets here and there, rusted rifles, scraps of cartridge belts, all nearly hidden among the flowers.
>
> There, beside his trench, facing the miles of open country,

alone with God and with the birds and flowers and butterflies all about his bed – there lay our only son . . . Over the wooden cross they had slung his helmet – bullet-riddled as we knew it must be. A few yards away are the graves of two Germans, as though he had shot them first.

The cornflowers will fade, the piteous trenches crumble gradually away, but that wide starry sky, that majesty of silent peace will still be there.

Sadly, her son, Lieutenant Colonel C. G. Buckle, DSO, MC, was not allowed to remain where he had fallen, with 'birds and flowers and butterflies all about his bed'. Shortly after his mother's visit he was exhumed and moved to the concentration cemetery at nearby La Ville-aux-Bois. But the wide starry sky and the majesty of silent peace remain.

Dropping down into the valley of the Aisne, past the huge French cemetery on the hillside at Craonelle, we turned west, riding into the late-afternoon sun with the stiff wind now at our backs. Our average speed increased to a more respectable 16mph, the temperature was up to 24°C, the sat-nav was working perfectly, and all was well with the world. Well, almost. My ribs were still aching like a bastard and after a tough afternoon battling the headwind, Phil and I were both running on empty. But the valley was picturesque and peaceful, and looking up at the high ground to our right gave a very clear view of what the French soldiers had to contend with as they struggled to gain a toe-hold on the ridge. At the huge Franco-German cemetery at Soupir we paused for a break and to walk amongst the 19,000 burials. It's a beautiful and peaceful spot, shaded by trees, and the grass is blanketed with clover and daisies.

The final run into Soissons was excruciating. Knackered after 75 tough miles, and with our pace dropping painfully, we could see Soissons in the distance, but it never seemed to get any closer. We got there, eventually, wind-blown, sunburned and on our last legs. I would have liked to look round Soissons, but we just didn't have the strength of will to get any further than the hotel restaurant. Dinner, though, was spectacularly good – *pavé de boeuf* with marrow-bone and a Béarnaise sauce, although Phil was most aggrieved that his marrow-bone clearly came from the shin of a mouse while mine was a thigh-bone from some kind of diplodocus. It was heavenly.

I couldn't wait to get to bed, but once there, it became another endless sleepless night of rolling, panting and groaning (and not in a good way). The hours dragged on. And on. 2 a.m. 3.17 a.m. 4.05 a.m. 5.37 a.m. The frustration, and tiredness. *Why can't I sleep, dammit?* Fitful napping, it turns out, just wasn't working for me. And it's so boring. I'd been trying to apply the unofficial cycling Rule #5 (harden the fuck up) for the last week, and even tried a version of retired pro cyclist Jens Voigt's famous catch-phrase – 'Shut up ribs!' But nothing was working. We had a rest day planned for Paris the following day, where Phil's wife Helen, and my wife Emma, would come out on the Eurostar to meet us. Phil, Helen and Emma would then head back to the UK while I carried on. I wasn't sure one rest day was going to be enough.

I got up and spent the usual half hour trying to pack everything into my bags without whimpering or passing out. It was agony. Then I phoned Emma and manfully snivelled, 'I just can't do this any more.' Filled with equal measures of self-loathing and self-pity, I asked her to book me and the bike on the Eurostar home with her. I needed some time to recover, and 70 miles a day on the bike was not the best way to do that.

It was another beautiful day as Phil and I set off for Paris, although the easterly wind we had been hoping for had swung round to the south and was now a cross/headwind. Oh well, we only had 55 miles to do because we were going to cheat again. The original race route took a wide anti-clockwise loop around the northern and western suburbs of Paris before coming into the city through Saint-Cloud to the Parc des Princes. One hundred years ago this may have been quite pleasant, but in the intervening century Paris has spread its concrete tendrils outwards and the route is now through some pretty crappy suburbs. So we were going as far as Chantilly, then getting a train into the Gare du Nord to meet Helen and Emma.

The countryside south-west of Soissons was preternaturally green and leafy, as spring had well and truly arrived. It was a beautiful morning spent riding among the fields and trees, with one or two tough little climbs to ensure we didn't have it too easy. To our right was (or, rather, wasn't) a vanished First World War cemetery. According to my 1919 Michelin guidebook, there was a large American cemetery here, near the Croix-de-Fer crossroads. There's even a photo of it and a brief description. But it isn't there now. I can only assume the burials were moved to one of the bigger American cemeteries at Belleau or Seringes-et-Nestels, or repatriated. Unlike the British, the Americans allowed repatriation of soldiers killed abroad.

We stopped at Longpont to look at the lovely old abbey, already partly ruined by the time the fighting came to this area. I didn't realise, but the French had their own dissolution of the monasteries, in the early days of the Revolution, and many of these lovely old buildings were damaged or destroyed. Amazingly, the Germans didn't blow this one up. The rest of the village was reduced to rubble, but the walls of the abbey remained standing. Continuing through the delightful sun-dappled greenery of the Forêt de Retz, we arrived at Villers-Cotterêts for coffee and to buy some baguettes for later, and then stopped in the shadow of another ruined abbey, the Abbaye Royale Notre Dame de Lieu-Restauré, for a leisurely lunch.

It was all going so well. Then the sat-nav led us a merry dance as we tried to avoid the N2, trying to take us up farm tracks and footpaths. Poor Phil tried quite hard not to laugh as I once again heaped Anglo-Saxon abuse on this stupid thing attached to my handlebars. I was becoming dangerously Cleesean (as in John Cleese) about this small lump of plastic. It did it again at Chantilly, although this time (and not for the first or last time) it was the fault of my route-planning software, which makes some outrageous assumptions about what routes are possible on a bicycle.

By mid-afternoon we were at the train station in Chantilly, chugging down cold Cokes and shoving Snickers bars in our faces. The tall buildings and narrow streets of Paris posed another challenge to the sat-nav, which was always about 50 yards behind where we actually were, but eventually we rolled to a stop outside our hotel, to be greeted by two lovely ladies sitting outside in the sun, who gave us beer. I suddenly felt stupidly emotional.

Ten doors down from where we were sitting drinking beer used to be the offices of *Le Petit Journal*, where Louis Ellner arrived to sign in at the end of Stage 4. He was now 46 hours and 9 minutes down on the leader, but he was still going. We raised a glass to those tough, determined men and their astonishing feats of endurance.

★

For the riders of the Circuit des Champs de Bataille, the two rest days in Paris must have been an absolute godsend. After almost 1,200km of racing across appalling roads in unspeakable weather, they finally got a decent amount of time to sleep, eat, and recover. At 4 p.m. on the first rest day the riders were expected to attend a Champagne reception at *Le Petit Journal*, and with free food and booze on offer they were happy to oblige. Oscar Egg, winner of the first stage, was there, as were the great and good from the cycling world – team bosses, journalists, bike manufacturers, tyre manufacturers, dignitaries from the Union Vélocipédique Française (the French cycling authority), and so on.

Louis Ellner stood to one side, on the periphery of the bustling reception, with a glass of Champagne in his hand, watching his fellow riders mingle with the reporters and team bosses. He was one of two true *isolés* left in the race (Marcel Mariellonny, from Switzerland, was the other), and he felt like a complete outsider. He didn't know any of these people, he had no experience of professional cycling, and he was in every sense an *isolé*. He wondered how much longer he would have to stay here.

'Louis, there you are.' Duboc, smiling, appeared by his side. 'Have you met Monsieur Able Henry, owner of *Le Petit Journal*? It's his Champagne you're drinking.'

Ellner turned to Duboc's companion and bowed. 'It's a pleasure, sir. And very fine Champagne it is, too.'

'You know your Champagne, then?' enquired a visibly sceptical Henry.

'A little,' conceded Ellner. 'My family owns a Champagne house in Épernay. Maison Charles Ellner.'

'Excellent! Duboc here has been telling me all about your extraordinary tenacity. Is it true that you are riding a pre-war *routière* bike, not a racer?'

'Yes, it's true. I had an old racing bike, but it had some serious problems and I couldn't get any spare parts, so I borrowed my cousin's *routière* instead.'

'Well, Monsieur Ellner, I salute you. Yours is exactly the sort of spirit and courage we wanted to encourage with this race. I hope to see you at the finish in Strasbourg. *Bon chance!*'

Duboc took Ellner by the elbow and led him towards the throng. 'Let's introduce you to a few people, eh, Louis?'

*

Emma and I spent our rest day loafing around Paris doing nothing in particular, much as the riders would have done in 1919. But I bet they didn't pay €6 each for a coffee in the Tuileries Gardens, or spend €40 a head on lunch by the Seine. But the weather was lovely, I could hobble slowly, and Paris has rarely looked so beautiful. We'd done the museums and the sights on previous visits, so we didn't feel the need to do the culture thing, so we just wandered about.

We met up with Phil and Helen for a wonderful dinner at Le

Relais de l'Entrecôte, a restaurant that only serves *steak-frites*, but which does them so unbelievably well. And as we meandered back to our hotel in the warm spring evening I could, for the first time, see why people find Paris so enchanting.

Back in London, I took myself off to the local Minor Injuries Unit where a kindly doctor poked my ribs until I yelped, and then diagnosed three cracked ribs and prescribed a month of not doing very much. I was gutted that I'd had to abandon in Paris, but I couldn't carry on in that state. I would head back to France in a couple of weeks to continue the trip, but in the meantime I needed to recover. Riding 400 miles in a week with three cracked ribs, and very little sleep, had taken its toll. On the up side, the house was well stocked with chocolate Hobnobs and the Giro d'Italia was on TV every afternoon. Result!

General Classification after Stage 4

	Rider	Time	Time gap
1	Charles Deruyter (B)	56hr 06min	00hr 00min
2	Paul Duboc (F)	56hr 16min	+00hr 10min
3	Urbain Anseeuw (B)	56hr 39min	+00hr 33min
4	Henri Van Lerberghe (B)	57hr 53min	+01hr 47min
5	Theo Wynsdau (B)	66hr 03min	+09hr 57min
6	Jean Alavoine (F)	66hr 06min	+10hr 00min
7	José Pelletier (F)	66hr 29min	+10hr 23min
8	Joseph Verdickt (B)	68hr 03min	+11hr 57min
9	André Huret (F)	69hr 07min	+13hr 01min
10	Charles Kippert (F)	69hr 14min	+13hr 08min
24	Louis Ellner (F)	96hr 15min	+40hr 09min

STAGE 5

Paris to Bar-le-Duc

333km

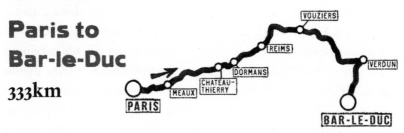

7 May 1919

To Louis Ellner's great surprise, there was no sign of Paul Duboc on the start line for Stage 5. He went over to a group of French riders that included Alavoine, Huret and Pelletier.

'Anyone seen Duboc?' he asked.

A pained expression passed across Alavoine's face. 'I heard a rumour he'd abandoned.'

'Abandoned? He seemed fine at the reception yesterday.'

'Hmmm . . . well, I heard there was a problem with his bike after Stage 4. Something to do with the lead seal. People are saying that he changed bikes, got caught, and that the commissaires gave him the option of abandoning rather than suffering the embarrassment of being thrown out.'

'Bloody hell! I can't believe it.' Ellner shook his head, sad that one of the people who had been friendliest towards him was out of the race.

'Nor can I,' replied Alavoine, sourly. 'If they'd disqualified him, I would've got his 600 Francs for finishing second.'

'And I would've got your 400 Francs for third, and Huret here would've got my 300 Francs for fourth,' complained Pelletier.

'I'm quite glad in some ways,' confessed Alavoine. 'He was looking bloody strong, and it puts the rest of us one place higher on GC.'

The group nodded their agreement.

The commissaires had indeed been busy that second rest day. They convened at the offices of the newspaper to discuss various infractions that had come to their notice. Lobeau was fined 25FF for refusing to get out of the car that was taking him to hospital, Chassot (despite the fact that he had abandoned) was given a warning for getting his team manager to take some spare tyres for him in his car, and a complaint by Alavoine that Deruyter had got a tow from a car, in order to pull out a gap, was dismissed.

Also, Guénot and Morel had been spotted in a car between Soissons and Senlis, and an investigation would be opened. Ali Neffati, who had abandoned at Saint-Quentin, asked to be re-admitted to the race for Stage 5, but the commissaires were having none of it. In those days it was not uncommon for riders who missed the time-cut to be allowed to continue to race for prize money but not to appear on the GC. There was even some business from Stage 3 – Arsène Pain was given a 1-hour penalty for getting a lift in a truck near Lille, and Wynsdau was given a 5FF fine for not signing on at the departure from Brussels.

Then there was Duboc, and the mysterious missing lead seal. Rumours had been circulating widely since the finish of Stage 4 that Duboc had swapped bikes at some point during that stage. As a result of the rumours, and possibly with hard evidence, the commissaires couldn't turn a blind eye even if they wanted to. He was the leading Frenchman, and a major figure in the peloton, and I suspect they would have loved to have kept him in the race if they could. We don't know the real truth, but *Le Petit Journal* reported two non-starters for Stage 5 – Verdickt ('injured') and Duboc ('suffering').

Due to the massively long 333km Stage 5, the riders had to sign in at the offices of *Le Petit Journal* between 11 p.m. and midnight on the evening of their second rest day. A caravan of riders, officials and supporters would then roll out to Noisy-le-Grand on the eastern outskirts of Paris for a 2.30 a.m. start. There was a carnival atmosphere as the convoy of riders, cars, trucks and spectators made their way through Paris to the start line, accompanied by a band and chanting from the crowds.

The reason they left from Noisy-le-Grand was because Paris had a blanket 12kmh speed limit and a lot of red-tape that precluded organising races within the Seine *département*. With their railway stations and good access, Noisy-le-Grand and neighbouring Villiers-sur-Marne (which were outside the city limits of Paris) became the default start/finish lines for races to the east of the capital. Villiers even boasted three cycling cafés on its main street before the war, one of which had been owned by Octave Lapize, the famous pre-war Tour winner and pilot who was shot down and killed during the war.

At 2.30 a.m. the remaining 22 riders set off on another mammoth stage across the battlefields, this time heading east across the Marne, Champagne, Argonne and Verdun battlefields. As usual, the first hour or so was spent riding *piano* behind the lead car, but as the sky in the east began to lighten the speculative attacks began. At the first checkpoint in Meaux, a place that had seen France's last-ditch stand against the Germans in September 1914 in the First Battle of the Marne, André Huret had a one-minute lead over the peloton. He was 13 hours behind the leading trio on GC, so no one was too interested in chasing him down. Besides, the peloton would catch him soon enough without having to put in too much effort.

The First Battle of the Marne was known to the French as the 'miracle on the Marne', so close had the Germans come to taking Paris. In the first months of the war the Germans had swept through Flanders and down towards Paris, and if they had stuck to the original Schlieffen Plan and encircled Paris from the west, they might even have taken the capital and won the war in the west before it had even fully started. But the German General Von Kluck swung his troops to the east of Paris in pursuit of the British Expeditionary Force and came up against the combined might of the French and the BEF near Meaux.

There followed a five-day battle that stretched along a line from Paris east to Verdun, during which the Allied and German armies engaged in a titanic struggle for supremacy. Unlike later the First World War battles, this was a mobile one, ebbing and flowing across the undulating countryside. At one point the general in charge of the defence of Paris commandeered 1,100 taxis (or 400 or 600, depending on your sources) and used them to ferry reserve troops to the front line. One of those drivers was Lucien Petit-Breton, two-times winner of the Tour de France before the war, who had enlisted as a driver in the transport corps. He was killed later in the war when his vehicle collided in the dark with a horse-drawn cart near the front.

The Allied forces finally pushed the Germans back from the Marne and pursued them 30 miles north to the River Aisne where the Germans had prepared a defensive line along the Chemin des Dames. Both armies then raced north, trying to turn the flank of the other, until they reached Diksmuide in Belgium, where the front stabilised into what we now know as the Western Front.

For the French, the First Battle of the Marne, which had forced half a million Parisians to flee and the government to relocate to Bordeaux, was a miraculous escape. And a significant victory because, for the preceding month, it had seemed as if the German army was invincible.

From Meaux the race headed north-east, following the River Marne as it winds its way through fertile farmland. Everywhere there were signs of war, although there wasn't the wholesale destruction found in Flanders, Artois and the Somme. The Second Battle of the Marne, in June 1918, had also been a moderately mobile one and although villages and farms were severely damaged, they hadn't been pounded to dust like they had been elsewhere on the Western Front. The roads, however, were in a shocking state, having been used by heavy military vehicles for more than four years. The *pavé* was smashed and subsiding, and the macadam was no more than rutted and potholed gravel, but the rate of progress in the race was still quite rapid (around 25kph) compared to previous stages, thanks mainly to the improved weather.

As the riders headed east under clear skies and a following wind, it looked like the organisers had just about managed to save their race, despite an appallingly hard *parcours*, abysmal weather, and the loss of 65 riders. They still had some big names in the race, and now they would be crossing battlefields more familiar to the French readership. They were reaching the apotheosis of the race as they headed for the hugely symbolic town of Verdun.

But then, just as it seemed that everything was going to be OK, that the race was back on track, something happened that would ensure the race was bumped from the front pages and became an irrelevance – the terms of the Treaty of Versailles were announced.

Terms of the Treaty of Versailles are announced on 8 May. Good news for the French, bad news for Le Petit Journal's *race*

This was what every French (and Belgian, and Luxembourgois) citizen had been waiting for, to see how Germany was going to pay for what it had done. And as a consequence everyone was buying newspapers, thus negating any slight gain in *Le Petit Journal's* circulation due to the race. With space at a premium in the paper (it was a four-page broadsheet), *Le Petit Journal* was forced to devote most of its pages to the Treaty of Versailles and squeeze the race report into just a couple of paragraphs of timings at various checkpoints on page four. It was another disaster for the newspaper, another stroke of terrible luck in a seemingly endless run of misfortune.

While a mainstream newspaper like *Le Petit Journal* was forced to devote itself to actual proper news, *Sportwereld* in Belgium was a sports newspaper and had no such restrictions. They had Karel Van Wijnendaele covering the race, and it is only because of his reports in *Sportwereld* and the reports in *L'Auto*, the French sports paper, that we have even the vaguest idea of what happened on Stage 5.

Huret's attack was, as expected, reeled back in and the peloton continued east as the sun rose on a pleasant spring day. Approaching Château Thierry, the evidence of war became more and more obvious. It was here that the German advance in late May and June 1918, their last throw of the dice before the Americans became fully operational, was brought to a halt. They had broken through the British lines on the Aisne and swept south, reaching the Marne in under a week. Two months of hard fighting in June and July eventually pushed the Germans back, but by then the landscape and villages were in ruins and the Americans had experienced a tough and bloody introduction to the war.

What the Americans lacked in battlefield experience, they made up for in terms of sheer grit, and the US Marine Brigade became famous for its attack on Belleau Wood, battling for several weeks to oust the Germans from their positions amongst the trees and then hold them against determined counter-attacks. The reputation of the Marines as an elite fighting force was forged amongst the shattered stumps and boulders of this small wood on the Marne. The Marines suffered nearly 10,000 casualties here, of which nearly 2,000 were killed.

Racing through the forlorn ruins of Vaux, a small village completely obliterated in 1918, the riders rounded Côte 204, the hill that dominates the west of Château Thierry, and plunged into the town. By this point Deruyter and Van Lerberghe were leading the 15-strong peloton, having dropped the usual suspects (Ellner, Asse, Leroy, Pain, etc.) along the way. With Duboc out, Deruyter, Van Lerberghe and Anseeuw were the only ones with a realistic chance of winning, but everyone knew that one crash or mechanical problem could change all that in a second.

They pushed on along the banks of the Marne, heading for Reims, dodging the potholes and craters, and sticking together for the time being. The hills to their left were a curious sight. So far the riders had seen little sign of agriculture, as few farmers had been able to return to their land, but on the south-facing slopes of the valley there were Champagne vineyards that had been cultivated throughout the war. In some places they were shell-torn and churned up, but the rest were relatively unscathed and under cultivation. The front line had twice swept over this area, but the grape harvest had been nurtured and brought in by the women, children and old folk of the area, sometimes under shell-fire. During the 1914 harvest, 20 children were killed by shelling and sniping (yes, they were actually sniping at children), and whole families had been wiped out by artillery fire. In several churchyards hereabouts you can see the headstones of entire families killed on the same day.

As it turned out, 1914 was one of the all-time great Champagne vintages, so good that it can still be drunk to this day (assuming it has been carefully rebottled, and that you can afford the €15,000 a bottle asking price). By the autumn of 1918 around 60 per cent of Champagne's vineyards were still intact and throughout the war cultivation never stopped.

At Verneuil the race left the Marne valley and turned north, almost exactly following the front line of June and July 1918. As before, the front had moved significantly over the course of those early summer months, so towns and villages were in ruins rather than obliterated. The peloton stuck together, with no one willing to attack Deruyter so far from the finish line, although some of the weaker riders began to drop away.

Approaching Reims, the leading riders must have once again found it hard to believe their eyes. This once-beautiful medieval city had been within range of the German guns for the entire war, and almost nothing was left standing. The stunning cathedral, where once the kings of France had been crowned, was a burned-out skeleton, having been hit by 300 German shells. By the end of the war only 68 of Reims' 14,000 houses were inhabitable.

In the space of four years, 300 German shells hit the beautiful medieval cathedral at Reims

At Reims, Deruyter, Anseeuw, Van Lerberghe, Alavoine, Heusghem, Huret, Wynsdau and Desmedt came in together, followed a few minutes later by Kippert, Nempon, Ménager, Hanlet and Pelletier, and then another few minutes later by Morel, Paul, Leroy and Guénot. There was no sign of the stragglers.

★

After three weeks slumped on the sofa at home watching the Giro d'Italia on the telly and reading obscure 1920s books about the post-war battlefields, I was desperate to get back on my bike – there's only so much of Carlton Kirby's astonishing TV commentary a man can take. Having said that, Eurosport's coverage of the Giro was perfect for a man in my position. Sean Kelly's soft Irish monotone would send me off to sleep on the sofa after about half an hour, and Carlton's rising hysteria would wake me up when the stage was 2km from the finish.

But the enforced indolence was slowly driving me mad. I had unfinished business in France and I wanted to get back on the road. I've never really had wanderlust, having travelled extensively for work, but during the first part of my trip I discovered that travelling by bike, day after day, is a rather wonderful experience. You see more, you hear more, you smell more, you experience more. Everyone should try it. Seriously. Riding 50 miles a day is not nearly as hard as it might sound. It may sound like a lot to a non-cyclist, but it really isn't – it's 5 hours at a sedate 10mph. Ride for an hour, stop for coffee. Ride for another hour, stop for cake. Ride for another hour, stop for lunch. And so on. At the end of the day you feed your face with whatever you feel like, guilt-free, and then sleep like a baby (assuming you haven't smashed your ribs to pieces) for 8 hours.

Towards the end of my incarceration I went out on my bike a couple of times to see how things felt. A little rusty, but otherwise fine. When I wasn't watching the Giro I spent time fettling my bike to prepare it for the second leg, and rethinking my riding gear in light of the fact that I would be back on the road in early June, so probably (hopefully) wouldn't be needing so much foul-weather gear.

By a stroke of luck a friend of mine happened to be heading to France in his car and agreed to drop me and my bike at Meaux, thus avoiding the necessity to book tickets for the Eurostar or dice with homicidal van-drivers in the eastern suburbs of Paris. I was ready, the bike was ready, and off I went with Emma's exhortations not to fall off again ringing in my ears.

It was 14°C and overcast as I rolled out of Meaux. There's a good museum next to the First World War memorial on the outskirts of town, but I had 85 miles to do and not a lot of time for museums. It was good to be back in the saddle, riding through the pleasant Marne landscape. There were poppies growing in the verges, and wheat was ripening in the fields. I breathed in great lungfuls of fresh, clean air and felt a wave of contentment wash over me. The only sounds were the gentle click of Campagnolo gears, the thrum of tyres on the road, and the larks singing above me. Occasionally a car would pass me, often giving a little beep of warning while still several hundred metres behind, then passing with at least two metres to spare. That little beep says, 'I've seen you, I am conscious of your vulnerability, and I will take care while passing you.' I absolutely LOVE those little beeps. At one point a little beeper stopped a mile or two further on and I was very tempted to stop and give them a hug. But I'm English, so of course I didn't.

After a couple of hours gently easing back into the rhythm of riding again, I took a detour off the Reims road to visit Belleau Wood where the US Marines fought so bravely in 1918. Again, the differences between Allied and German cemeteries is brought into stark relief here – the German cemetery is neglected and leaf-strewn, almost brutalist in its grey appearance, while the American one is immaculately tended and laid out in an unusual semi-circular arrangement around a commemorative chapel built over the front-line trenches. There were 8,600 German dead crammed into their small cemetery, while 2,300 American dead lay in a cemetery three times the size.

The wood itself is quiet and peaceful, sitting atop a small hill covered with trees and large boulders. I was the only one there among the old artillery pieces and memorials and birdsong. This must have been a hellishly difficult place to take from a well-dug-in enemy. I was reminded of the bizarre story of Ernest Strickler from Wisconsin who came here in 1928 and shot himself in the head. In his pocket was a suicide note that explained that he couldn't carry on living while so many of his comrades had died, and requested that he be buried alongside them. Unfortunately there was no trace of an Ernest Strickler in the official US Marines records, so he was buried in the local civilian cemetery nearby. Even so, kind-hearted American visitors often visit him there and leave flowers on his grave.

A few miles further on, on Hill 204 above Château Thierry, there is a colossal US memorial that overlooks the town and the River Marne, with spectacular views of the rainclouds building from the south-west. I didn't linger . . . lunch in Château Thierry beckoned.

The rain that had threatened never materialised, and I continued east along the banks of the Marne, with vineyards up to my left and the slow meander of the Marne down to my right. At Dormans I stopped at the French national memorial to the Marne dead, an imposing chapel on the slopes of the river's south bank. It's an impressive place, no doubt, but it lacks the intimacy and emotion of some memorials. Its scope is so wide, and the carnage so terrible, that all I felt was a very distant, abstract sense of sadness.

From just beyond Dormans the route turned north and headed directly towards Reims, along the front line of the Second Battle of the Marne in 1918. The road rose and fell gently and a soft tail-wind helped me along at a respectable 16mph average. The skies were overcast, but the temperature was a pleasant 18°C and it was good being back on the road. My legs felt strong, my ribs didn't hurt, and the bike was running smoothly. But the real shock – the sat-nav was behaving impeccably.

At Bligny I came across something I really didn't expect – an Italian First World War cemetery. And a sizeable one, too, with 3,550 burials. Two divisions of Italian infantry had been transferred to the Western Front in 1918 and fought alongside the French during the Second Marne. Another 60,000 Italians, unsuitable for front-line duty, had also been transferred to the Western Front in late 1917 to act as labour battalions. Apparently some of these were men who had taken part in mutinies and were deemed unreliable for fighting.

The cemetery is rather stark by the standards of the nearby Chambrecy Commonwealth War Graves Commission cemetery, with concrete crosses fitted with metal name-plates, and gravel walkways, rather than the CWGC's carved headstones, flowers and grass. A faded Italian *tricolore* ribbon tied around one head-stone is almost the only sign of colour in this sad, grey place. It feels a long way away from the sun-washed slopes of the Apennines or the bustling chaos of Naples, and I rather wished these men had been afforded a more sympathetic and aesthetically pleasing place in which to spend eternity.

From Bligny I took another detour, this time south-east for a couple of miles, where in late July 1918 the New Zealand Cyclist Battalion (with quite a lot of help from the Highland and West Riding Regiments) took the villages of Marfaux and Chaumuzy in a few days of tough fighting. There's a small memorial in the CWGC cemetery to those cyclists who have no known grave.

It's tempting to think of cyclist battalions as super-fit young chaps pedalling around the Western Front plugging gaps in the line, undertaking perilous missions, and acting as rapid-response units. But they weren't. The minute trench warfare became the norm, bicycles were pretty much useless for anything other than delivering messages, and cyclist battalions were used as labour battalions or fought as regular infantry.

The original idea had been for cyclists to be used for scouting, reconnaissance and communications, as well as being able to move quickly to where they were needed. By the end of 1914 this was no longer possible, and it wasn't until mid 1918 that the war became mobile again. A quote from the New Zealand Cyclist Battalion diaries gives you an idea of what things were like for them:

Cyclists battalions were conceived as rapid response units, but when trench warfare became the norm they usually ended up as labour battalions. This is a Belgian one at the beginning of the war

The roads were particularly bad, and very congested with the traffic necessary to an advancing army, and riding was impossible, the cycles having to be pushed all the way – a heavy task with a full pack up.

Private W. G. Bell of the 9th Battalion, Army Cyclists Corps, when asked about his experiences during the war, had this to say:

We dug up half of France! We used to cycle up as near to the front line as we could and dump our bikes. 300 of us there was. We stacked our bikes in the field and then we went to where there was a dump of pick-axes and shovels, and we'd follow the officer single-file. Mind you, it was pitch dark by now . . . You'd dig like fury. And if your spade hit a stone old Jerry would put up the Very lights [flares] and round would come his machine-guns, raking along the line . . . I think we had about three months of that.

I read somewhere that Hitler hated bicycles (apparently he introduced a lot of anti-bike legislation in the 1930s), and that his hatred stemmed from his time in the First World War as a cycle messenger. He wanted to be a motorcycle messenger, but the army only gave him a bicycle, and he was livid.

With 70 miles in my legs, I was beginning to fade, so I stopped in Chaumuzy for a Coke and a rather ancient chocolate éclair, the only things left in an otherwise empty *patisserie*. Sitting on the bench at the bus-stop outside, I was soon surrounded by curious French children getting off the school bus. It was to become a bit of a theme during this trip.

'*Bonjour monsieur, d'où venez-vous?*' said a precocious eight-year-old, eyeing me with undisguised curiosity and wanting to know where I'd come from.

'*Je viens de Londres, en Angleterre.*'

'*Sur votre velo?*'

'*Oui.*'

'*Vous êtes Anglais?*'

'*Oui, bien sûr.*'

A small girl on the edge of the group started jumping up and down, chanting 'God save ze queen, God save ze queen!'

'*Et vive la France!*' I proclaimed, to the delight of my giggling fan club.

There followed quite a lot of chatter, most of which I didn't understand. But it was nice to have contact with people (other than waiters and hotel receptionists), and young French kids seem rather engaging. When they get to 14 they're selfie-taking, hormonal monsters like teenagers the world over, but the under-10s are rather fun.

The sugar-rush from my Coke-éclair combo had the desired effect, and I kicked on to Reims with renewed vigour, arriving in the late afternoon. I was delighted to find that my hotel had proper coat-hangers – ones with actual hooks rather than the crappy unstealable ones. This allows you to hang your washing up around your room and gives it a half-decent chance of drying by the morning. Yes, it's sad being pleased by coat-hangers, but these things become important when you're bike-packing. It's the same with hairdryers. Ones with a switch that stays on (as opposed to ones that turn off if you take your finger off the button) allow you to dry out your cycling shoes quickly and easily, as well as filling your room with a curious damp fug of wet Spaniel and Roquefort cheese.

After wandering around town, admiring the cathedral, having a bite to eat, and a few drinks, I meandered back to my hotel. In the gutter outside I noticed what looked like an old pair of cycling shorts that had clearly been run over multiple times. *That's odd*, I thought to myself, *who would throw an expensive pair of cycling bib-shorts into the street? And why?* I looked up at my hotel-room window on the third floor, where an empty coat-hanger was blowing in the breeze of the open window. Bugger.

Back in my room, I washed my bib-shorts again, and hung them up to dry well away from the window.

⋆

Leaving the sad ruins of Reims behind, the leading group of riders set off north-east along the road towards Sedan. They normally would have gone due east to reach Verdun, via Suippes and Sainte-Menehould, but that road had ceased to exist. During four years of war, the front line between Reims and Verdun had barely moved and so a great swathe of countryside 35 miles long by 25 miles deep had been shelled to oblivion. There were no roads, no villages, no trees, no farms, no nothing. So the *parcours* took them around the northern edge of this devastated wasteland, on the only road east that was still passable.

Even so, the road had been used continuously by German troops travelling to and from the front for four years, so it was in a terrible state, not helped by the Germans mining it as they withdrew north in 1918. To make matters worse, the warm, dry weather that the riders had enjoyed earlier that morning was now making life unpleasant. The temperatures soared (relatively), the sun blazed, and the peloton and convoy threw up clouds of dust. A week earlier the riders had almost frozen to death, now they were being roasted alive, and choked.

Wynsdau punctured just after Witry-lès-Reims and spent a frustrating 10 minutes changing his tyre. He would then have to chase like fury to catch up with the peloton. He knew they were taking it relatively easily on these terrible roads, so he had a choice – push on and risk an accident, or take it easy and maybe lose time. He pushed on, his sweaty, dust-smeared face a picture of concentration as he made his way through and around the potholes, shell craters and ruts.

By midday the leading group, now consisting of ten riders, had reached Vouziers at the northern edge of the Champagne front nearly 3 hours later than scheduled. Not without incident, though – Nempon had abandoned with heat exhaustion and Huret had fallen asleep (or passed out) in the saddle and crashed. Fortunately his bike was undamaged and he managed to ride back up to the leaders.

The riders were greeted at the checkpoint by the legendary, and diminutive, figure of Monsieur Talibard, one-time trainer of Hippolyte 'The Terrible' Aucouturier. Aucouturier was one of the villains of the 1904 Tour, an event characterised by crowd violence and wholesale cheating. The top four finishers of that Tour, including Aucouturier, were subsequently disqualified and Henri Desgrange nearly didn't bother organising another Tour de France because of it.

Talibard was in charge of a squad of German prisoners of war, to whom he'd assigned water duties – some PoWs refilled *bidons*, others supplied buckets of fresh water so the riders could sluice themselves to remove as much of the dust and grime as possible. Although there was a great deal of anti-German feeling in France and Belgium after the war, many of the riders who fought are unlikely to have felt any great antipathy towards the PoWs dispensing water . . . Most soldiers recognised that the enemy were men just like themselves, forced into a war they didn't want, enduring the same miseries and privations.

With no one ahead, and with the top GC riders all in this group, they were in no hurry to get on their way when the time-keeper signalled their 5 minutes were up. An unofficial truce had been called by Alavoine, the new *patron* of the peloton, and the riders were grateful of it. After 15 minutes Alavoine stretched, picked up his bike and motioned to the others. 'Let's go.'

The route now turned south-east and headed across the Argonne battlefields towards Verdun. The land here was like that at Ypres, the Somme and Champagne – churned, blasted and poisoned by millions of shells, a scene of total devastation. The Argonne Forest was no longer a forest, merely a vast swathe of uprooted trunks, splintered branches and dense undergrowth, interspersed with concrete gun emplacements, bunkers and twisting belts of barbed wire.

Just before Varennes-en-Argonne disaster struck. Van Lerberghe, Hanlet and Huret all punctured at the same time. Alavoine sat up and gestured for the rest to do the same. Deruyter clearly wasn't happy about it, eager to push on, but the peloton soft-pedalled until the unfortunate trio rejoined them. 'Sabotage,' grumbled Hanlet to no one in particular. It wasn't unusual in those days for fans to sabotage their favourite's main competitors, or even for locals to sabotage the race out of sheer bloody-mindedness.

As they neared Verdun the roads became worse and worse, but at least the dry weather meant there was little mud to contend with. Of the six official cars that started from Strasbourg, three had so far succumbed to broken suspension springs due to the state of the roads. Off to their left, just past Varennes, the riders could see a large hill pockmarked with dozens of huge craters, while all around was churned and blasted chaos. For four years the French and Germans had fought for control of this vital observation point on the Argonne front, and the result was that the village of Vauquois, which used to sit atop it, had disappeared off the face of the earth.

Alavoine, Deruyter, and the others pressed on, their pace often reduced to a crawl by the terrible roads and the dust kicked up by the race convoy. All the riders were wearing goggles, and most had a handkerchief tied over their nose and mouth to keep the dust out and the ether in. This wasn't so much a race as an exercise in survival, so no one attacked, no one made life difficult for the peloton, and everyone just concentrated on getting to the end in one piece. There would be time enough for the attacks to begin once they were south of Verdun.

Several hours behind the leaders, the stragglers were suffering from the heat and the roads. Morel and Ménager had teamed up for mutual support, as had Ellner and Asse. As a *poilu*, Robert Asse had seen active service for four years and had fought somewhere near here. He looked around him, hoping to recognise some landmark, but everything looked the same back then, and now it was just a slightly greener vision of hell. His regiment had been in and out of the line on the Aisne, near Suippes, and around Verdun. Most of the time he'd had no idea where he was, and had cared even less. He'd been so far removed from his home on the coast of Brittany that he might as well have been on a completely different planet.

As he and Ellner slogged on, Asse looked at the graves in the fields on either side and wondered if any of them marked the last resting place of Pierre, or Jacques, or Étienne, or any of the other friends he had lost. Being on these battlefields had unleashed a tide of emotions Asse had thus far kept tightly bottled up inside. But now he was exhausted and thirsty, and he ached, physically and emotionally. The past came crashing in on him, dragging him reluctantly back to the horrors of Mont Cornillet, the pitiless bombardments, the futile attacks, the unspeakable savagery of hand-to-hand fighting in muddy trenches.

Asse didn't seem to notice as the kilometres rolled by. The mindless physical toil and endless discomfort took him back to another time. He was trudging up a dusty track to the front line, laden with boxes of ammunition; he was cowering in a roadside ditch while wounded men and horses screamed in the mud; he was gagging from the cloying stench of rotting corpses that lay unburied for weeks in no man's land. And, worst of all, he was dragging his best friend's badly wounded brother from muddy shell-hole to muddy shell-hole as the shells rained down and the bullets whipped around him. Not even the white noise of the bombardment could drown out his inner dialogue – *leave him, save yourself; get him back, don't leave him to die like this.* Back and forth. Robert kept going, until it became obvious that René was dead. At the bottom of a muddy shell-hole Robert closed René's eyes, took his personal effects and paybook, and made his way back towards the French lines as the barrage lifted to target the reserve lines.

The city of Verdun stood, scarred and mauled, amongst a landscape of hills and valleys utterly devastated by shelling. The city itself had fared better than some places, such as Ypres or Albert, but in 1916 the area north and west of Verdun, 27km wide and 16km deep, was systematically shelled by both sides for ten months. On the first day of the battle alone the Germans fired more than 1 million shells onto French positions on the east bank of the River Meuse.

For the French riders in the peloton – Alavoine, Huret, Guénot, Muller, Asse, Morel and Ellner – Verdun was a source of national pride and also immense sorrow. Around 75 per cent of the French army fought here at some point during the ten-month battle, and the French suffered around 400,000 casualties in 300 days of unrelenting fighting. Everyone knew someone who had fallen at Verdun, and the city became the centre of French remembrance after the war.

The lead group stopped at the checkpoint in the middle of town, took a short breather, and readied themselves for the final 55km south to the finish in Bar-le-Duc. Deruyter was desperate to

By the end of the war Verdun was another forlorn ruin, like so much of the Zone Rouge

get away from the bunch, convinced he was the strongest on the road if not necessarily in a bunch-sprint. But Alavoine was keeping a very close eye on him, knowing that Deruyter would attack when the opportunity presented itself. There was a nervousness in the group, each wondering if he might grab a top-three place on the stage and earn a few hundred Francs.

★

My bib-shorts hadn't suffered unduly from becoming road-kill the night before, and I was looking forward to 70 miles and 3,600ft of climbing through some interesting countryside. I was now seriously off the route of the race, but that was OK because (a) the race route has vanished under the A34 motorway, and (b) I wanted to see the Champagne and Argonne battlefields. While the race did a wide loop north of the Champagne front via Vouziers, I would just head due east along the old road to Verdun, through parts of the Zone Rouge that are still out of bounds to the public.

Just east of Reims is Fort de la Pompelle, commanding a small hill, and one of the key forts held by the French throughout the war that protected the eastern approach to Reims. Getting to it by bike proved to be slightly problematic – the choice was either along a horrendous dual carriageway full of speeding trucks and with no hard shoulder or bike path, or along some country roads and small lanes. Obviously I opted for the latter, and ended up carrying my bike across a ploughed field, through a copse of particularly spiky trees, over a barbed-wire fence and then down a steep 30ft bank onto the aforementioned dual carriageway of doom. I made a mental note: never, ever, EVER click the 'cycling' button on the on-line route-planner.

By the end of the war La Pompelle was a heap of ruins, but it held out against determined German attacks for four years and is now an excellent museum. As usual, I was pretty much the only person there, and I spent an interesting hour meandering around looking at the exhibits and reading about the 'frightfulness of the beastly Hun'. The French were absolutely outraged by what the Germans had done to the cathedral at Reims and viewed this as yet another attempt by the Germans to destroy the culture and history of France.

Under increasingly heavy clouds I rode north-east to Nauroy, one of the many *villages détruits* (destroyed villages) in the Zone Rouge. Except that this is no longer Zone Rouge, it's 'normal' farmland under cultivation. There's nothing much to see at Nauroy except an information board and signs saying *Terraine Militaire, Défense D'entrer* (military land, do not enter) and quoting Articles 413–15 and R644-1 of the penal code. Obviously I took no notice and wandered (carefully) around, trying not to step on anything explosive.

A mile or two east I came across the Zone Rouge proper . . . a fenced-off, high-security area of about 30km² around the destroyed village of Moronvilliers. The road runs east through the

The remains of a French 75mm field gun outside Fort de la Pompelle, near Reims

middle of this area, which was handed over to the military in 1919 and planted with Bavarian pines. For 50 years the French military tested nuclear weapons here, adding radioactive waste to the unexploded First World War shells, poison-gas residue and unrecovered bodies. According to some sources the land here is contaminated with depleted uranium and beryllium, several thousand times the safe level, and a significant number of people working here in the 1950s and 1960s subsequently developed thyroid cancer.

I'm not exactly an eco-warrior, but the more I read about the Zone Rouge the more horrified I am by the ecological damage caused by the First World War and subsequent military operations. Moronvilliers is an exception in that it was used for 'cold-shot' nuclear testing after the Second World War, but elsewhere in the Zone Rouge the land is still toxic even a century after the First World War. Billions of shrapnel balls have leached lead into the soil and ground-water, areas where artillery was sited are saturated with toxic perchlorates (used as propellant for shells), areas where large numbers of shells landed are polluted with heavy metals such as mercury (used in percussion caps), copper and zinc, and the soil of the Zone Rouge has been found to contain up to 1,000 times the safe level of arsenic in some places.

In 2012 the French authorities declared the tap water of 544 communes in the Pas-de-Calais region unsafe for consumption by children and pregnant or breastfeeding women. In 2015 the French authorities ordered farmers near Spincourt, north-east of Verdun, to destroy their crops and pour away hundreds of thousands of litres of milk due to high levels of heavy metals found in them. Analysis of local wildlife in the Zone Rouge by German scientists in 2004 found animals with hundreds of times the safe limit (for humans) of lead, cadmium and arsenic in their organs.

After the First World War France and Belgium faced a serious problem . . . what to do with all the unused or unexploded ordnance? Much of the unexploded stuff was detonated *in situ* (polluting the land still further), but the unused ordnance amounted to millions of tonnes of lethal shells that needed to be dealt with. The Belgians loaded it onto ships and dumped it in the North Sea off Zeebrugge, while the French tended to dump it in lakes or deep gorges. Lac Bleu at Avrillé in the Loire is a beautiful blue-green colour because of 3,000 tonnes of ordnance that were dumped into it after the war and which are now corroding prettily away.

A hundred years ago we had little knowledge of the long-term environmental impact of artillery on the soil or ground-water, so in many places the Zone Rouge was reduced in size to enable farmers to return to their land, unaware that they were growing crops in dangerously contaminated soil. People refer to the collection of unexploded shells from the fields as the 'iron harvest', but for generations this land has also been producing a toxic harvest.

These were just some of the cheerful thoughts running around my head as I rode through the Moronvilliers militarised zone. This particular part of the Zone Rouge is abandoned now, and should probably remain so for thousands of years. But all around it are fields of wheat and oilseed rape, barely yards from the military warning signs and barbed-wire fences. I wondered who, back in 1919, decided which 'field' was too dangerous to farm, and which was safe.

Not all of the Zone Rouge is fenced-off military land. Here at Navarin Farm there's just a warning sign

To my right, hidden by the trees and protected by fences and CCTV, are the *'monts de Champagne'* – Mont Cornillet, Mont Haute, Mont Blond and Mont Sans Nom – low hills where the Germans dug in at the end of the First Marne in September 1914, and where they remained until September 1918. Except for a period of relative quiet during the battle of Verdun in 1916, this area saw almost constant action throughout the war and suffered horribly as a result.

Ten miles further east brought me to Camp Suippes, a larger area of Zone Rouge now used by the army as a firing range. A dozen villages on this front were destroyed during the war, and five of them (all within the boundaries of Camp Suippes) were never rebuilt. On the western edge is the Navarin Farm memorial, an impressive pyramid topped by a sculpture of three soldiers. Apart from being cleared of ordnance and bodies, the area around the pyramid remains as it was in 1918, complete with hundreds of shell-holes, belts of rusting barbed wire and signs warning of 'vestiges of war'. I sat on the steps of the pyramid and ate an energy bar while staring across this brutalised landscape, trying to imagine what it must have been like here in 1915.

Skirting Camp Suippes to the north, I was now in search of water. It was quite a warm day and my *bidon* was empty, but the countryside offered nothing by way of a shop or petrol station, just endless fields and deserted hamlets. By the time I reached Cernay-en-Dormois I was gasping, and resorted to knocking on doors, hoping to scrounge some water. Eventually I came across a family digging some kind of pit in their front garden, and for a moment I wondered if they had just finished burying the last cyclist to come asking for water. As it turned out, they were charm personified. While mum went to fill my *bidon*, the rest gathered round and quizzed me about my trip:

'Two thousand kilometres by bike?'

'Yes.'

'Noooo!'

'Yes.'

'That's all your luggage?'

'Yes.'

'Noooo!'

'Yes.'

'For three weeks?'

'Yes.'

'Noooo!'

'Yes.'

'You have an arse of steel, yes?'

'Yes,' I conceded, not liking this latest line of questioning.

Mum returned with my *bidon* of iced water, and I tried not

to think about the beryllium, perchlorates and heavy metals it probably contained. *'Un sandwich, peut-être?'* she asked. I politely declined and explained I had many more miles to cover. They waved me off with cheery cries of 'Good luck, mad English-man.' It was another of those interactions that make travelling by bike so enjoyable and rewarding. I grinned like an idiot for the next five miles, until a biblical rain-storm and an errant sat-nav brought me back down to earth with a squelch.

La Main de Massiges, the next stop on my tour of the Champagne battlefields, was at the top of a gently sloping one-mile dirt track. At least it would have been a dirt track, had 17 million litres of rain not just fallen on it in ten minutes, turning it as slippery as an ice-rink. Picking myself up for the second time in five yards, I decided pushing was the better option. Halfway up, I passed a sign that read *'Danger. Depot Explosifs'*, beneath which was stacked a pile of unexploded First World War shells. These things always send a shiver down my spine, even though I know they're fairly unlikely to explode at the precise moment I pass by. But these rusting shells tell a story – they were shoved into the breech of a French 75mm field gun and fired up here by some poor French gunner 100 years ago, sweating under the intense labour while the guns roared for hour after hour. Sometimes worn-out artillery pieces exploded, sometimes the guns came under counter-battery fire, sometimes the gunners had to wear gas masks as they fed the insatiable guns.

La Main de Massiges, a plateau near Massiges village that is shaped like an open hand and rises 200ft above the land to the south, formed part of the German front line in 1915. Here, for the last eight years, local volunteers have been excavating the trench system dug into the chalky plateau, restoring around 400 yards of German trenches and dug-outs. It's an astonishing place, and as I sloshed through the trenches I genuinely felt like I'd travelled back in time – all around was rusting barbed wire, old pots and pans, discarded helmets and rusty weapons. In the dug-outs were broken chairs and collapsing beds. It felt as if the German soldiers had only just left. Nowhere else on the Western Front gives such an apparently authentic feel of a First World War trench system. And yet there is no one there, not even anyone official, nor any fencing around it.

The extraordinary excavations at the Main de Massiges, on the Champagne Front

I stood on a fire-step and looked across the wire to where the French trenches would have been as the rain began to fall again. Away to the east there were heavy black clouds and lightning, probably near Verdun. The last 20 miles were completed in horrible weather and I arrived at my hotel soaked to the skin. But after 70 miles and 3,500ft of climbing, and little by way of food, I was ready for some serious dinner, and my hotel (a delightful place on the southern edge of the Argonne Forest) obliged with one of the best meals I've ever had in France. And then they brought the cheese trolley. Rarely have I seen or smelled anything so divine.

Breakfast wasn't too shabby, either. Having almost died of malnutrition in the bleak emptiness of the Zone Rouge yesterday (well, been a bit peckish), I ate as much as I could and stuffed as much as I could into my jersey pockets. Although it was only 20 miles on the direct road to Verdun, I was planning on mooching around the Argonne battlefield and had no idea whether I'd be able to find anything to eat or drink.

Less than three miles into my day, at Les Islettes, I got pulled over by the police. Sigh. Apparently I had failed to come to a complete stop at a Stop sign, and was duly admonished. My first ever encounter with French police had resulted in me getting tear-gassed by the CRS (the French riot police, not the Co-op), so I'm unfailingly polite in my dealings with *les flics*. I played the stupid Englishman card, tortured them with my schoolboy French for a while, and was sent on my way with instructions to unclip and put a foot down at *all* Stop signs. 'Vous êtes vraiment un cockwomble énorme,' I replied, although maybe not quite loud enough to be heard.

The Argonne sector was another place where the front line barely moved between September 1914 and September 1918. After the First Marne the front stabilised, running east–west from Reims to Verdun, and this 10-mile section of the front settled down across the valley of the Aire River. Thick forests and steep slopes either side of the Aire meant that the only real progress that could be made by either army was in this valley.

Riding through the forest between the valleys of the Aire and the Biesme (the river valley on the western edge of the Argonne sector), you can understand why so little progress could be made – the hills and ravines are seriously steep-sided and very heavily wooded, and the well-dug-in Germans had constructed concrete bunkers with interlocking fields of fire. The artillery had blasted the trees into burned, shattered trunks and the ground was treacherous and chaotic with branches, undergrowth, shell-holes and trenches. After a couple of extremely bloody and unsuccessful attempts to oust the Germans from the forests, the French shifted their attention to Vauquois, a small village on a hill that dominated the Aire valley. In the forests the French and Germans settled down and spent four years sniping, trench-raiding, firing trench mortars, and digging mines under the enemy positions. With the front lines often as close as ten metres apart, nerves became shredded and men were stretched to breaking point.

But it wasn't always like that. In his book *Poilu*, Louis Barthas describes how, when the front lines were particularly close together, unofficial truces were sometimes called and a live-and-let-live attitude prevailed. There were whispered conversations between French and German troops in listening posts only a few metres apart, and even exchanges of rations or alcohol. Sometimes shared suffering and a sense of humanity gave both sides a much-needed break from the horror and death.

Turning off the road between Le Four de Paris and Varennes, I followed a dirt track for half a mile into the woods, in search of the Abri du Kronprinz, a group of German command bunkers situated a mile or so behind their front line. And again, like at La Main de Massiges, I was the only person there amongst the bunkers and craters and trenches. There are four or five concrete bunkers in a remarkable state of preservation, one of which is believed to have been used by Crown Prince Wilhelm, eldest son of the Kaiser and the man in charge of this sector. And it's certainly not your average bunker, with its bay-window and elaborate fireplace and chimney.

This place was fascinating, and I spent half an hour or so exploring among the shell-holes and bunkers. As I was preparing to leave, an official-looking bloke with a clipboard arrived and seemed to be checking the site. Any dead tourists? No. Any unexploded ordnance? No. All good. This appeared to be Health & Safety, French-style. He nodded towards my bike and began the usual where-have-you-come-from-and-where-are-you-going conversation.

'*Toutes les champs de bataille – Liège, Ypres, Lille, Cambrai, Somme, Saint-Quentin, Chemin des Dames, Marne, Champagne, Argonne, Saint-Mihiel et Les Vosges.*'

'Noooo!'

'Yes.'

'By bike?'

'Yes.'

'*Fantastique!!*'

He then pointed to something high in a tree above us, about 45ft up. It was a massive chunk of rusting iron that had been blasted out of the ground and embedded in the tree trunk at some point during 1918. It's still there 100 years later. I stared at it in awe, considering the strength of the blast that threw it up there, and what effect that would have on a human body.

At Varennes the rain started again with a vengeance, so I took cover in the bar by the bridge. Opposite is where Louis XVI and Marie-Antoinette were captured while trying to escape the Revolution in 1791. This is pretty much Varennes' claim to fame, but the entire town was flattened in 1918 so there's almost nothing to see from the old days. The occupants of the bar were more interested in bickering about their Lotto syndicate than a soggy Englishman nursing his coffee, so I was spared the yes–nooo conversation (not that I really minded . . . it was a decent showing-off opportunity).

With the rain showing no sign of letting up, I splashed my way north-east to Montfaucon, another vital piece of high ground from which the Germans could direct their artillery onto French positions on Côte 304 and Mort Homme near Verdun. There's another huge American memorial here, surrounded by the remains of the old village and assorted bunkers, but it was too wet to spend much time exploring so I adjourned to the village café (it was open!) and had some lunch.

The owner of the café was a Belgian bloke who moved to Montfaucon so he could spend his spare time walking the battlefields and filling his café with the rusty First World War stuff he finds. Of all the people I encountered on my trip, he was the only one not to be even remotely surprised that someone should want to cycle the length of the Western Front, twice. He looked at me dripping muddy water onto the floor of his café, nodded understandingly, and went away to make me a huge sandwich and a pint of hot chocolate.

It was still raining as I made my way back to Varennes. I stopped en route and visited one of the saddest places I've ever been . . . the German cemetery at Cheppy. Tucked away up a remote country lane, the cemetery contains 6,165 burials and doesn't look as if anyone has been there since 1919, except for the bloke who cuts the grass every few months. There are no flowers, no signs of remembrance, no colour, no indication that anyone has visited. Some of the crosses are a bit wonky. A damp gloom lies over this forgotten corner of the Argonne, and I wondered about the way different nations remember their war dead.

The German cemetery at Cheppy, on the Argonne Front, drips with sadness and neglect. Twenty years after the war it became a crime in Germany to commemorate the deaths of Jewish soldiers who died in the First World War

Perhaps unsurprisingly, the Germans don't commemorate their war dead the way the British or French do. Very few people visit the First World War cemeteries back in Germany, let alone the ones in France and Belgium. And I suppose that's understandable in some ways, but also very sad. These young German lads were no different to their French, British, Australian etc. counterparts ... they were all young men, frightened out of their wits, hungry and thirsty, just struggling to stay alive. They saw the same horrific things, experienced the same miseries, and died the same brutal deaths. Just because they fought on the losing side, does that make them any less deserving of remembrance, or pity?

Particularly sad was the Jewish headstone of Fritz Kaufmann, killed in April 1916. He was one of 100,000 Jews who fought in the German army in the First World War, and one of the 12,000 who died fighting for their country. Whether he was one of the 30,000 German Jews awarded a medal, I don't know. But I do know that 20 years after he died for his country, it became a crime in Germany to commemorate his death.

I left a pebble on the top of Fritz Kaufmann's headstone and carried on my way.

At Vauquois the rain eased off and I meandered around the craters of this hilltop site. Vauquois has the dubious distinction of being the only place in the First World War to be completely destroyed ... from underground. With the French occupying the southern part of the village, and the Germans the northern part, both sides began underground mining operations in 1915, and over the course of four years more than 500 mines were detonated beneath the village. It's reckoned that around 10,000 men were buried by these explosions, never to be found, and the village completely disappeared. Beneath the hill there are an estimated 24 miles of tunnels dug during the war.

The sheer effort involved in trying to take this small hill beggars belief. Four years of fighting, four years of shelling, four years of digging, tens of thousands dead, hundreds of thousands wounded. Families devastated, young men traumatised, hopes and dreams snuffed out. It's difficult to reconcile the pre-war photos of a sleepy rural village with the craters and wire you see today.

A couple of miles to the west I went in search of the Kaiser-tunnel, a 300-yard-long tunnel dug by the Germans to allow them sheltered access to their front line. It lies near Côte 285 and the La Haute-Chevauchée, an old Roman road that runs through the middle of the Argonne Forest, in the cheerfully named Mort Fille (dead girl) sector. The tunnel, one of two dozen dug by the French and Germans in this sector, contains a telephone exchange, a first-aid station, an operating theatre and an electricity-generating station, but sadly is only open to the public on the ninth Sunday of alternate months from September to August, excluding March and October (or something equally confusing).

At the French ossuary I passed a clapped-out old Opel in which lurked two very dodgy-looking young men. They didn't look like typical battlefield tourists and seemed very out of place. My mind went back to a conversation I'd had with a security guard at the Newfoundland Memorial Park on the Somme, who told me that so many tourist cars were being broken into that they now employed security guards in the car park. I obviously wasn't going to leave my bike unattended, so I rode down through the forest on a muddy path that took me through trenches and shell-holes to the (closed) tunnel entrance.

I was not encouraged to discover that the two lads, in their trackies, hoodies and baseball caps, had got out of their car and followed me into the woods. My vague feelings of unease now turned into full-on paranoia. I hadn't seen anyone else for about an hour, and I had visions of being robbed of all my possessions at knife-point. The two blokes appeared to have no interest in the trenches and shell-holes around them as they advanced towards me in a disconcertingly concerted manner. I swung a leg over my bike and pedalled off up another track, trying to look as nonchalant as possible. Back on La Haute-Chevauchée I set an uncomfortably brisk pace back towards civilisation, expecting to hear the rattle of an ancient Opel behind me at any moment.

I have no reason, apart from my own middle-class and middle-aged prejudices, to suspect that I was about to become the victim of a felonious assault, but it was still rather unnerving. Maybe I've lived in London for too long. However, this was the only unsettling experience (except for the feral kids of Metz) in a plethora of very pleasant encounters with the locals on my journey.

The last 20 miles to Verdun were completed in an horrific downpour. It was a very miserable hour and a half. By the time I reached my hotel and stripped off in the bathroom, I had been so wet for so long that I resembled a pallid, white prune. It's not a good look.

*

Heading south from Verdun, the racers joined the Voie Sacrée (the sacred way), the only road to and from Verdun that wasn't under direct enemy fire. With both the railway lines to Verdun under observation and within range of German guns, the only way for the French to get men and supplies to the Verdun front was along this 65km road from Bar-le-Duc to Verdun. General Pétain decreed that only motor transport was allowed to use the road, so troops were forced to march either side of it while a fleet of 3,500 trucks and 800 ambulances carried weapons, munitions, food and the wounded.

This macadam road had been used day and night, for nine months, and required 13 labour battalions (around 10,000 men) to keep it in good repair and keep the trucks moving. If one broke down it was pushed off the road, where teams of mechanics would try to get it going again. Nothing could be allowed to disrupt the resupply of Verdun, and it is said that for the duration of the battle for Verdun, a truck would pass any given point on the Voie Sacrée every 14 seconds, day and night, for nine months.

By the end of the war this famous road was in a poor state of repair but the riders pushed on as hard as they dared. It was now late afternoon and they'd been riding since well before dawn. Nerves were frayed, bodies tired and absolute concentration was required not to get stuck in a rut or crash into a pothole. But even so, the pace increased and the lead group began to split apart.

With around 15km to go Deruyter, riding at the front, punctured. Alavoine needed no encouragement, and immediately attacked, taking Desmedt and Heusghem with him.

'*Merde!*' cursed Deruyter, jumping from his bike and frantically waving to one of the tail-enders. 'Hey, Guénot,' he shouted, 'want to earn some money?'

Guénot stopped beside him. 'How much?' he asked.

'Fifty Francs to pace me to the finish,' said Deruyter, already busy changing the tyre.

'One hundred.'

'Seventy-five, and that's a damn sight more than you're worth,' spat Deruyter. Guénot laid down his bike and started to help Deruyter with the tyre.

If Deruyter had known it was only 15km to go he probably wouldn't have bothered recruiting Guénot, but they had no real idea how far there was left to race. After eight or nine minutes they were under way, with Guénot setting as furious a tempo as he was able to muster . . . 75FF was a decent incentive.

Alavoine, Desmedt and Heusghem arrived in Bar-le-Duc together, and there was a straight three-up sprint for the line. Alavoine won by a length from Heusghem, with Desmedt fading to third. It was just before 6 p.m. and they had been racing for almost 16 hours. Deruyter powered across the line 9 minutes later (with Guénot a minute behind him), no doubt annoyed that he couldn't get the win but pleased he hadn't lost too much time. He was probably a bit peeved that he'd agreed to pay Guénot to pace him for a measly 15km, but a deal's a deal and he'd have to pay up. Riders who reneged on these deals soon got a reputation and found it difficult to recruit help when they needed it.

For the next few hours riders arrived singly or in pairs. The long-suffering Ernest Paul arrived at 7.50 p.m., along with

Pelletier; Kippert and Leroy came in together at 8.10 p.m.; and the last man to finish that day was Séraphin Morel at 11.30 p.m. It had been an unbelievably gruelling day for all of them, not least for Hanlet, who had suffered seven punctures, and Huret was forced to cover much of the stage standing on his pedals due to two severe saddle-sores.

Word from the checkpoint at Vouziers seemed to suggest there were three more riders still out on the road: Ellner, Asse and Pain. The commissaires, knowing that Ellner was never likely to give up while there were wheels on his bike and breath in his body, sat tight in the Grand Café de Commerce and waited. And waited.

Out on the road Asse and Ellner, who had teamed up for moral and mechanical support, kept going as long as they could. The clear skies meant that as the sun dipped below the horizon the temperatures fell sharply, adding frozen fingers to their suffering. But at least the clear skies meant they were able to see, just, by the light of the near-full moon. The roads around the Verdun battlefield were roads in name only, and after several hours of smashing through unseen craters in the dim moonlight, Asse fell once again, for the umpteenth time that day. Ellner stopped and waited.

'That's it! I've had enough of this shit!' spat Asse, rubbing his already scabby elbow. 'I'm going to find somewhere to rest for a few hours. You carry on, if you want.'

Ellner looked up at the moon, then along the road snaking off into the gloom. He didn't want to carry on alone. He was exhausted, and having to play catch-up the whole time was dispiriting. Starting and finishing every stage in the middle of the night, without the chance to rest up properly, was wearing him down.

'Yeah, good idea,' he said.

Together they walked their bikes for another kilometre or so across this barren desert until they came across some crumbling trenches dug by the side of the road. In a cold, damp dug-out they curled up and huddled together for warmth.

At 7.50 a.m. the next morning Arsène Pain arrived in Bar-le-Duc, having taken refuge somewhere on the Verdun battlefield. And at 9.25 a.m. Ellner and Asse rolled in after their cold and uncomfortable night in a trench. The commissaires, who had spent the rest day visiting the remnants of Fort Douaumont near Verdun, had effectively abandoned the time-cut rules and convened later in the afternoon to penalise Deruyter 15 minutes for being paced by Guénot, and an investigation was opened into Guénot's behaviour (they'd previously penalised him for getting a lift in a car, so he had 'form'). Normally they would have thrown Guénot out of the race, but with so few riders remaining, they eventually just docked him an hour.

★

My Verdun 'rest day' was spent on the battlefield. It's a strange, sepulchral place quite unlike any other battlefield I've been to. The dense forest planted over it after the war makes it hard to understand the lie of the land, and as you ride around you get sudden glimpses through the trees of abandoned fortifications, endless shell-holes, and trenches, all mossy and overgrown. If some British memorials further north seem quietly triumphalist, French memorials tend to convey a sense of sadness and sorrow, and that's certainly the case at Verdun.

It was at Verdun that the Germans attempted to bleed the French army white with a deliberate policy of attrition. The Germans suspected that the French would never give up Verdun, so they set about trying to get the French to commit endless resources to its defence. The 300-day battle in 1916 became a microcosm of the First World War, with horrific artillery barrages, hopeless ground offensives, mud, gas, dust and blood-letting on an industrial scale.

During this battle, 1.14 million Frenchmen stood toe-to-toe with 1.25 million Germans, and won (just). But the battle resulted in nearly 1 million casualties, of which around 350,000 were fatalities. Around 60 million shells were fired during the battle, and in the 10 years after the war, each hectare of land around Verdun gave up 12 tonnes of metal per year. Verdun is to the French what the Somme is to the British.

Relieved at not having to spend 20 minutes wrestling with my bags, I had a leisurely breakfast, pinched sufficient rations for lunch (the Verdun sector isn't well supplied with hotels or cafés), and then made my way north-east up onto the battlefield on the right bank of the Meuse (after a surprisingly tough little climb of 6 per cent over 3 miles). The weather was grey but dry, the temperature was a decent 16°C, and there were few visitors to be seen.

The battlefield is criss-crossed with tracks through the forests, mostly barriered off to prevent numpties in 4×4s from going where they're not supposed to and getting stuck. Happily, the barriers don't prevent numpties on road bikes from going cyclo-crossing on 25mm road tyres, so I slipped and slid my way up a muddy track to the remains of Fort Souville, where I poked around in the dank darkness until a rudely awakened colony of bats whirled around my head. Not wishing to disturb what was probably the last nesting colony of the world's rarest bat (or something), I left them in peace and rode across to Fort Vaux.

The defence of Fort Vaux by Major Reynal and a handful of soldiers against increasingly determined German assaults is the stuff of legend. For six days and seven nights Reynal and his men fought off the Germans, who had got into the upper levels of the fort. With grenades, flame-throwers and rifles, the French and Germans fought for every inch of every corridor and tunnel. With no food, no water, increasing numbers of wounded, and dwindling ammunition, Reynal and his men fought on. It was only when the ammunition ran out that Reynal finally surrendered. The Germans afforded him and his remaining men a guard of honour as they left the fort.

Walking through those same tunnels is a sobering experience, and when you come to one of the barricades thrown up by the French you are very aware that this is where desperate men fought for their lives a hundred years ago. Reynal became a national hero, and *Le Petit Journal* pulled off an impressive scoop early in 1919 by serialising his account of the defence of Fort Vaux.

The story at Douaumont, a few miles to the north-west, could not have been more different. Douaumont was the most important fort on the Verdun battlefield, and yet four days after the battle started it was occupied by just a maintenance crew of 54 men (mostly elderly French reservists). A squad of ten German engineers stumbled up to the fort, found it virtually unoccupied, and captured the entire garrison without a shot being fired. One hundred thousand soldiers died in the fight to get it back. At one point during the German occupation a couple of soldiers decided to brew up some coffee using fuel from a flamethrower. One of them knocked something over, starting a small fire which set off some ammunition. The resulting conflagration caused a blast that killed 679 German soldiers in the fort. Their bodies are still in there, bricked up behind a wall.

I arrived at Fort Douaumont in time to see three coach-loads of school children disappearing inside. Not wishing to get entangled with 150 chattering, giggling, selfie-taking French teenagers, I gave the fort a miss and carried on to the Tranchée des Baionnettes, another site of bizarre events in 1916. It was here, allegedly, that an entire company of French soldiers was buried alive standing in their trench. After the battle all that could be seen was a row of rifle barrels sticking out of the ground, bayonets still attached. After the war a memorial was built over the trench, but sadly the bayonets have subsequently been pilfered.

Just up the hill the Douaumont Ossuary is an astonishing building, looking like something out of a Fritz Lang movie. Resembling a submarine with a lighthouse stuck on the top, this monument occupies the ridge in the centre of the battlefield, overlooking a huge cemetery containing 16,000 graves. Within the ossuary are the bones of 130,000 unidentified French and

The cost of Verdun: 16,000 men lie buried in the French cemetery at Douaumont, and a further 130,000 unidentified bodies lie in the ossuary (top left of photo)

German soldiers, piled up in alcoves and visible through the windows on the lower level. To us Brits, the sight of piles of human bones is quite unsettling, and as you look at some bloke's skull, or femur, or pelvis, the appalling reality of war hits you firmly between the eyes. This was someone's son, someone's husband, someone's father. They died in hell, their bodies pulverised, their mangled, unidentifiable remains slung in a truck and transported to an ossuary where they mingled with 130,000 other rotting corpses. French or German, the experience was the same, the end was the same. I sat on the grass bank above the cemetery and shed another tear for those poor bastards.

Near the Froid Terre fortifications I came across flooded shell-holes from which bulrushes and other wetland plants were growing. There's a sign warning people away, not because they're going to get blown up or drown, but because these flooded craters are now the habitat of rare species of amphibians and insects. After walking around the sites of such carnage and horror all morning, it was reassuring to see that at least something of value had come of it, even if that was just rare newts and dragonflies.

Human bones in the Douaumont Ossuary. There are few places on the Western Front that give us such a stark reminder of the human tragedy of this conflict

Heading west, I dropped down off the plateau and crossed the meandering Meuse River, aiming for the battlefields of the left (west) bank. The sun had come out, and I stopped in the little square of Charny-sur-Meuse to contemplate the war memorial while I sat on a bench and ate the rolls I'd surreptitiously made at breakfast. Gradually a collection of kids, aged about eight, gathered around (they were waiting for the school bus, apparently) and one particularly earnest young lad of about seven stepped forward and introduced himself to me. Then he introduced me, one by one, to all the other kids. We politely shook hands, exchanged pleasantries, and then they stood in a semi-circle around me, as if waiting for something. I looked at them, they looked at me.

Then the questions started. Who, what, when, where, why? I may have exaggerated some of my answers for dramatic effect. Of course I can ride at 100kph. Yes, my bike really did cost €25,000. No, I've never won the Tour de France, but I did finish fourth ten years ago. Yes, I met the Queen when I got my knighthood. The kids were saved from even more outrageous lies by the arrival of the bus, and off they went, waving cheerily. It was another of those delightful and unexpected encounters.

At Chattencourt I turned north and slogged up the 12 per cent incline that is the southern slope of Mort Homme. At the bottom of the hill is an old tiled sign attached to a farm building, pointing the way to Mort Homme. It's an original Michelin one from the 1920s, and there are still a fair number of them scattered about the French battlefields, a reminder of the boom in tourism after the First World War as old soldiers and widows flocked to the battlefields to pay tribute to the fallen.

The hills of Mort Homme, and neighbouring Côte 304, were vital to both sides and were bitterly contested throughout 1916 and 1917. They became the focus of huge artillery barrages so intense that the height of Côte 304 was reduced by four metres by the end of the war. As I struggled up Mort Homme the skies darkened, the rain started, and within a couple of minutes I was caught in the middle of a massive thunderstorm. Lightning crackled and fizzed all around, followed almost instantly by deafening thunder-claps. Hurling my bike to the ground next to the monument to the 69th Division, I sprinted into the woods and sheltered beneath what I hoped was a particularly short tree. For ten minutes the wind blew and the rain pounded, as thunder and lightning rumbled and crashed in frightening proximity. It was an incredibly visceral experience.

Shivering under my tree, I looked at the 69th Division memorial. I think it's possibly the most extraordinary memorial that exists from the First World War. It's a sculpture of Death, the figure of a partially decomposed skeleton standing draped in a funeral shroud, holding the 69th Divisional standard in one hand and raising the flame of victory aloft in the other. Except that the flame of victory is missing now, probably struck by lightning at some point in the distant past. I'm not reassured. The words engraved on it (*Ils n'ont pas passé* . . . They did not pass) are a reference to Nivelle's exhortations to his troops to stand firm.

The powerful and moving memorial to the French 69th Division on Morte Homme near Verdun

For me, this haunting, disturbing monument cuts right to the heart of war memorialisation. There's no sense of sentimentality or nationalistic triumphalism about it, it's a stark reminder of the realities of war, as well as a suitable memorial to the men who fought and died here in their tens of thousands. Even the words *Ils n'ont pas passé* have a grim finality about them. This memorial effectively says, 'We did our duty here, but death was the only victor.' I think it's a very brave piece of work, and as I stood in the rain I mentally saluted the veterans of the 69th Division who commissioned it.

As the thunderstorm moved eastwards and the rain eased off, I went exploring the old shell-holes and collapsing trenches amongst the trees. The endless Bavarian pines deprive you of any views, sadly, and it's hard to get an idea of how important (and exposed) this little hill was.

Côte 304 a mile to the west, now Côte 300, is another rarely visited site that was the scene of unimaginable horror. To take Mort Homme, the Germans first had to capture Côte 304 to prevent flanking fire from the French, so the troops here experienced the same relentless drumfire of artillery, gas shells, infantry assaults and counter-attacks.

Our old friend Louis Barthas, irascible barrel-maker from the Midi and author of *Poilu*, served here in May 1916, and his descriptions of the battlefield are harrowing: 'For several months the hill had been disputed as if it had diamond mines on its slopes. Alas, all it contained now were thousands of shredded, pulverised corpses.'

In the woods around the more traditional Côte 304 memorial were more trenches and craters, and long-forgotten tunnels. You don't have to search for long to find rusting ammunition, pieces of bone and bits of shrapnel, although you'd be mad to pick any of it up.

Back in Verdun, I ditched the bike at the hotel and walked into town for another dinner for one. By far the worst thing about travelling alone is this daily humiliation, but at least social media and a Kindle help take the edge off the pitying looks and having to occupy the Table of Shame in every restaurant. On the way back to the hotel that night I realised why Verdun has so few hotel rooms – under the walls of the citadel is a huge motorhome park, and it was absolutely rammed with RVs. Dozens and dozens of them. But do people bring their RVs because there are no hotels, or are there no hotels because everyone comes here in an RV?

With only 60 miles and 3,000ft of climbing, the following day felt like another rest day. It was spitting with rain as I set off south for Bar-le-Duc along the Voie Sacrée, but I was looking forward to this bit because if ever a road was special, this one was it. This road, recently and appropriately renamed the D1916, was the lifeline of Verdun. So many men travelled along (or alongside) it, to and from the charnel house that was Verdun. So much *matériel*. It was on this road that Pétain, newly appointed commander of

Verdun, experienced something that shook him to his core – the sight of his filthy, wounded, bedraggled and emotionally shattered troops trudging away from the front line. Ghosts of men with dead eyes and thousand-yard stares, stumbling along. For an officer who genuinely had an affinity with his men it was heartbreaking, and Pétain subsequently ensured that regiments were rotated in and out of the line with far more frequency.

So there I was, on the Voie Sacrée. And it did feel special. Emotional. Either side there were poppies growing in the fields and verges, and all along the road there are small markers topped with a *poilu*'s helmet. I pedalled slowly along this gently undulating road, imagining the columns of men marching alongside, and the road packed with endless columns of trucks and ambulances. As I rolled into the small town of Souilly, the road up ahead was packed with a column of trucks and ambulances. Grey, First World War vintage trucks and ambulances. I genuinely could not believe my eyes. Had I pedalled into some kind of time-warp? Of course not, but here I was on the Voie Sacrée with three First World War trucks, two First World War ambulances, a First World War staff car and a First World War motorbike, all manned by people in period military uniforms. It was genuinely astonishing, and I felt very emotional for some strange reason.

The convoy had stopped at a bar in Souilly and were doing that French thing of drinking spirits at 11 a.m., so I stopped too (for a coffee). The bar was full of people in uniform and I got chatting (well, mangling the French language) to a lady dressed as a First World War nurse, who told me that they were driving from Verdun to Bar-le-Duc to commemorate the centenary of the battle of Verdun and the role of the Voie Sacrée in the battle. I was absolutely blown away by stumbling on this amazing event. Proper, genuine First World War vehicles on the Voie Sacrée!

I mingled, I talked to various people about their vehicles, and I talked about the Circuit des Champs de Bataille to anyone who would listen. No one had ever heard of it, and they were astonished that a bike race crossed these battlefields early in 1919. One

A collection of First World War vehicles on the Voie Sacrée. They were there in 2016 to pay tribute to the extraordinary men who kept Verdun supplied during the battle

kind chap offered to take me and my bike to Bar-le-Duc in his truck. I would have loved to have taken him up on his offer, but the convoy travelled at a much slower pace than me on my bike, and I wanted to be in Saint-Mihiel that evening, so I had to decline. But before I left I was interviewed by French TV (who were covering this event) about my trip. I offered to attempt it in French, but the producer blanched visibly and said it would probably be better in English.

I was still buzzing from this encounter when I arrived in Bar-le-Duc for a late lunch. I did a quick lap of the town where Stage 5 ended, grabbed a bite to eat, and then headed on to Saint-Mihiel, 20 miles to the north-east. The weather, which had been rainy and cold, went mental as the sun came out and the temperature rocketed to 25°C. Suddenly I was drenched in sweat inside my waterproof layers, so I stripped down to my base-layer and continued on my way. In one village I caught sight of myself reflected in a shop window and realised I looked exactly like one of those eccentric old men on a touring bike. The only things missing were a beard and sandals. I was quite relieved when the clouds reappeared and the rain started again, as the temperature dropped from 25°C to 12°C in the space of 5 miles (if the sat-nav is to be believed), and I could put my MAMILicious Castelli clobber back on.

Saint-Mihiel was *en fête* when I arrived, celebrating '100 Years of Life'. It was a sort of First World War centenary, but concentrating on the life-goes-on aspect rather than the death-and-destruction. There was a band, there was dancing, there were traditional crafts being demonstrated, there were old cars and wagons, there were people in period costume, there was food and drink. Despite the rain it was a joyous occasion, and a reassuringly French affair.

I ducked into the bar at the centre of things, dripping water and shivering, where a Cognac and a couple of hot chocolates soon restored me. I didn't ask for them, they just appeared, the landlady perfectly anticipating the needs of a cold, wet cyclist. There was another touring cyclist in the bar, drinking beer and watching the football on the TV in the corner. He was a Belgian called Bart, on his way home from northern Spain, and we sat and talked cycling and touring for a while. In my three weeks on the road, he was one of the few 'proper' cyclists I came across. It felt good to spend an hour or so in the company of a like-minded soul.

My hotel in Saint-Mihiel was deserted when I rolled up. I dinged the bell, and waited. Then I dinged some more, and waited. Then I noticed a note on the reception desk: 'We're all at the *fête*' it read. Next to it was a list of names and room numbers, and a pile of keys.

General Classification after Stage 5

	Rider	Time	Time gap
1	Charles Deruyter (B)	71hr 24min	00hr 00min
2	Urbain Anseeuw (B)	72hr 39min	+01hr 15min
3	Henri Van Lerberghe (B)	73hr 53min	+02hr 29min
4	Jean Alavoine (F)	81hr 59min	+10hr 35min
5	Theo Wynsdau (B)	82hr 14min	+10hr 50min
6	José Pelletier (F)	84hr 18min	+10hr 54min
7	André Huret (F)	86hr 06min	+14hr 42min
8	Albert Desmedt (B)	86hr 07min	+14hr 43min
9	Hector Heusghem (F)	86hr 10min	+14hr 46min
10	Henri Hanlet (B)	87hr 11min	+15hr 47min
21	Louis Ellner (F)	127hr 40min	+56hr 16min

STAGE 6

Bar-le-Duc to Belfort

313km

9 May 1919

With Deruyter leading the race by an hour and 15 minutes from Anseeuw, and with Van Lerberghe a further hour and 15 minutes back, the superior condition of the Belgians was telling. Jean Alavoine, now the leading Frenchman in the absence of Duboc, was over 10 hours behind Deruyter and had little chance of a podium finish unless one of the leading trio suffered an insurmountable problem. One crash or unfixable mechanical issue could end anyone's race at any moment, so Alavoine wasn't giving up hope. And there was still one more battlefield to be negotiated, not to mention a substantial mountain in the Vosges – the Ballon d'Alsace. It wasn't over yet.

The rest day in Bar-le-Duc was spent doing the usual things – sleeping, eating, carrying out bike maintenance and attending to sores and injuries. For the trailing triumvirate of Pain, Asse and Ellner, all of whom arrived in Bar-le-Duc on the morning of the rest day, sleeping and eating were of paramount importance because they would need to be back on the start line in 16 hours' time.

In the real world, the peace negotiations were occupying most French newspapers and the race rarely got a mention. Any space the papers had left over was devoted to two juicy news stories . . . an investigation into a particularly grisly serial killer in Paris, and the trial of four newspapermen for treason. Henri Landu, 'the Bluebeard of Gambais', spent the war years in Paris advertising in the lonely hearts columns for widows (and there were many), whom he would then fleece of their money and kill. He chopped up the bodies and burned them in his stove at home. He murdered ten in total (plus the son of one of them), but was caught in April 1919 and guillotined in 1922. If you really want, you can see his severed head in the Museum of Death in Los Angeles.

The Lenoir/Desouches/Humbert/Ledoux treason trial centred around a group of Frenchmen who used secret German state money during the war to buy a French newspaper for the purposes of spreading defeatist propaganda. It was all part of the *Bonnet Rouge* conspiracy that also involved Bolo Pasha (subsequently executed), a crooked pre-war French prime minister, and the sultry female spy Mata Hari (also executed). You used to be able to see Mata Hari's severed head in the Museum of Anatomy in Paris, but someone stole it in 1954.

The riders in the race were only vaguely aware of events unfolding elsewhere, concentrating instead on preparing for the next stage, a hefty 313km slog south through the Vosges mountains. They were particularly concerned about their gearing for the three significant climbs of the day – the Col de Martimpré (10km at 5 per cent), the Col de Grosse Pierre (6km at 5 per cent), and the Ballon d'Alsace (10km at 7 per cent). These weren't monstrous climbs like those of the Alps and Pyrenees that were introduced to the Tour de France just before the war, but nonetheless they were significant obstacles if you were on a heavy bike with limited gearing.

In the *parc fermé* Hector Heusghem sat on a bench in the sun, the rear wheel of his bike on his lap as he worked in silence. He removed the rear sprocket from the 'climbing side' of the wheel and set about replacing it with a 23-tooth sprocket he had brought with him, hoping it would get him over the Ballon d'Alsace. He would have liked a lower gear for the mountains, but couldn't risk dropping the chain while riding on the flat in the higher gear due to the lack of chain tension. Running skilled hands around the rim, he took a spoke key and carefully adjusted the spoke tensions, truing the wheel in readiness for tomorrow's stage.

'Afternoon, Hector,' said Van Lerberghe, sitting down next to him with his own pair of wheels. 'That was a good day for you, yesterday, wasn't it.'

'Yeah, I was pretty pleased with that, although I think I could've beaten Alavoine if he hadn't come across me like that.'

Van Lerberghe grunted, his attention focused on a minute inspection of his tyres. 'The roads yesterday really cut up my tyres,' he remarked. 'Think I'll change them both, just in case.'

They worked in silence, enjoying the warm sun on their backs. 'Is it true,' asked Heusghem after a few minutes, 'what they say about the Ronde this year?'

Van Lerberghe glanced up at him. 'I don't know. What do they say?'

'That you and Van Hevel had a bust-up before the race. That you conned Buysse's *soigneur* into giving you his *musette*. And that you stopped for a beer outside the velodrome in Ghentbrugge.'

Van Lerberghe laughed. 'They were taking the piss, calling me the Death Rider of Lichtervelde. Van Hevel was being a right smug bastard. He spent most of the war lazing around in a British hospital while I was up to my neck in mud and bullets on the Ijzer, so I thought I'd show him.' He grinned slyly. 'But you don't want to believe everything you hear.'

'So you didn't have to be helped across the finish line by your *soigneur*?'

Van Lerberghe laughed again. 'That was because of the "finishing bottle" I took, not the beer. Anyway, I was fine. And I beat Van Hevel by 14 minutes, so that shut him up.'

The two men returned to their tasks, tweaking and fettling in preparation for the next day's stage.

In fairness, Van Lerberghe's nickname as the Death Rider was thoroughly deserved. Before the war he had become famous for his lone, and almost always doomed, solo breakaways. He had a habit of riding off the front of the peloton with 100km to go, only to be reeled back in before the finish, but at the Ronde van Vlaanderen (Tour of Flanders) that year the peloton had left its chase much too late. If he had indeed stopped for a beer, it was probably to make a point to those who had mocked him on the start line. The newspaper *L'Auto* referred to Van Lerberghe as 'swollen-head', so it would seem he wasn't the most popular man in the peloton.

Or, the story of the Ronde could be a complete fabrication (there are those who say it is). Like many of these cycling tales, they have been told, expanded, retold and embellished to the point that no one knows for sure what is fact and what isn't. Certainly, the journalists of the day, who rarely glimpsed riders for more than a minute or two, were more than happy to wax lyrical about extraordinary exploits they had not actually witnessed. Personally, in the absence of first-hand documentary evidence, I'm more than happy to believe these extraordinary tales. I *want* to believe these tales. These myths and legends, stories of staggering fortitude and courage, are part of what makes bike racing so enthralling.

At 3 a.m. the next morning the riders gathered at the Café du Commerce in Bar-le-Duc to sign on for the penultimate stage. It was a cold, crisp night under starry skies that promised another bright day ahead. There was a palpable sense of relief amongst the riders, with the prospect of good roads and nice weather ahead of them. A small group had formed around Alavoine who, as a veteran of four pre-war Tours, had climbed the Ballon d'Alsace twice in each direction and was answering questions about the severity of the gradient.

Asse, Pain and Ellner weren't among them. They stood separately, knowing that it didn't matter what advice Alavoine gave them – none of them had the gearing or the strength to make it over the Ballon on their bikes, and that they would be pushing most of the way up. They were resigned to their fate, but knew that on particularly steep climbs you could walk almost as fast as you could ride. No one knew it at the time, but everyone would end up pushing their bikes up the Ballon d'Alsace that day.

Just before 4 a.m. most of the riders gathered for the start, but in the outside toilet of his lodgings José Pelletier was bent double, gripped by debilitating stomach cramps that threatened an eruption from either end. He hadn't been feeling well for a couple of days, but had awoken this morning feeling even worse. The potent cocktails of stimulants, ether and other drugs were known to cause stomach problems, and he'd suffered similar discomforts in the past.

As he made his way back into the house there came a frantic hammering on the front door. 'Monsieur Pelletier! Monsieur Pelletier! Quickly. The race is about to start!'

Pelletier threw open the front door. 'Tell them I'll be there in a few minutes.' He turned, barged past his alarmed host, and went to gather his things.

There was still no sign of Pelletier as the starting pistol fired and the peloton rolled out of Bar-le-Duc, bound for the Saint-Mihiel battlefields and the Vosges mountains. Ten minutes later, as the commissaires were packing up and preparing to leave, Pelletier arrived. He scrawled his name on the start sheet, leapt onto his bike, and took off in pursuit of the pack. His guts were still performing somersaults, but he pushed on, knowing that he should be able to catch them quite quickly.

Pelletier wasn't the only one suffering that morning. Heusghem crashed in the first 10 miles, but remounted and chased back on. Deruyter was also experiencing 'gastric distress' and was obliged to stop behind a bush, losing 10 minutes to a peloton that was now pushing hard to take time out of him. As Anseeuw and Van Lerberghe set a punishing pace towards Saint-Mihiel, the weaker riders were soon dropped and a group of a dozen powered away. They arrived at the remains of Saint-Mihiel as the sun was beginning to rise, by now unsurprised by the ruin and destruction that greeted them. A few *sinistrés* watched curiously as the riders and the race convoy passed, before returning to their scavenging and reconstructions.

The First World War front line formed a salient at Saint-Mihiel, where the German lines jutted out into French territory. Annoyingly for the French, it stuck out far enough to cut off the railway line from Nancy to Verdun (hence the French need of the Voie Sacrée) and dominate the Meuse River crossing there. But for four years the French, despite their best efforts, could not dislodge the Germans from their salient and the front line became static. So the Germans did what they did in those days . . . they reinforced their carefully chosen lines, poured thousands of tons of concrete, and made the salient into a fortress. They were there to stay.

It wasn't until September 1918, in the final months of the war, that the Allies were able to oust the Germans from the Saint-Mihiel salient. The Americans, under General Pershing, were given the job and amassed more than 500,000 troops to do it. The combination of overwhelming numbers of men and *matériel*, combined with the German willingness to abandon the salient and withdraw to prepared positions further back, meant that in 36 hours the Americans had achieved what the French hadn't managed in 4 years. Having said that, these were the last months of the war and the Germans didn't put up much of a fight – 16,000 of them surrendered in one day.

The most extraordinary thing about the Saint-Mihiel battle was that the American attack was to be followed 12 days later by an American attack on the Argonne front 110km away. The Americans had less than two weeks to pinch out the Saint-Mihiel salient and then transport half a million men, artillery and ammunition across to the Argonne in preparation for a combined French and American assault. There was so little time that as soon as the first wave of troops had gained their objectives at Saint-Mihiel, they were withdrawn and transported straight to the Argonne front to begin preparations there. As a feat of logistics, it was extraordinary.

Not that the riders in the Circuit des Champs de Bataille were aware of much of this. They were trying to stay with Anseeuw, Van Lerberghe and Alavoine at the front of the peloton as they pressed on, hoping to make sure Deruyter didn't get back up to them. The more pressure they put on him, the more likely it was that he would crash or suffer a mechanical problem, so they turned the screw as hard as they could.

All around the signs of war were everywhere, and very recent signs at that. There had been fighting in this area right up until the armistice in November 1918, and here they were, just six months later. The direct route from Saint-Mihiel to Nancy had disappeared during the fighting in 1918, so the race looped around the northern edge of the salient to Pont-à-Mousson, and then south to Nancy. Military vehicles of all descriptions lay broken and abandoned in the fields, and by the roadside were piles of munitions, discarded weapons, and rolls of barbed wire collected up by the labour battalions. The woods were bleak, smashed and chaotic, heavily fortified and criss-crossed by trenches.

On the rough roads crashes and punctures were inevitable, and by the time the leaders reached Pont-à-Mousson they had lost Pelletier, Desmedt and Hanlet. Behind them, Deruyter's stomach cramps had eased and he was riding like a maniac to catch back up. With a 75-minute lead over Anseeuw, Deruyter could afford to take it reasonably easy, but he wasn't that kind of rider – he wanted stage wins, not just because his wife had expensive tastes in furs but also because he liked winning.

As the sun came up and the war-torn countryside disappeared behind them, the peloton once again felt the sun on their faces and dust in their throats. With one final push Deruyter made it onto the back of the peloton and tucked in behind the leading trio. They cannot have been happy to see him. Approaching Nancy, Charles Kippert rode up alongside Alavoine and asked if he might be allowed to lead the peloton into his home town. This was something of a tradition in those days, and riders were 'allowed' to clip off the front of the pack so they could stop briefly to greet friends and family at the roadside. Alavoine nodded, and signalled to the others to back off the pace slightly so that Kippert might have his moment of glory. And what a moment it was. Hundreds upon hundreds of spectators turned out to cheer the local boy as he led the race through the town, an emotional moment for him.

The roads were good, the weather was good, and the peloton was making decent progress, even if they were an hour behind the anticipated schedule. By Lunéville the 11-strong peloton had dropped the weaker riders, who arrived at the checkpoint in dribs and drabs over the following 2 hours. Ellner was already so far behind that he didn't feature on the timing sheets that morning.

*

Clearly the '100 Years of Life' festivities in Saint-Mihiel had gone on long into the night, because when I wandered into the hotel dining room the following morning breakfast was notable by its absence. On the 'buffet' table there was a half-empty bottle of red wine and some dirty glasses, a box of tea bags, a three-day-old croissant, a broken VHS player, and a loaf of bread that was so hard, it obviously dated back to when the Americans were here in 1918 (they were, after all, doughboys). The staff were still sleeping off their hangovers, and my breakfast was AWOL. Unimpressed, I left my key at the deserted reception desk and made my way into town in search of something to eat that wouldn't reduce my dental work to ruins.

For anyone who is interested in poking around the First World War battlefields, the Saint-Mihiel salient is astounding. It's another forested area that has just been left to nature, so the locals didn't bother dynamiting the pill-boxes or filling the trenches. This is proper Zone Rouge, and as a result there's loads of stuff to look at, if you can find it amongst the trees. It's also advisable to stick to the paths (well, narrow, muddy tracks) because this area was not systematically cleared after the war and there is still plenty of dangerous stuff lying about.

First stop was the Tranchée de la Soif (trench of thirst), a well-preserved section of German trenches and concrete shelters among the trees. In May 1915 a French attack by the 172nd RI (*regiment d'infanterie*) broke into these trenches, but 7th Company were then cut off from their regiment. For three days, without food or water or sleep, this small band of men held a short section of this trench against constant German counter-attacks. They finally surrendered when their ammunition ran out. Picking my way along this section of trench, I was surrounded by the remains of shattered concrete, barbed wire and rusting iron, the gnarled trees heavy with moss and lichens, the squelch of my shoes in the mud the only sound. It was eerily beautiful, and incredibly peaceful, and desperately sad. Around 60,000 French soldiers were killed in these woods in 1915 alone.

A little further along the road to Apremont, set back among the trees, I stopped at an imposing bunker around 35m in length, a fortified German field hospital complete with narrow-gauge railway for evacuating the wounded. The scale and solidity of buildings like this are a reminder that the Germans were convinced they were here to stay, and built accordingly. During the four years they occupied this salient they constructed miles of concreted trenches, hundreds of deep concrete shelters, and all the infrastructure that an occupying army needed. Outside Apremont they built an entire concrete village in an old quarry, complete with terraced gardens. One German officer even had the decorative ceilings from Ligier Richier's house (he was a famous Renaissance sculptor from the sixteenth century) in Saint-Mihiel ripped out and installed in his concrete bunker in the quarry. Richier's most famous sculpture, *Le Transi de René de Chalon*, is so strikingly similar to the 69th Division memorial on Mort Homme that it must have been the inspiration.

French trenches in the Bois Brûlé on the Saint-Mihiel salient, scene of bitter fighting for four years

At the Bois Brûlé you can still walk among the astonishingly well-preserved concrete trenches and dug-outs, and it's here that you can really appreciate the full horror of this sector. The front-line trenches here are, in places, only seven metres apart. Imagine being on duty just seven metres away from an enemy with a rifle and a bag of grenades. Or a flamethrower. There's an excavated and reconstructed section of French trench here which vividly illustrates the difference between the French and German ones. While the German trenches are deep, solidly built concrete affairs, the French ones are shallower and less well constructed, because the French had no intention of spending four years in them. But they did.

Another of France's First World War heroes found fame in these woods. During an attack in April 1915 Jacques Péricard, a sergeant-major with the 95th RI, led his section into the second line of German defences before they were swept back by a heavy

German counter-attack. Surrounded by the bodies of his men, he stood up and urged the dead and the dying to get up and fight. *'Debout les morts!'* he cried. Arise, you dead! It became a rallying cry throughout France, and after the war Péricard compiled a superb book about Verdun from eyewitness accounts. I bought a copy recently from an antique bookseller in France, and tucked inside was an original French ration card from April 1919, coinciding precisely with the Circuit des Champs de Bataille. Another of those odd coincidences that became a theme of this story.

Having spent far too long (and yet not long enough) mooching around trenches and bunkers, I now needed to put in some proper miles if I was to make it to my hotel in Lunéville before dark. So that's what I did, crossing a wide, flat valley of fruit orchards and then following a line of hills south-east towards Toul. It was in Toul that Octave Lapize, the great pre-war Tour de France winner, died in 1917. His plane was shot down over the Saint-Mihiel salient and he was taken to a hospital in Toul, where he died of his wounds.

Cruising along at a steady 20mph, the bike felt smooth and comfortable, I felt fairly strong and comfortable, and the weather was warm and dry. Shifting down for a slight incline, I felt an almost imperceptible lurch from the rear shifter. *Hmmm . . . that didn't feel right.* I downshifted again, and the action felt worse. *Arse! That's the unmistakable feeling of a cable about to break.* I used to own a Laverda Jota (a prehistoric Italian motorbike) back in the day, and that used to chew through clutch cables every few months, so I know that sickening sensation as the cable frays and then starts to pull apart. My rear derailleur cable was definitely giving me that feeling.

I resolved to keep going, reduce gear-changes to a minimum, and sort things out when I got to Nancy, a town big enough to have a bike shop that could sell me a spare cable. So obsessed was I with my failing derailleur cable that I inadvertently rode onto a French motorway. *No,* I thought to myself, *there were no toll-booths, this must be a dual carriageway.* A crescendo of tooting, beeping and parping from passing motorists persuaded me that maybe this was actually the A31 motorway. If you get a bollocking for not unclipping at a Stop sign, I wondered how the police would react to me riding my bike on the motorway. I'd probably get Tasered. Still, better that than a €500 fine.

Anyway, it was too late now, I was committed. There would probably be a junction in 10 or 15 miles, so I cracked on as fast as I could, hoping not to end up like all the road-kill smeared across the hard shoulder. As it transpired, after a mile or two there was another junction and I turned off there before *les flics* were alerted. I've often laughed at the monumental stupidity of cyclists who end up on motorways, scarcely able to conceive of how such a thing is possible. Let me tell you, it's easier than you might imagine. But staggeringly stupid, nonetheless.

As I rode into the middle of Nancy I became aware that none of the shops was open. *Balls . . . it's Sunday, therefore there's no chance of finding a bike shop open.* I stopped in Place Stanislas for a coffee and to consider my options. I sat in the sun in this beautiful square, marvelling at the incredible architecture and the nerve of the café proprietor to charge €6 for a really crappy cup of coffee. OK, so I would nurse the bike as far as Lunéville (20 miles away), find a bike shop first thing the next morning, replace the cable, job's a good 'un.

Just outside Nancy the cable finally pulled apart, the chain dropped down the block due to the lack of cable tension, and I was left struggling up a slight incline in my biggest gear (50×12). Even dropping onto the front inner ring only gave me a 34×12. Hmmmm. Looking at the elevation profile for the rest of the day, I could see that there were no significant climbs to come, so I'd persevere with my two available gears until Lunéville.

Needless to say, the bike shop in Lunéville closed some time in the 1970s, so at my hotel I set about trying to effect some kind of bodge. In the hotel's bike storage facility (aka the conference room) there were three other road bikes, one of which was a

Colnago sporting a Campagnolo Record mechanical groupset and a lovely-looking rear derailleur cable. Hmmm . . . tempting, but perhaps not. Anyway, I had zip-ties and a multi-tool. By holding the rear derailleur in the desired position, and wrapping a zip-tie round it to hold it in place, I could select any one of the 11 gears on the rear block.

The question was, which one? If I couldn't get a replacement cable at the bike shop in Saint-Dié-des-Vosges the next day, I had two days in the Vosges mountains coming up, so obviously I needed something to get me up and over those, but not something that would cause my legs to spin-out at 15mph. The first day only had a couple of gentle climbs, so I opted to use the 23-tooth sprocket (it's a bit like driving over the mountains in your car and only being able to chose one gear to do it in). I had enough zip-ties to allow for eight changes, if I needed them. A quick spin around the conference-room table confirmed that all was in order.

Satisfied with my zip-tie bodgery, I meandered into town for some dinner. There was some kind of equestrian event going on at the chateau, and the place was full of horsey women with jodhpurs and riding crops. I kept my male gaze to myself and drank beer in the early evening sunshine. In a small brasserie there were three cyclists having dinner, and they kindly invited me to join them, thus sparing me from the Table of Shame. Cyclists can identify fellow cyclists by their spindly upper bodies, bizarre suntans, and curious off-bike clothing, so we immediately clocked each other as fellow roadies.

One of the trio turned out to be the owner of the Colnago in the hotel, and I was quite glad I'd decided against stealing his rear derailleur cable. They were financiers from Luxembourg who go on an annual cycling trip together, and we spent a very pleasant evening talking about bikes, nice places to ride, gearing, the Circuit des Champs de Bataille, and Andy Schleck.

★

From Lunéville Stage 6 still had another 160km and 2,000m of climbing to go. The sun was shining from a crisp blue spring sky and the roads, which had been well behind the First World War front lines, were generally in good condition as Deruyter led the 11-man peloton south. At St-Dié-des-Vosges they paused at the *parc fermé* for some food and to wash off some of the dust. Punctures and mechanical issues were still plaguing some riders, with Kippert and Leroy dropping off the back of the peloton while Hanlet and Pelletier took their places in the leading group.

The road, which had been climbing gently for the last 30km, now ramped up at Anould to over 5 per cent. The riders pulled over to swap their rear wheels round onto their climbing gear, and then pressed on. It was hard going on the macadam road, and with pitches of up to 8 per cent some of them began to struggle. Heusghem was happy with his choice of a 23 on the back, and soon a group of the strongest climbers – Heusghem, Alavoine, Desmedt, Van Lerberghe, Deruyter and Anseeuw – began to pull out a lead on the others. The road twisted up through the pine forests that clad the foothills of the Vosges. Over the Col du Plafond and the Col de Martimpré they rode, the temperature dropping as they climbed higher into the mountains.

Just outside Chalgoutte they passed a large convoy of army trucks parked along the roadside. The trucks, adorned with *'Danger High Explosives'* signs, were being guarded by a platoon of fearsome-looking Colonial soldiers. They were on their way to Gérardmer, where tonnes of unused ammunition was being disposed of.

By the checkpoint in Gérardmer the six leading riders had put 4 minutes into the remains of the peloton, which was slowly disintegrating behind them. But the two climbs they'd ridden were just a prelude to the main event – the Col de Grosse Pierre and the Ballon d'Alsace were still to come. The temperature continued to drop, but the riders barely noticed as they struggled to turn their huge (by modern standards) climbing gear on some of the steeper pitches of Grosse Pierre. The top of the Col is 950m above sea level, and when they got there they were surprised to find snow on the ground.

Alavoine, the lone Frenchman in this leading group, must have been worried. He knew the Ballon was higher than this; there would be snow up there for sure. He'd only ever ridden it during the Tour, in July, but it would be very different at this time of year, especially after the weather they'd had in the last few weeks. The others looked at each other grimly and then focused their attention on the slippery descent down into La Bresse.

For many riders these descents were almost worse than the climbs ... the unmade, gravelly mountain roads were treacherous at the best of times, and on a heavy bike with very poor brakes (using cork brake pads on wooden wheel rims) they were terrifying. There were often no guard-rails, either, so riding off the road would have catastrophic consequences. Cycle tourists before the First World War were advised, in these conditions, to tie a tree branch to their seat-post with a length of rope and to drag it down mountains to keep their speeds down. But this was a race, and the riders took the risks necessary to descend as quickly as they dared.

Up ahead, the lead vehicles in the race convoy had reached Saint-Maurice-sur-Moselle and had turned onto the climb over the Ballon d'Alsace. It was a tough climb in those days, even in a car, and slowly they chugged their way up. When Henri Desgrange included the Ballon in the Tour in 1905 he didn't think any riders would be able to cycle all the way to the top, and confidently expected them to have to walk at least some of the way. But René Pottier, one of the greatest climbers of the pre-war generation, managed it without walking in 1905 and again in 1906, and became a legend in cycling, hailed as one of the greatest climbers of all time. Sadly, he committed suicide early in 1907 when he discovered that his wife was having affairs while he was away at the Tour. In an uncharacteristic show of empathy and respect, Henri Desgrange erected a memorial to Pottier at the top of the Ballon, which is still there today.

Snow on the lower slopes of the Vosges mountains in 1920, a scenario that the racers must have cursed as they struggled upwards

As they continued upwards the cars encountered more and more snow, slipping and lurching as they struggled for grip. A kilometre from the top the cars were forced to a halt by snow that lay more than a metre deep. The commissaires got their shovels (which, apparently, they had salvaged from the Saint-Mihiel battlefields earlier in the day) from the boot and began to clear the snow in front of the convoy. They worked for an hour, but cleared no more than a few cubic metres of snow before giving up any thought of going further up the mountain. After more digging they managed to turn the vehicles around and descend back to Saint-Maurice-sur-Moselle, where they waited for the riders.

Heusghem, Alavoine, Deruyter, Desmedt and Van Lerberghe arrived at Saint-Maurice-sur-Moselle together, and were surprised to see the commissaires' cars parked at the side of the road. Degrain flagged them down.

'There is snow at the summit, and the Ballon is impassable by car,' explained Degrain, 'but you should get through with your bikes. We're going around, via the Col des Croix, and we'll wait for you on the other side. Good luck!'

And with that, they drove off. The riders looked at each other, shrugged, and started their ascent of the Ballon, wondering what fresh hell awaited them at the summit. Up to this point the leading five riders had ridden *tempo* together, but on the steeper slopes of the Ballon they split apart. Heusghem pulled out a lead over Deruyter and Van Lerberghe, while Desmedt dropped ever further behind and was caught by Anseeuw (who had been having mechanical problems all afternoon). By following the wheel-tracks of the vehicles, sometimes riding, sometimes pushing, they struggled upwards. The bright sunshine, which earlier had been such a pleasant blessing, was now reflecting off the deep snow, causing the riders to squint in order to make out the route ahead.

When Heusghem reached the point at which the cars had turned back, he came to a stop. The snow ahead was waist deep and unbroken. He looked back down the mountain, but there was no one in sight. Wearily he hoisted his bike over his shoulder, cyclocross style, and began to force a way through the snow. It was exhausting work requiring an immense effort to push himself and his bike towards the summit. He was pouring with sweat, yet chilled to the bone the minute he stopped for a rest, as he slipped and heaved his way upwards. At one point he collapsed exhausted in the snow and wondered whether to wait for the others – they could take it in turns breaking a trail through the snow. But he had no idea where they were, and he didn't want to surrender any time he had gained, so he struggled on.

Behind him, the others weren't having much more luck. Yes, Heusghem had forced a sort of trail through the snow, but it was still a hellish job carrying their bikes on their shoulders. They slipped and cursed and heaved their way through the snowdrifts, past the shuttered *auberge* at the top and then down the other side.

It was several kilometres, and several hours, before Heusghem was able to get back in the saddle and actually ride his bike, and even then it was a terrifyingly sketchy descent. The hairpins on the south side were incredibly slippery and there was nothing except a few rickety wooden hand-rails to stop him sliding several hundred metres down the side of the mountain. By the time he was on the lower slopes, Heusghem was physically and mentally exhausted. The commissaires were waiting at the *auberge* in Le Puix, where he stopped briefly to flip his rear wheel back onto the higher gear, and the lead car then preceded him as he put in a final push to Belfort, 20km distant.

A couple of minutes behind, Van Lerberghe and Deruyter were riding hard to catch him. Deruyter had a large enough lead on GC that he could afford to freewheel all the way to Belfort, but he wanted the stage win, he wanted the money.

The crowds in Belfort had been waiting for more than 2 hours by the time Heusghem swept into town. On the run in to the finish line the crowds were so deep, and so enthusiastic, that only a small corridor remained between them. Hector Heusghem crossed the line at 5.18 p.m. to tumultuous applause, after 13 hours and 18 minutes of racing. Nine minutes behind him came Deruyter and Van Lerberghe, who sprinted for second place. Van Lerberghe won by a length from an intensely frustrated Deruyter, who came in third. Over the next couple of hours more riders arrived individually, shattered by their exertions over the Ballon. Shortly after midnight Henri Ménager and Arsène Pain came in together, having spent 20 hours and 23 minutes on the road.

Muller, Asse, Leroy and Ellner were still unaccounted for, but the commissaires assumed they would appear in due course. The skies were clear, there was a full moon, and with snow on the ground, visibility was actually quite good on the Ballon.

Up on the mountain, Ellner slogged on. With hopelessly inappropriate gearing, he had been walking almost since Saint-Maurice-sur-Moselle, pushing his bike in the tracks left by the 20 riders ahead of him. When night fell the temperature plummeted and he began to shiver uncontrollably. Somewhere near the summit he noticed tracks leading away from the 'road', towards what looked to be a mountain *refuge*, from which he could see a glimmer of light. He made his way towards it, and when he got there he saw a bicycle leaning against the outside wall.

Inside the *refuge*, Camille Leroy had, after a lot of fumbling around, found an old oil lamp, a box of matches, and a stack of fire-wood. After much cajoling he had just got the fire going when Ellner stumbled in, wet and frozen. While Ellner crouched in front of the fire Leroy went outside to fill an ancient kettle with snow to put over the fire . . . a drink of hot water would help restore them both. As Leroy sipped the hot water from his *bidon*, Ellner fished in his *musette* for something to eat. At the feed station in Saint-Dié a kindly helper, with a surreptitious wink, had slipped a couple of extra mutton chops into Ellner's bag when the commissaires weren't looking. He handed Leroy a chop, which was devoured with appreciative grunts. Huddling as close to the fire as they dared, under a couple of threadbare blankets, they both got a couple of hours' rest.

Joseph Muller arrived at the finish at 6 a.m. the next morning, followed 8 minutes later by Robert Asse. They had stopped at the *auberge* at the foot of the Ballon and rested there for a few hours. We don't know what time Leroy and Ellner crossed the finish line, as their times were never recorded. But they did make it to the finish some time that morning and would be on the start line for Stage 7.

*

I expected to see my new-found Luxembourgois friends at breakfast the next morning, but they still hadn't appeared by the time I'd stolen all the breakfast buffet (you snooze, you lose) and got on my way. With the 50 × 23 gear I could maintain around 16mph on the flat before my legs became a blur. It was a bit slow, but it was manageable.

The race route headed south-east along the banks of the River Meurthe, rolling gently along and devoid of too much traffic, thanks to the nearby N59 motorway. It was another lovely spring morning and although the Meurthe valley isn't particularly pretty, I was feeling at peace with the world as I spun along. The rhythm of days on the road was reassuring, combining well-drilled routines at either end of the day with unexpected surprises in the middle.

I stopped in Baccarat for a coffee. For a moment I considered visiting the crystal-glass museum there, before remembering that I actually detest decorative glassware (probably something to do with being abandoned by my family on the island of Murano when I was a young lad – long story). I reached Saint-Dié-des-Vosges by late morning and made my way to the bike shop to buy a derailleur cable. Obviously, the bike shop was closed. It was Monday, of course they were closed.

I spent a moment or two considering my options. Basically, I didn't have any. Yes, I could have gone in search of a cable, put in loads of extra miles and lost loads of time, but I really didn't fancy that. So I just kept going. I had zip-ties, I had a multi-tool and I had some duct-tape – there was nothing I couldn't fix! Actually that's not quite true, because I didn't have any WD40 or a sledgehammer, but I had everything else necessary to effect a top-quality bodge.

By early afternoon I was approaching the foothills of the Vosges and took a short detour at Saulcy-sur-Meurthe to visit the grave of René Fonck. Fonck is the greatest fighter pilot you never heard of. Von Richthofen? Yes. Guynemer? Yes. Bishop? Yes. Fonck? Not so much. But René Fonck shot down 75 enemy aircraft during the First World War, only five fewer than the Red Baron. Fonck was awarded the Medaille Militaire, the Legion d'Honneur, the British Military Cross and the British Distinguished Conduct Medal. The man was, and remains, the highest-scoring Allied air ace of all time.

But Fonck didn't fit the hard-living, hard-drinking, womanising image of an air ace and so never captured the public's imagination like Guynemer, who was the darling of the French press. Fonck was calculating, intelligent, and an expert flyer. He rarely got involved in dogfights with other fighter pilots and instead concentrated on seeking out and bringing down the reconnaissance planes that directed enemy artillery, which he considered a far better use of his time and skills. While some flyers engaged in what were effectively aerial duels between gentlemen pilots, Fonck just got on with his job.

After the war Fonck became friends with several of his old adversaries, including Ernst Udet (a member of Von Richthofen's Flying Circus) and Hermann Göring. During the Second World War Fonck was arrested by the Gestapo and interned at Drancy, the camp north of Paris from which most of France's Jews were deported to the concentration camps. Bizarrely, despite his arrest and internment by the Gestapo, after the war Fonck was accused of being a collaborator due to his friendship with Udet and Göring, but his close ties to the French Resistance meant the charges were dropped.

I sat on a bench in the civilian cemetery where Fonck is buried (he died in 1953), eating a cheese roll, enjoying the warmth of the sun and thinking about the astonishing life of René Fonck. I also wondered about the front lines hereabouts. During the Battle of the Frontiers in 1914 there was a certain amount of action around the River Meurthe, specifically the battle of the Col de la Chipotte, but the line settled down in 1915 and nothing happened thereafter. Literally nothing. The Germans sat in their trenches, the French sat in theirs, and apart from a bit of trench-raiding from time to time, that seemed to be it.

After the initial skirmishes in 1914 the front line settled down and ran parallel to the Meurthe, around 10 miles to the north-east, and so there is little evidence of the war along the race route. In 1918 the Americans took over this part of the line and used it for training in preparation for the Saint-Mihiel offensive slightly further north. The build-up of American troops along the Meurthe persuaded the Germans that an attack was imminent, and they moved some of their troops away from the Saint-Mihiel salient to the Meurthe in readiness. As a result, the Americans pinched out the Saint-Mihiel salient far quicker and more easily than they might have expected.

Back in the saddle, the road tilted upwards towards the mountains and I clicked down to my lower 34 × 23 gear and started climbing into the Vosges. It was a pleasant, warm afternoon, there wasn't much traffic, and the road up the Col du Plafond climbed through the pine trees at a gentle incline, averaging only 4 per cent over 4.5km. The Col de Martimpré was next, another gentle climb at 4 per cent for 10km, topping out at 800m. My climbing gear appeared to be spot-on but I suspected I'd have to change to the 26-tooth cog for the longer and steeper climbs over the Grosse Pierre and Ballon on the following day.

To my surprise, I arrived in Gérardmer much earlier than I'd expected, so I went for a ride around the beautiful lake there. Since the 1920s Gérardmer has been a playground – in the winter there's skiing, and in the summer there's hiking – but prior to that it was just a quiet backwater in the Vosges. Strangely, there's no fishing or swimming allowed in this lovely mountain lake. That's because after the First World War (and again after the Second World War) the French authorities dumped hundreds of tonnes of unexploded ordnance into it, which is now leaching its toxins into the lake, a situation not helped by the slightly acidic nature of the water.

In 1918 and 1919 convoy after convoy of trucks brought ordnance from all over France to be dumped into this lake, an isolated spot far from human habitation. Divers have been down in recent years to assess the possibility of clearing the ordnance, but it's deemed too dangerous to disturb. I sat outside a lakeside café having an ice cream and a coffee, looking over this picturesque scene, struggling to understand the environmental catastrophe lurking beneath the tranquil water.

The blue skies and sunshine had been replaced with mist, drizzle and low cloud when I awoke the next morning. I'd be riding up to nearly 1,200m above sea level, and it was likely to be cold as well, so I dressed accordingly. After breakfast I went down to the hotel basement and tweaked my gearing for the day ahead, shifting the rear derailleur onto the 26-tooth sprocket and securing it with a zip-tie.

The climbing starts almost as soon as you leave Gérardmer, and before long I was winding my way slowly up the Col de Grosse Pierre. The low cloud and drizzle reduced visibility to a few hundred metres, so there was nothing to see . . . I just put my head down and got on with it. By late morning I was in Saint-Maurice, at the foot of the Ballon, feeding my face with pains-au-chocolat and coffee in a roadside café before heading for the top. The mountain was wreathed in mist which blotted out what views might have been available.

My slog up the Ballon d'Alsace was wreathed in mist and fog, but at least there wasn't a metre of snow like in 1919

The Ballon d'Alsace is an 'iconic cycling climb', the first proper mountain to be included in the Tour de France, making its first appearance in the 1905 edition. At this point we can pause for a moment while the Tour pedants argue that the Col de la République or the Col du Pin-Bouchain count as proper mountains and appeared in the race before the Ballon. I don't care. But I do like an iconic cycling climb. Over the years my boy Joe and I have climbed a dozen or so Alpine and Pyrenean climbs that have witnessed extraordinary feats of endurance and courage on two wheels, and I've loved them all.

Unfortunately I didn't feel that love for the Ballon. Yes, I was riding in the wheel-tracks of the great René Pottier, and many other legends of cycling, but the climb itself is just a bit 'meh' by modern standards. It's not long, it's not steep, and there's no great sense of achievement unless you race up it as fast as you can. Which I didn't. So when I got to the top after nearly an hour of climbing, and was unable to see more than 100 metres in any direction due to the mist and cloud, I was a bit underwhelmed. And bloody cold.

But as I sat huddled over a coffee in the café at the top I decided I was being a bit unfair on the Ballon. No, it doesn't have sweeping vistas of snow-clad peaks, or beautiful meadows full of wild flowers and mountain streams, but it has appeared in 20 editions of the Tour, and was the first real test of man and machine against gradients of up to 8 per cent. It was here that the tragic figure of René Pottier spread his metaphorical wings and flew, it was here that Gino Bartali first revealed his climbing prowess to the world, it was here that Eddy Merckx took his first Tour stage win. And it was here that Louis Ellner, just some bloke with a bike, struggled on foot through a metre of snow to the finish of Stage 6 of the Circuit des Champs de Bataille.

Annoyingly, I must have ridden right past the Pottier memorial in the mist without realising it. But by the time I remembered about it I was halfway down the other side, trying not to slide out on the wet hairpin bends awash with grit and diesel. In the dry this would have been a sensational descent, but in the mist and rain it was just a bit frustrating.

An hour or so later I rocked up at my hotel in Belfort, an

exuberant *fin de siècle* building in the middle of town with a fabulously ostentatious lobby. The sight of a sodden, filthy and cold *rosbif*, along with his bicycle, sent the receptionist into a frenzy of horrified tutting and bell-dinging as she summoned a man with a mop to follow me around. The bike was consigned to a dungeon in the basement and I was put in a room as far away from the other guests as possible.

Belfort, like pretty much everywhere I'd been in France, was *en fête*. I do like the way the French seem so happy to sack off work and have a festival instead, and this one was a music festival. Which meant two dozen competing groups of musicians dotted around the town centre, and a Euro-pop DJ with a 3,000-gigawatt sound-system making the mother of all cacophonies. My favourite was a band of nutters that comprised four accordions (obviously), five pipasso bagpipes and two hurdy-gurdies. The sound was indescribable, but I loved it.

I supposed I should have had a look around the historic bits of Belfort. The town is dominated by an enormous fortress that resisted German occupation in 1870 and 1914, and Belfort is justly proud of its refusal to capitulate. But the late-afternoon sun had come out, there were pavement cafés filling up with music-lovers, and I had beer on my mind. Followed by *steak-frites* and a *pichet de vin rouge*. That evening I meandered back to my hotel accompanied by a medley of '90s handbag house, '70s prog rock, and whatever the French equivalent of a ceilidh is. It was all rather charming.

General Classification after Stage 6

	Rider	Time	Time gap
1	Charles Deruyter (B)	85hr 01min	00hr 00min
2	Urbain Anseeuw (B)	86hr 55min	+01hr 54min
3	Henri Van Lerberghe (B)	87hr 30min	+02hr 29min
4	Jean Alavoine (F)	95hr 40min	+10hr 39min
5	Theo Wynsdau (B)	97hr 06min	+12hr 05min
6	José Pelletier (F)	98hr 25min	+13hr 24min
7	Hector Heusghem (F)	99hr 28min	+14hr 27min
8	Albert Desmedt (B)	100hr 18min	+15hr 17min
9	André Huret (F)	100hr 44min	+15hr 43min
10	Henri Hanlet (B)	101hr 07min	+16hr 06min
21	Louis Ellner (F)	157hr (est)	+74hr (est)

STAGE 7

Belfort to Strasbourg

163km

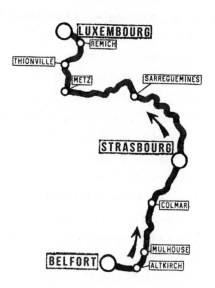

11 May 1919

Victory was so close that Charles Deruyter could almost taste it. All through the rest day he was like a cat on a hot tin roof, unable to settle to anything, pacing, fretting. His wife, Adrienne, who had come to see her husband triumph in Strasbourg, did her best to calm him, but to no avail. For the third time that day he set to work on his bike, checking every nut, every bolt, even though he knew it was ready. Did he have a big enough gear for the final stage? It was a 160km sprint, almost all of it downhill, so he could afford to run a 15 on the back. He hoped. There was a short little climb on leaving Belfort, but thereafter the riders faced a long, shallow descent all the way to Strasbourg. If he could hang on up the climb he'd be set for the rest of the stage.

Anseeuw and Van Lerberghe were similarly preoccupied. Anseeuw only had a 35-minute lead over Van Lerberghe, and he knew that could disappear in an instant. All he had to do was keep Van Lerberghe in sight to secure second place overall, and he might even grab first if anything happened to Deruyter.

Van Lerberghe knew it would be hard to make up 35 minutes on Anseeuw, but it wasn't impossible. Should he throw the dice and attempt one of his infamous lone breakaways? With Alavoine 8 hours behind him on GC, Van Lerberghe had nothing to lose by attempting one of his 'Death Rides', but the others wouldn't let him disappear up the road if they could help it.

As Deruyter checked and rechecked his bike, his mind went back to the arguments he used to have with his father about cycling. His father had desperately wanted him to be a cabinet-maker, but ever since Charles had been to see the Paris–Roubaix race as an adolescent, he had had his heart set on a career in cycling. There had been huge family rows, he'd been banished to a boarding school for three years, but when he returned he had got a job with a small bicycle manufacturer. When he told his father he was going to be a bike racer his father exploded. 'Never at all, ever!' yelled his father. 'You will die on that ugly contraption, and within a few months all we shall have for consolation is to come and weep in the cemetery.'

Deruyter smiled at the memory. His parents had finally relented and allowed him to buy a *routière*, which he rode everywhere. He even raced it at a couple of local events, finishing near the front on each occasion. Unfortunately, quite by chance, his father saw him in one of the local races and went ballistic. He locked Charles' bike in the shed and forbade him to ride it any more. So, after work and at weekends, Charles secretly built himself a race bike, which he kept at a friend's house. From then on he never raced closer than 20km from his home, and raced under the name of Gobert.

Unfortunately his father twigged and confiscated this bike as well, slashing the tyres for good measure. Charles was distraught and the moment his dad's back was turned he stole his bike back, keeping it at an aunt's house. The game of cat and mouse continued for a few months until his exasperated father gave in. From the 1908 season onwards Charles had devoted himself to bike racing, and in 1909 he gave up his job at the factory and moved to Brussels to ride full-time. That year he won the amateur classification of the Liège–Bastogne–Liège, and was on his way.

Deruyter's father finally came around, possibly thanks to the generous prize money Charles was now earning. In 1912 Charles was recruited by the Peugeot team on a two-year contract and had a fair degree of success (1st in the Grand Prix de Namur, 2nd in Paris–Tours and 16th in the Tour de France in 1912, 2nd in Paris–Roubaix in 1913) before the First World War brought a halt to most of the racing.

As he fettled his bike, Deruyter thought back to those successful pre-war days and wondered if they would ever return. Four years later the world was a very different place, but the war had been relatively kind to Deruyter. He enlisted in the Belgian air force in 1914 and worked as an aircraft mechanic, but was allowed time off to continue racing in parts of France. He won the Paris–Orléans and the Criterium de Lyon Républicain in 1916, and in 1917 he won Tours–Paris (not Paris–Tours), beating Eugène Christophe, Henri Pélissier and Jean Alavoine in the process. Deruyter was a rising star, but he had lost his best years to the war. He hoped that the Circuit des Champs de Bataille would put his career back on track.

While the favourites worked on their bikes, the rest of the peloton ate, rested and took care of their aches, pains and wounds. Wynsdau, who had crashed near Amiens, was nursing an injured and very swollen foot which made every pedal-stroke torture. Marcel Mariellonny, the Swiss *isolé*, was suffering from terrible saddle-sores that seemed to defy all efforts to deal with them. And Joseph Muller was nursing what he suspected was a broken collarbone, sustained when he fell heavily near Verdun. Everyone was covered in scabs and abrasions, the result of multiple crashes throughout the last two weeks. And some, like Ernest Paul, were like walking skeletons – thin, exhausted and malnourished. The *forçats de la route* (convicts of the road) were a very rag-tag bunch as they prepared for the final push.

But the good news was that the final stage didn't start until 10 a.m., an unheard-of luxury for riders accustomed to starting in the early hours of the morning. The bad news was that it was pouring with rain as they assembled at the Grande Taverne for the sign-in. Despite their rivalries, this band of 21 survivors was also bound by shared suffering, an experience so tough that none of them would forget it. And none of them would experience anything as tough during the rest of their racing careers. Despite the weather there was an almost cheerful atmosphere in the peloton as they chatted in the bar. On such a short stage there was almost no chance of anyone outside the top three improving their overall standings, so for most of the riders there was little to play for.

From the gun the peloton set a furious tempo, averaging 35kmh for the first hour. They had reached Altkirch by 11 a.m. and for the first time in the race the peloton was actually ahead of its anticipated schedule. Poor Desmedt had yet another puncture, a result of the poor-quality tyres he'd been obliged to use throughout the race. Fortunately it happened in a small village where an obliging spectator held an umbrella over him while he fixed his tyre and then raced to catch back up, until he got another puncture at Colmar.

But the furious pace meant that the likes of Ellner, Muller, Asse and a couple of others were dropped by the time the peloton turned north towards Mulhouse, and the rampaging group of 15 riders blew apart under pressure from Van Lerberghe, Alavoine and Deruyter. By the time they reached Mulhouse the lead group was down to seven riders, and surprisingly Anseeuw was not among them. He could afford to lose a few minutes to Van Lerberghe, but not too many. Van Lerberghe could see an opportunity to grab second overall, and he and Deruyter took turns pushing hard on the front while Alavoine, Kippert, Hanlet, Wynsdau and Leroy fought to stay in touch.

The rain continued to fall, but there was a following wind, the temperatures were bearable and for once no one cared much about the weather. Just beyond Colmar poor Leroy crashed heavily, and then there were six. Deruyter and Van Lerberghe were the only two forcing the pace, taking it in turns to lead the six-man group. Alavoine and the others just didn't have the strength to take their turns on the front, or maybe Alavoine was too canny to put his nose in the wind.

With around 30km to go, the rain eased off and the sun came

out. Van Lerberghe flicked an elbow (a sign used by pro cyclists to indicate that the person behind should come through and do a stint on the front of the group) and drifted back through the group to take a breather at the back. At this moment Deruyter attacked, catching Van Lerberghe unawares and before he could recover. Only Kippert was alert enough, and strong enough, to jump onto Deruyter's wheel. For a moment Van Lerberghe tried to persuade the others to give chase, but none of them had the strength or the inclination to organise a concerted pursuit. Unless something terrible happened to Anseeuw, Van Lerberghe's attempt to snatch second place on GC was over.

Deruyter powered on, with Kippert on his wheel. Behind, the heart had gone out of the chase and the Van Lerberghe group eased the pace sufficiently for Leroy to catch them, followed by Heusghem, Morel and Anseeuw. As the two-man breakaway approached Strasbourg the crowds along the roadside became deeper and deeper, cheering home the two leading riders. The organisers, quite sensibly, arranged a motorised escort to clear a way through the throng to the Place Tivoli (now home to the European Parliament) where Deruyter and Kippert, just before 3 p.m., sprinted it out for the stage win in front of tens of thousands of baying, cheering fans.

Charles Deruyter beat Charles Kippert by a length to take the stage win and the race. Just over 2 minutes later Alavoine and Hanlet, who had escaped from the chasing group, sprinted for third, with Alavoine taking it by a wheel, to the noisy appreciation of the French crowd. Over the next hour the riders came home in ones and twos, with Anseeuw and Van Lerberghe finishing together. The bands played, the spectators cheered, Marcel Allain gave another speech, and slowly the crowds dispersed.

At 7.15 p.m., long after most people had gone home, Louis Ellner arrived at the finish line where race commissaires Perrine, Degrain and Lecomte were still waiting for him. They knew he was coming. They knew he would make it. They stood and gave him a round of applause as he rolled across the line with a

The front page of Le Petit Journal, *on 12 May 1919, continued to be dominated by the peace talks, but they made room for a short race report*

sheepish, slightly self-conscious grin on his face. After he'd signed in, each commissaire shook his hand and congratulated him. For riders like Alavoine and Van Lerberghe, finishing this race was a massive achievement. For someone like Ellner, finishing it was an incredible feat of mental strength and physical endurance.

★

Although Stage 7 was the easiest by far for the racers, it would probably be my hardest day. I was determined to do at least one stage in one go, and Stage 7 was the only one I could feasibly manage in a day. The problem was that most of that stage route is now under the A35 motorway, so I needed an alternative. I could head through the Belfort Gap and then follow the Rhine to Strasbourg, or I could take the scenic route along the eastern foothills of the Vosges, along something called the Route des Vins d'Alsace. The former was downhill all the way and involved little in the way of effort, or scenery. The latter would involve 5,000ft of climbing, up and down all day, but would be very pretty. Both were around 105 miles. I put both routes into the sat-nav and would wait to see how I felt when I got up in the morning.

And I felt good. Having only ridden 50 miles a day for the last two days, I felt rested and refreshed, and the weather was glorious when I got up, so I opted for the harder but prettier route. Breakfast was a frenzy of carb-loading and pastry-theft, and I then tempted fate by dressing in my lightest summer riding gear, in preparation for sunshine and a day of temperatures in the mid-20s. By doing so I was almost certainly guaranteeing snow, flooding and plagues of locusts, but I would deal with that when it happened.

My only other concern was my gearing. If I left it on the 26 at the back I could spin up any of the hills easily, but would struggle to maintain a decent speed on the descents and flats. Taking advantage of the comfortable facilities in the hotel foyer, I flipped my bike upside down and set about snipping off the zip-tie, moving the derailleur down onto the 23-tooth sprocket and fixing it in place. The receptionist looked aghast, and I pretended not to notice. I considered lubing the chain as well, but decided against making any more mess. The man with the mop reappeared.

On the road, the weather was glorious, the temperature was a pleasant 17°C, and I was making decent progress north-east with a gentle following breeze. My gearing was mostly OK, too, even if I rarely seemed to be in the exact gear I would have liked. I stopped in Thann mid-morning for my second breakfast and to admire the rather lovely half-timbered Alsace architecture. This part of the world definitely feels more German than French, something that's reflected in the road signs and place names as well as the architecture.

A little later I started to see signs on my left to Hartmanns-willerkopf, the southern-most battlefield of the Western Front. After the Franco-Prussian war in 1871, when Germany annexed

Alsace, the new border between France and Germany ran right through the middle of the Vosges mountains and the summit of the Ballon d'Alsace sat on that border. With the outbreak of war the French attempted to push the Germans off the Vosges and back across the Rhine near Mulhouse. The French managed to force them several miles eastwards, but the Germans dug in on the heights of the eastern Vosges and could not be shifted.

Throughout 1915 the French made repeated attempts to improve their positions, at a cost of 10,000 French dead on Linge Ridge and 30,000 French dead at Hartmannswillerkopf. The tough Alpine conditions in the winter, and the rocky mountainous terrain, led to horrible fighting conditions. Artillery bombardments were much more deadly here than on the muddy battlefields further north because shells exploding onto rock blasted lethal stone fragments in all directions. Gas and flamethrowers were also used extensively here in some of the nastiest fighting seen on the Western Front. By the end of 1915 an inevitable stalemate ensued, and both sides decided little progress could be made in this sector.

I would have loved to have taken a detour to look at the huge French memorial at Hartmannswillerkopf, and to visit some of the well-preserved trenches and emplacements there, but there was the small matter of an extra 2,500ft of climbing and an extra 20 miles to cover. I looked wistfully up at the mountains to my left and kept going. Maybe next time.

The road meandered onwards, through the vineyards and impossibly picturesque villages of Alsace, while the sun climbed higher. By lunchtime it was hot, surprisingly hot, 30°C hot. I stopped in a shady restaurant in Somethingheim (Eguisheim, Wettolsheim, Wintzenheim, Ingersheim, Lunchtheim, who knows . . . everything around here is Somethingheim). Anyway, I ordered the local speciality, as recommended by the waitress – an exciting-sounding *tart flambée*. A rather less-than-exciting cheese-and-onion pizza turned up. But I ploughed my way through it, knowing it would sustain me for the rest of the day.

The sun continued to roast me alive as I pedalled on, registering over 30°C for the next few hours. It seemed an appropriate book-end to my trip. The day I left Strasbourg it was 3°C and sleeting; the day I returned to Strasbourg it was 33°C and blisteringly sunny. It was so hot and sunny that I stopped often for Coke, water, and ice cream, and each little town was more picturesque than the one before. Places like Riquewihr, Ribeauvillé, Bergheim and Obernai are so pretty, with their cobbled streets, stone archways and brightly painted half-timbered buildings (all adorned with millions of geraniums), that you feel like you're on some kind of Disney film-set. The downside is that coach-loads of generously proportioned sightseers in bright-yellow shorts descend on these places and make them feel even more Disneyesque.

By late afternoon I was cooked, literally and metaphorically. After 75 miles, mostly in boiling-hot temperatures, I could feel my skin tightening and my legs fading as the sweat poured off me. At Heiligenstein, 80 miles down and after the final climb of the day, I stopped and moved the rear derailleur down the block to something that would give me more speed. And for the next 25 miles I managed to maintain a respectable 20mph. But it was a pretty flat and boring 25 miles, with nothing much to look at. I passed through Duttlenheim, home town of Arsène Wenger (the legendary Arsenal manager), and then spent the next 10 miles fantasising about my very own *Ice Cold in Alex* moment, where I would sit at a bar and drink an ice-cold beer after a tough day in the blistering sunshine.

At 6.17 p.m. I rolled back into the Place Broglie, having ridden 105 miles in 8 hours. A passing French lady kindly took a photo of me flaked out on the same bench I had started from many weeks earlier, and I then set off to find beer. And food. And more beer.

Back where I started, in the Place Broglie in Strasbourg, after a punishing 108 miles on the final day

General Classification after Stage 7

	Rider	Time	Time gap
1	Charles Deruyter (B)	85hr 01min	00hr 00min
2	Urbain Anseeuw (B)	86hr 55min	+01hr 54min
3	Henri Van Lerberghe (B)	87hr 30min	+02hr 29min
4	Jean Alavoine (F)	95hr 40min	+10hr 39min
5	Theo Wynsdau (B)	97hr 06min	+12hr 05min
6	José Pelletier (F)	98hr 25min	+13hr 24min
7	Hector Heusghem (F)	99hr 28min	+14hr 27min
8	Albert Desmedt (B)	100hr 18min	+15hr 17min
9	André Huret (F)	100hr 44min	+15hr 43min
10	Henri Hanlet (B)	101hr 07min	+16hr 06min
21	Louis Ellner (F)	166hr (est)	+78hr (est)

THE AFTERMATH

The 21 survivors of the Circuit des Champs de Bataille were treated to a decent meal and a few drinks by the organisers that evening in Strasbourg. The celebrations were already well underway when Louis Ellner pushed open the door of the restaurant and slipped inside. The place was small, and packed out with riders and race officials. Ellner was, literally, late to the party. He was scanning the room for somewhere to sit when Ernest Paul spotted him.

'Louis!' he shouted. 'Over here!'

Ellner still couldn't quite get used to being here, among these people. He had read about Alavoine and Van Lerberghe in the papers before the war; now here he was, riding with them, eating with them, celebrating with them. These were legends, the celebrated hard men of bike racing. They were like gods to Ellner, a different species to the club cyclists he knew back home.

'Everyone!' shouted Paul, banging his fist on the table to silence the crowd. 'Please stand and raise a glass to our esteemed colleague, and *Lanterne Rouge*, the inestimable Louis Ellner. *Salut*, Louis!'

'*Salut*, Louis!' yelled the crowd. There seemed to be genuine affection for this odd-ball club cyclist from Épernay as they applauded his courage.

Paul cleared some space for Ellner at his table. 'Will you be doing the Bordeaux–Paris, next weekend?'

Ellner laughed out loud. 'I don't think so. I need to go home and sleep.'

Bordeaux–Paris was a 580km non-stop race due to be held the following weekend, and it always attracted the big-name riders. Several of the riders present would be heading off to Bordeaux (Deruyter, Wynsdau, Desmedt, Asse and Alavoine), as well as a few who had dropped by the wayside such as Duboc and Dejonghe. There would also be a few notable riders who weren't at the Circuit des Champs de Bataille – Eugène Christophe, Henri Pélissier, Firmin Lambot and Philippe Thys, all superstars of cycling at that time.

The party went on late into the night, despite the fatigue most of them felt. There was a shared bond between these men now, a bond that ran deeper than in most bike races. These 21 men had suffered unbelievable hardships over the last two weeks and experienced something that few other racers could imagine. The physical hardships were one thing, but the emotional hardships of racing across the Zone Rouge were something else completely. For many of them the battlefields brought back painful memories of fighting for their lives, of friends dying by their sides, of sights and sounds and smells that would haunt their nightmares for years to come. Even those who had been spared front-line action were profoundly shocked by the carnage and devastation they rode through, scarcely able to believe what they were seeing.

At the end of the night the riders bade farewell to their colleagues and staggered back to their lodgings. Many of them would meet up at subsequent races, some would ride together at Six Day events or on the Tour de France, all with varying degrees of success. Except Louis Ellner. He stumbled back to his room, certain in the knowledge that he would never be a professional bike rider, and certain he would never see these men again, unless it was from the side of the road at a bike race near Épernay.

★

My final evening was spent shovelling food and drink into my face, while staring vacantly into the middle distance. Around me the cafés and restaurants were busy with students from the university, and there was music and laughter in the warm spring air. My mind wandered back and forth through the last few months, alighting on moments of pain and joy and astonishment and sadness, contemplating my journey and the exploits of the riders a century earlier.

For the first time on my trip, the hotel breakfast buffet went un-looted. But I do have one last crime to which I have to confess. As well as a rather lengthy rap-sheet that includes trespass, pastry-theft, lying to small children, contravention of Articles 413–15 and R644-1 of the French penal code, and crimes against the French language, I must also confess to this: train fraud. Not knowing precisely when I would finish my *circuit des champs de bataille*, I hadn't booked a ticket from Strasbourg to Paris, nor from Paris to London. The Eurostar ticket I bought online over breakfast, and then I made my way to the station in Strasbourg to get a train to Paris.

'Of course, Monsieur,' said the bloke in the ticket office. 'But you cannot take your *velo* on the train. It is not allowed. The next train that accepts bikes is in three days.'

'No problem,' I said. 'Just a ticket for me. I will travel *sans velo*.'

I then lugged my bike to the appropriate platform, hid it behind a magazine kiosk, and waited for my train. Watching other TGVs come and go, I observed a routine: a train would arrive, and several guards would supervise people getting on and off. When the doors started beeping the guards disappeared and about 10 seconds later the automatic doors of the train would begin to shut.

When my train arrived I hid behind the kiosk with my bike. Once the guards had vanished and the doors began beeping, I heaved my bike over my shoulder and sprinted across the platform to the train, bundling myself and my bike through the closing doors. Phew! And it's a non-stop service to Paris, so they couldn't even throw me off at the next station. Result!

Needless to say, the ticket inspector wasn't pleased to find my bike on board. Positively livid, he was. I played the charming but stupid and apologetic Englishman card, and not only did he not fine me €200 as he should have done, he even wished me a *bon route.* I should probably feel a bit bad about my illicit behaviour, but a large part of me wonders why the hell you can't take bikes on TGVs. It's just so stupid. So, SNCF, I'm sorry. But probably not as much as I should be. *Je suis rosbif.*

★

Louis Ellner didn't give up racing altogether after the Circuit des Champs de Bataille. He had clearly developed a liking for it, and incredibly, he was back amongst the pros only six months later, on the start line of the Grand Prix de l'Armistice, a single-stage race from Strasbourg to Paris on 10 and 11 November 1919. Among the 42 entrants were Jean Alavoine, Urbain Anseeuw, Georges Gatier, Joseph Muller, Camille Leroy, Jean Bauer, and Lucien Buysse, all veterans of the Circuit des Champs de Bataille. In addition, the Pélissier brothers were there, along with Firmin Lambot and Honoré Barthélémy. Ellner isn't mentioned in the reports or the results; he probably rolled in long after everyone else had packed up and gone home.

Ellner reappeared in April 1920, on the start list for the Paris–Roubaix on 4 April. Again, he doesn't appear in any of the race reports, or in the results list, so it may have been too much for this enthusiastic *isolé*. A month later he was on the start line for the Paris–Nancy race, alongside Paul Duboc, but again he didn't make it onto the results sheet and probably finished hours behind the winner.

Bless him. He was obviously a decent club cyclist, and had more grit and determination that most of us can even begin to imagine, but he clearly wasn't a pro-level cyclist. But he tried. And tried. After 1920 he disappears from the record, except to appear in a list of (not-cycling-related) competition winners, where he is recorded as a teacher at a boys' school in Épernay. Then, in 1927, Louis Ellner reappears on the cycling scene, this time at the Trophée de Champagne (he finished 12th), and then in half a dozen local races between 1927 and 1931. He is last heard of in the 1951 Paris–Brest–Paris race, where he finished 136th in a time of 82 hours 1 minute. He must have been a relatively old man by then, but he still clearly loved riding his bike.

Astonishingly, the Circuit des Champs de Bataille made another appearance in September 1920, but this time as a single-day race around Compiègne and Soissons. Organised by a different newspaper, *L'Echo des Sports*, and called Le Petit Circuit des Champs de Bataille, this was an absolute breeze by comparison – better weather, better roads, fewer battlefields, less distance, and only one day long.

Ellner didn't compete in Le Petit Circuit des Champs de Bataille ... he was racing at the Grand Prix d'Épernay that same weekend (he came 15th). But René Chassot was back, as were José Pelletier, Henri Wynsdau, Jules Nempon and Ernest Paul. The bad news (for the peloton) was that two of the three dreaded Pélissier brothers had signed up for it. At a mere 180km, it was a sprint, the prize money was a generous 10,000FF, and clearly the Pélissiers thought this would be easy money. It was. Henri Pélissier won a six-man sprint, beating René Chassot into second and José Pelletier into fifth. Wynsdau and Nempon both abandoned, and Ernest Paul struggled in an hour behind the winner.

And so the Circuit des Champs de Bataille gave its final shudder, breathed its last breath, and expired, never to be repeated. *Le Petit Journal* didn't want it. *L'Echo des Sports* didn't want it. And the riders certainly didn't want it. Ordinary races were tough enough without throwing in diabolical weather and non-existent roads. But the Circuit des Champs de Bataille did help to start the process of getting cycling back on its feet after four years of war, although it took a while.

The Tour de France in 1919 had the dubious distinction of being the slowest in its history; 69 riders started and only 11 finished, and the average speed was slower than before the war. But 14 of our battlefield refugees made it to the start line of that Tour: Alavoine, Ménager, Buysse, Duboc, Asse, Heusghem, Chassot, Dejonghe, Anseeuw, Matthys, Huret, Verdickt, Nempon and

Verstraeten. Alavoine, Nempon and Duboc were among the 11 that finished. That Tour was also famous for being the first time the yellow jersey was awarded, and for Eugène Christophe breaking his forks (again).

It took several more years for cycling to return to normal in Europe as roads and velodromes were rebuilt, riders regained their strength, and bike manufacturers got back on their feet. And although bike racing carried on as before, an entire generation of riders had lost some of their best years to the war. Aside from the unfulfilled promise of riders killed or maimed in battle, for those in their prime the war deprived them of earnings and glory. Take Jean Alavoine. He was 28 when war broke out, an age when cyclists are normally at their peak. In four pre-war Tours he had won six stages and finished third on GC three times. After the war he won 11 stages of the Tour, finished second on GC twice, won the mountains jersey once, and finished second on GC at the Giro d'Italia. Imagine what he might have achieved had war not intervened. It was the same with Lucien Buysse, Hector Heusghem and a handful of others, all of whom could have been even more successful were it not for the outbreak of war.

Ernest Paul offers us a slightly different example. Before the war he enjoyed considerable success at the Tour, finishing in the top ten on GC three times, winning a stage, and showing great promise. But by the end of four years of war he was a different man, physically and perhaps emotionally, and was unable to get anywhere near his pre-war exploits ever again.

And who knows what might have become of the Circuit des Champs de Bataille had misfortune not been heaped upon misfortune. An essentially interesting race and moving tribute to the fallen, the Circuit des Champs de Bataille was scuppered by an unfortunate series of events that no one could have foreseen. Although Le Petit Journal proclaimed the race to have been a triumph, it really wasn't. The unseasonably bad weather made life hellish for the riders and the organisers, and the roads were also much worse than had been expected.

And if that wasn't bad enough, the terms of the Treaty of Versailles were announced halfway through the race, which knocked the race off the front page of *Le Petit Journal*.

The whispering campaign against the race was also unfortunate; there were hints of all sorts of behind-the-scenes shenanigans. The lucrative Grand Prix de l'Heure, organised by *L'Auto* and held at the same time as the Circuit des Champs de Bataille, meant that riders such as Henri Pélissier and Eugène Christophe preferred the relative comfort, safety and generous prize money of track racing. Did *L'Auto* stage the Grand Prix de l'Heure as a spoiler for the Circuit des Champs de Bataille? We don't know, but they might have expected to attract track specialists like Oscar Egg, Maurice Brocco, and Ali Neffati, all of whom raced the Champs de Bataille instead.

It's rather sad in some ways. The Circuit des Champs de Bataille could have become a significant addition to the cycling calendar, an annual reminder of the futility of war, a tribute to the millions of men who fell. Instead it was briefly an object-lesson in bad planning and bad luck, and was soon forgotten by the cycling world. Except, it seems, by Karel Van Wijnendaele of *Sportwereld*, who continued to rant about the terrible conditions and hopeless organisation for decades to come. He was later banned from journalism for life for collaborating with the Germans during the Second World War.

Interestingly, *Le Petit Journal* didn't completely give up on bike racing. In 1933 they organised a one-week stage race from Paris to Nice (the owner of *Le Petit Journal* also owned a newspaper in Nice), and now the Paris–Nice is a well-established and prestigious part of the cycling calendar.

But the Circuit des Champs de Bataille sank into oblivion, barely rating a mention in cycling history books more focused on the Tour and the Classics. And it's such a shame, because it was one of the most extraordinary bike races ever staged. At a time when the world was picking itself back up after the most horrific war in human history, a war that allowed engineering knowhow to develop machines capable of killing millions of people, the super-human efforts of these 87 riders have been all but forgotten.

Or maybe not. Maybe they will finally get the recognition and plaudits they deserve, thanks to a new race that made its debut in August 2018 – The Great War Remembrance Race. Organised by Flanders Classics, the people who put on the prestigious Ronde van Vlaanderen, the Gent–Wevelgem, and the Het Nieuwsblad races, the GWRR is a one-day race across the battlefields of Flanders that commemorates those who fought and died in the First World War. It is the natural successor to the Circuit des Champs de Bataille, and attracted many of the big-name racers from the pro peloton. Fernando Gaviria, Fabio Jakobsen, Yves Lampaert and Niki Terpstra were among the star riders who raced in the 1919 wheel-tracks of Deruyter, Anseeuw and Ellner.

★

My own 1,200-mile *circuit des champs de bataille* was an absolute breeze by comparison to what they put up with in 1919. Yes, I cracked a few ribs and got a bit scabby. Yes, I got very cold and wet on occasion. And yes, there were (brief) moments when I wondered what the hell I was doing. But riding around France, Belgium and Luxembourg on a modern road bike, on modern roads, doing 70 miles a day, isn't hard. It really isn't.

The hardest bit was trying to decide what to take with me – clothing, spares and tools – and then trying to get it all into a saddle-bag and bar-bag. That required a certain amount of thought and discipline, but I think I got it right. And I loved being on the road day after day, stopping where and when I wanted to visit some incredible places. I was concerned, before I left, that three weeks on my own would be challenging. Having Joe and Phil along for some of the time certainly helped, but it turns out that I can be left alone with my own thoughts for days on end without turning into a gibbering idiot or resorting to self-harm.

As a *forçat de la route*, I experienced a kind of tranquillity I didn't expect to find on what was basically a tour of the Western Front. The daily routine of packing, riding, washing and sleeping brought me simple pleasure. It didn't matter that the scenery was generally not very pretty, or that the weather was often foul, or that I spent every day considering death and destruction on an unimaginable scale. I was, for some reason, content.

But my *circuit des champs de bataille* has also led me to places I didn't really want to go to. My liberal upbringing in the 1960s and '70s had made me think of the First World War in terms of *Oh What a Lovely War* and 'lions led by donkeys' – an unnecessary war instigated by incompetent and idiotic generals hell-bent on 'moving their drinks cabinet six inches closer to Berlin', whatever the cost. But the more I read about the rape of Belgium and the systematic destruction of French and Belgian culture, industry and agriculture, the more appalled I became. This wasn't collateral damage, this was deliberate theft and wanton destruction, designed to ensure that Germany remained a powerful economic force in Europe, whatever the outcome of the war, while her neighbours were obliged to rebuild completely.

And I find myself increasingly irritated by John Maynard Keynes' assertion that the Treaty of Versailles was too harsh on the Germans and somehow led inevitably to the Second World War. He described it as 'one of the most outrageous acts of a cruel victor in civilised history'. Versailles was far less harsh than the treaties the Germans had inflicted on the French and the Russians in recent years, and Germany ultimately paid less than 2 per cent of what was agreed in the Treaty. But Keynes' lamentations were music to the ears of Germany's far-right nationalists, who pinned Germany's downfall on intellectuals, politicians, and ultimately the Jews.

Far worse than the terms of the Treaty of Versailles was the Allied naval blockade of Germany and the slow starvation of German civilians. More than 250,000 German civilians died of hunger and malnutrition in 1918 alone, and the blockade continued until the Germans had actually signed the Treaty in June 1919. This, it seems to me, is far more of an 'outrageous act of a cruel victor'. But by maintaining the blockade the Allies were able to force a quick settlement.

But this probably isn't the place to get into a why-and-wherefore discussion about the origins of the Second World War. Marshal Ferdinand Foch, the great French general and military strategist, presciently said of Versailles: 'This isn't peace. This is an armistice for 20 years.' Sadly, he was right, almost to the day, and the world was once again plunged into war.

I completed my *circuit des champs de bataille* in a time of 101 hours 46 minutes, a time that would have put me in fifth place on General Classification, an hour behind Jean Alavoine and 30 minutes ahead of Theo Wynsdau. I would have won the equivalent of around £20,000, and almost certainly bagged myself a professional contract. I would probably have gone on to ride to a top-ten finish in the Tour de France, and won Paris–Roubaix the following year. Or probably not.

Obviously, I would never even have made it to the finish of Stage 1. For a start, I would have had to get up at 3 a.m., and that's never going to happen. Then I would have had to ride for 275km on muddy roads in the snow, on a bike made of pig-iron, while wearing a woollen jumper and some shorts. I would have abandoned at Haguenau, 29km from the start.

But I loved riding in the wheel-tracks of these extraordinary men. They were so tough, so dedicated, so indomitable, that you can't help but love them. They were survivors, forged in the furnace of a world war, toughened by hunger and thirst and fatigue. And when they'd done their duty they put down their rifles, picked up their bikes again, and raced.

There were moments when I raced with them, battling with my own injuries and horrible weather, lost in the snow, passing a convoy of First World War ambulances driving along the Voie Sacrée, exhausted and yet unable to sleep. There was a (very) small level of authenticity I experienced along the way that gave me a (very) large level of satisfaction. I could imagine riding these roads alongside Maurice Brocco or Ernest Paul, I could almost feel Hector Heusghem and Henri Van Lerberghe clattering along the *pavé* beside me. And when I looked at old buildings along the route I was experiencing a little bit of what they saw as they ploughed on through the wind and the snow.

For me, the scene at the Café de L'Est in Amiens epitomises this race. Of all the moments I've read about in the Circuit des Champs de Bataille, this is the one that really haunts me. The contemporary descriptions of Charles Deruyter arriving at the end of Stage 3 in a state of complete collapse paint a vivid picture of human endurance and emotion laid bare.

Out of the darkness and howling wind and rain appeared a man who had spent 18 hours riding at the absolute limit of his endurance, in conditions that defied belief. Hypothermic, physically and mentally exhausted, filthy and unable to stand unaided, this was bike racing at its most brutal, and most attritional. And there was Deruyter's devoted wife Adrienne, in this dilapidated candle-lit café amongst the post-war ruins of Amiens, waiting for her sobbing, broken husband to complete his toughest ever day on a bike, in the toughest ever bike race.

GLOSSARY

auberge: Wayside inn.

bidon: Water bottle.

block: Group of sprockets/cogs on the back wheel, cassette.

bottom bracket: The bearings where the pedals attach to the frame.

cassette: See **block**.

Classics: The big, established one-day races: Paris–Roubaix, Milan–Sanremo, Liège–Bastogne–Liège, Amstel Gold, Flèche Wallonne, Tour of Flanders, Het Volk, etc.

commissaire: Race judge, usually one of three on a race.

CWGC: Commonwealth War Graves Commission, the people who look after all the Allied cemeteries.

derailleur: Part of the gear system that moves the chain onto a different cog.

domestique: A member of a team who rides in the service of others.

dossard: Race number, pinned to the jersey.

GC: General Classification, the leader-board of a stage race.

Grand Tour: A three-week stage race, either the Tour de France, the Giro d'Italia, or the Vuelta a España.

groupset: Gears.

isolé: An independent rider, one with no team or support.

matériel: Military equipment and supplies.

Monuments: The five biggest and most important Classics.

musette: A light canvas shoulder bag for carrying food.

palmarès: The CV of a racing cyclist, list of wins and achievements.

parcours: Route of a bicycle race.

patron: The unofficial leader and spokesman for the peloton.

pavé: Carved granite cobbles, aka setts.

peloton: The main group of riders in a bike race; collective name for bike racers.

piano: Riding *piano* means taking it easy, soft-pedalling.

poilu: Slang name for French infantryman (literally, a hairy person).

regions dévastées: The parts of northern France affected by the war.

RI: *Regiment Infanterie* (French infantry regiment).

rosbif: French for roast beef; a slang expression for the English.

routière: A standard, upright road bike. Not a race bike.

sinistrés: The returning inhabitants of the *regions dévastées*.

sportive: A mass-participation cycling event, not a race.

tempo: Riding *tempo* means at a brisk, steady pace.

Zone Rouge: Areas of France too badly affected by the war to cultivate.

BIBLIOGRAPHY

Author's note: The dates shown below are those of the editions that I have consulted, not necessarily the dates of the first editions of those books.

Battlefield clearances and tourism
Blanchard, David, *North West France: Aisne 1918*, Pen & Sword, Barnsley, 2015

Brice, Beatrix, *The Battle Book of Ypres*, John Murray, London, 1927

Buckle, Elizabeth, *A Kingly Grave in France*, Unknown, London, 1919

Clout, Hugh, *After The Ruins*, University of Exeter Press, Exeter, 1996

Coombes, Rose, *Before Endeavours Fade*, After the Battle, Harlow, 2006

Gordon-Smith, Jeremy, *Photographing The Fallen*, Pen & Sword, Barnsley, 2017

Graham, Stephen, *The Challenge of the Dead*, Cassell, London, 1921

Hanson, Neil, *The Unknown Soldier*, Doubleday, London, 2005

Holt, Major and Mrs, *Battlefield Guide to the Somme*, Pen & Sword, Barnsley, 1996

Holt, Major and Mrs, *Concise Illustrated Battlefield Guide – The Western Front – South*, Pen & Sword, Barnsley, 2011

Holt, Major and Mrs, *Ypres Salient: Battlefield Guide*, Pen & Sword, Barnsley, 2007

Holstein, Christina, *Verdun: The Left Bank*, Pen & Sword, Barnsley, 2016

Holstein, Christina, *Walking Verdun*, Pen & Sword, Barnsley, 2009

Jones, Nigel, *The War Walk*, Cassell, London, 2004

Lloyd, David W., *Battlefield Tourism*, Berg, Oxford, 1998

Michelin, *Guides Illustrés Michelin des Champs de Bataille*, Clermont-Ferrand, 1919–22

Middlebrook, Martin and Mary, *The Middlebrook Guide to The Somme Battlefields*, Pen & Sword, Barnsley, 2007

Miles, Stephen, *The Western Front: Landscape, Tourism and Heritage*, Pen & Sword, Barnsley, 2016

O'Shea, Stephen, *Back to The Front*, Robson Books, London, 1997

Pulteney, Sir William, *The Immortal Salient*, John Murray, London, 1925

Reed, Paul, *Walking The Salient*, Pen & Sword, Barnsley, 1999

Reed, Paul, *Walking The Somme*, Pen & Sword, Barnsley, 1998

Smith, Corinna Haven, *Rising Above the Ruins of France*, Putnam's, New York, 1920

Summers, Julie, *British and Commonwealth War Cemeteries*, Shire, Oxford, 2010

Uffindell, Andrew, *The Nivelle Offensive and The Battle of The Aisne 1917*, Pen & Sword, Barnsley, 2015

Williamson, Henry, *The Wet Flanders Plain*, Faber and Faber, London, 1929

Belgium

Giles, John, *Flanders Then and Now*, After The Battle, Harlow, 1987

Lloyd, Nick, *Passchendaele: A New History*, Viking, London, 2017

Macdonald, Lyn, *They Called it Passchendaele*, Michael Joseph, London, 1978

Pauly, R. and Lierneux, P., *The Belgian Army in World War I*, Osprey, Oxford, 2009

Prior, Robin and Wilson, Trevor, *Passchendaele: The Untold Story*, Yale University Press, New Haven, 1996

Sheldon, Jack, *The German Army at Passchendaele*, Pen & Sword, Barnsley, 2007

Steel, Nigel and Hart, Peter, *Passchendaele: The Sacrificial Ground*, Cassell, London, 2000

Van Basten, Daniel, *The Battle of Liege*, Van Basten, 2016

Van Pul, Paul, *In Flanders Flooded Fields*, Pen & Sword, Barnsley, 2006

Wolff, Leon, *In Flanders Fields*, Penguin, London, 1979

Zuckerman, Larry, *The Rape of Belgium*, New York University Press, New York, 2004

France

Barbusse, Henri, *Under Fire*, J. M. Dent, London, 1926

Barthas, Louis, *Poilu*, Yale University Press, New Haven, 2014

Brown, Malcolm, *The Imperial War Museum Book of The Somme*, Pan, London, 1997

Clayton, Anthony, *Paths of Glory*, Cassell, London, 2003

Greenhalgh, Elizabeth, *The French Army and The First World War*, Cambridge University Press, Cambridge, 2014

Hart, Peter, *The Somme*, Weidenfeld & Nicolson, London, 2005

Herwig, Holger H., *The Marne, 1914*, Random House, New York, 2009

Horne, Alistair, *The Price of Glory: Verdun 1916*, Penguin, London, 1993

Kuklos, *Across France in War-Time*, J. M. Dent, London, 1916

Lynch, E. P. F., *Somme Mud*, Doubleday, London, 2008

Macdonald, Lyn, *Somme*, Macmillan, London, 1984

Middlebrook, Martin, *The First Day of The Somme*, Penguin, London, 1984

Murphy, David, *Breaking Point of the French Army*, Pen & Sword, Barnsley, 2015

Norman, Terry, *The Hell They Called High Wood*, Pen & Sword, Barnsley, 2016

Ousby, Ian, *The Road to Verdun*, Jonathan Cape, London, 2002

Péricard, Jacques, *Verdun 1914–1918*, Librairie de France, Paris, 1933

Robb, Graham, *The Discovery of France*, Picador, London, 2007

Rogerson, Sidney, *The Last of The Ebb: The Battle of the Aisne 1918*, Greenhill, London, 2007

Sheldon, Jack, *The German Army in The Spring Offensives 1917*, Pen & Sword, Barnsley, 2015

Sumner, Ian, *They Shall Not Pass*, Pen & Sword, Barnsley, 2012

Wharton, Edith, *Fighting France*, Amberley, Stroud, 2014

General First World War and Franco-Prussian War

Badsey, Stephen, *The Franco-Prussian War 1870–1871*, Osprey, Oxford, 2003

Blaker, Richard, *Medal Without Bar*, Hodder & Stoughton, London, 1930

Borden, Mary, *The Forbidden Zone*, Hesperus, London, 2008

Bull, Stephen, *The Old Front Line*, Casemate, Havertown, 2014

Caidin, Martin, and Barbree, Jay, *Bicycles in War*, Hawthorn, New York, 1974

Chapman, Guy, *Vain Glory*, Cassell, London, 1937

Corrigan, Gordon, *Mud, Blood and Poppycock*, Cassell, London, 2003

Doughty, Simon and Kerr, James, *Silent Landscape*, Helion, Solihull, 2016

Dunn, J. C., *The War The Infantry Knew 1914–1919*, Janes, London, 1987

Gerwarth, Robert, *The Vanquished*, Penguin Books, London, 2017

Hamilton, Robert, *The Great War: Unseen Archives*, Atlantic, Herts, 2014

Hastings, Max, *Catastrophe*, William Collins, London, 2013

Haythornthwaite, Philip, *The World War One Source Book*, Cassell, London, 1992

Holborn, Mark, *The Great War*, Jonathan Cape and IWM, London, 2013

Jones, David, *In Parenthesis*, Chilmark, New York, 1961

Macdonald, Lyn, *The Roses of No Man's Land*, Penguin, London, 1993

McCrery, Nigel, *The Extinguished Flame*, Pen & Sword, Barnsley, 2016

Neillands, Robin, *The Old Contemptibles*, John Murray, London, 2004

Saunders, Nicholas, and Cornish, Paul, *Contested Objects*, Routledge, Abingdon, 2009

Early bike racing

Augendre, Jacques, *Le Dictionnaire des Coureurs*, Maison du Sport, Paris, 1988

Becuwe, Frank, *Omloop van de Slagvelden*, Davidsfonds, Leuven, 2013

Bobet, Jean, *Lapize . . . Now There Was an Ace*, Mousehold Press, Norwich, 2010

Bourgier, Jean-Paul, *1919: Le Tour Renait de L'enfer*, Editions Le Pas d'Oiseau, Toulouse, 2014

Cossins, Peter, *The Monuments*, Bloomsbury, London, 2014

Cossins, Peter and Best, Isabel, *Le Tour 100*, Cassell, London, 2013

Dunne, Kieran J., *The Tour de France, 1903–1998*, Common Ground, Illinois, 2013

Foot, John, *Pedalare! Pedalare!*, Bloomsbury, London, 2011

Gallagher, Brendan, *Corsa Rosa*, Bloomsbury, London, 2017

Healy, Graham, *The Shattered Peloton*, Breakaway Books, New York, 2014

Horton, Shelly and Brett, *Goggles and Dust*, Velopress, Boulder, 2014

Kirsch, Colin, *Bad Teeth No Bar*, Unicorn Publishing, London, 2018

Leonard, Max, *Lanterne Rouge*, Yellow Jersey Press, London, 2014

Maso, Benjo, *The Sweat of The Gods*, Mousehold Press, Norwich, 2005

McGann, Bill and Carol, *The Story of the Giro d'Italia: Volume One, 1909–1970*, McGann, Cherokee, 2011

Moore, Richard and Benson, Daniel, *The Racing Bicycle*, Universe, New York, 2003

O'Brien, Colin, *Giro d'Italia*, Pursuit, London, 2017

Rapley, David, *Racing Bicycles: 100 Years of Steel*, Images Publishing, Victoria, 2012

Reid, Carlton, *Roads Were Not Built for Cars*, Island Press, Washington, 2015

Seray, Jacques and Lablaine, Jacques, *Henri Desgrange, l'homme qui créa le Tour de France*, Editions Cristel, Saint Malo, 2006

Sykes, Herbie, *Maglia Rosa*, Rouleur, London, 2011

Thompson, Christopher S., *The Tour de France*, University of California Press, Berkeley, 2006

Van Wijnendaele, Karel, *Het Rijke Vlaamsche Wielerleven*, USDZ, Gent, 1942

Woodland, Les, *Paris–Roubaix: The Inside Story*, McGann, Cherokee, 2013

Woodland, Les, *The Unknown Tour de France*, Cycle Publishing, San Francisco, 2000

Woodland, Les, *Tour of Flanders: The Inside Story*, McGann, Cherokee, 2014

Woodland, Les, *Tour de France: The Inside Story*, McGann, Cherokee, 2014

Newspaper reports

L'Auto: http://gallica.bnf.fr/ark:/12148/cb327071375/date1919

Le Petit Journal: http://gallica.bnf.fr/ark:/12148/cb32895690j/date1919

Sportwereld: http://www.nieuwsblad.be/sportwereld

INDEX

Illustrations are denoted by the use of *italics*.